The Struggle for South Africa

A Reference Guide to Movements, Organizations and Institutions

Volume One

Robert Davies, Dan O'Meara
and Sipho Dlamini,
Centre of African Studies,
Eduardo Mondlane University

Zed Books Ltd., 57 Caledonian Road, London N1 9BU.

The Struggle for South Africa was first published in two
volumes by Zed Books Ltd., 57 Caledonian Road, London
N1 9BU, in 1984.

Copyright © Centre of African Studies, Eduardo Mondlane
University, 1984

Copyedited by Mark Gourlay
Typeset by Jo Marsh
Proofread by Louise Hoskins
Cover design by Simon Acuah
Printed by The Pitman Press, Bath

British Library Cataloguing in Publication Data

Davies, Robert H.
  The struggle for South Africa.
  Vol. 1
  1. Pressure groups—South Africa
  I. Title   II. O'Meara, Dan
  III. Dlamini, Sipho
  322.43'0968   JQ1969.P7

  ISBN 0-86232-224-3
  ISBN 0-86232-225-1 Pbk

US Distributor
Biblio Distribution Center, 81 Adams Drive, Totowa,
New Jersey, 07512

The Struggle for South Africa

Robert Davies, Dan O'Meara and Sipho Dlamini

Dedication

At 4.30 p.m. on Tuesday 17 August 1982, Ruth First was killed in a parcel bomb explosion in her office at the Centre of African Studies, Eduardo Mondlane University, Maputo. She was murdered by the South African apartheid regime.

Ruth had been a militant in the South African liberation struggle for almost 40 years. Her contribution to the theory and practice of the ANC and South African Communist Party was immense.

And in the four years in which she was Director of Research at the Centre of African Studies, Ruth worked tirelessly to create a research and teaching institution which would directly serve the process of socialist transformation in Mozambique. For Ruth, Marxism was the theoretical and practical political tool of this transformation. Hers was a Marxism not of texts and quotations, but of deep analysis of Mozambican reality — what Lenin called 'the living soul' of Marxism, the 'concrete analysis of concrete conditions'.

Ruth was always determined to relate Mozambican research to the wider regional context, for she believed profoundly that the struggle for socialism in Mozambique is a central part of the struggle for liberation in Southern Africa.

This book is dedicated to her memory and the ideas she fought and died for.

A luta continua!
Amandla Ngawethu!

Contents

Volume One

Volume Two

Tables, Figures and Map

List of Abbreviations

AAC	Anglo American Corporation of South Africa Limited
AB	*Afrikaner Broederbond* (Afrikaner Brotherhood)
AECI	African Explosives and Chemical Industries Limited
AET	*Aksie Eie Toekoms* (Action Own Future)
AFCWU	African Food and Canning Workers' Union
AFL-CIO	American Federation of Labor-Congress of Industrial Organizations
Amaprop	Anglo American Properties Limited
Amcoal	Anglo American Coal Corporation Limited
Amgold	Anglo American Gold Investment Company Limited
Amic	Anglo American Industrial Corporation Limited
Anamint	Anglo American Investment Trust Limited
ANC	African National Congress (of South Africa)
ANS	*Afrikaans-Nasionaal Studentebond* (Afrikaner National Students' League)
Anti-CAD	Anti-Coloured Affairs Department
APDUSA	African People's Democratic Union of South Africa
APRP	Azanian People's Revolutionary Party
ARM	African Resistance Movement
ARMSCOR	Armaments Corporation of South Africa
ASB	*Afrikaner Studentebond* (Afrikaner Students' League)
ASSOCOM	Associated Chambers of Commerce
ATI	Anglo Transvaal Industries Limited
AWB	*Afrikaner Weerstand Beweging* (Afrikaner Resistance Movement)
AYRC	Azanian Youth Revolutionary Council
AZAPO	Azanian People's Organisation
AZASO	Azanian Students' Organisation
Bankorp	Bank Corporation of South Africa
BAWU	Black Allied Workers' Union
BC	Black Consciousness
BCC	Black Consultative Council of Trade Unions
BCM	Black Consciousness Movement

BCMA	Black Consciousness Movement of Azania
BENSO	*Buro vir Ekonomiese Navorsing en Staatsontwikkeling* (Bureau for Economic Research and State Development)
BIC	Bantu Investment Corporation
BLS	Botswana, Lesotho and Swaziland
BMWU	Black Municipal Workers' Union
BOSS	Bureau for State Security
BPA	Black Parents' Association
BPC	Black Peoples' Convention
BUF	Black Unity Front
CAHAC	Cape Areas Housing Action Committee
CCAWUSA	Commercial, Catering and Allied Workers' Union of South Africa
CED	Corporation for Economic Development
CIA	Central Intelligence Agency
CIWW	Council of Industrial Workers of the Witwatersrand
CNA	Central News Agency
CNETU	Council of Non-European Trade Unions
COD	Congress of Democrats
COM	Chamber of Mines
COMPRA	Combined Mitchells Plain Residents' Association
CONSAS	Constellation of Southern African States
COPE	Congress of the People
COSAS	Congress of South African Students
COSAWR	Committee of South African War Resisters
CRC	Coloured Representative Council
CP	Communist Party
CPSA	Communist Party of South Africa
CUSA	Council of Unions of South Africa
CYL	Congress Youth League (of the ANC)
D & H	Darling and Hodgson Limited
DMI	Directorate of Military Intelligence
DNP	*Dikwankwetla* (Strong men) National Party
DONS	Department of National Security
DP	Democratic Party
DPP	Democratic Peoples' Party
DRCs	Dutch Reformed Churches
DSAG	*Deutch-sud Afrikanische Gesellschaft* (German-South African Association)
DTA	Democratic Turnhalle Alliance
ESCOM	Electricity Supply Commission
FAK	*Federasie van Afrikaanse Kultuurverenigings* (Federation of

	Afrikaans Cultural Associations)
FCI	Federated Chambers of Industry
FCWU	Food and Canning Workers' Union
Fedfoods	*Federale Voedsel Beperk* (Federal Foods Limited)
Fofatusa	Federation of Free African Trade Unions of South Africa
FOSATU	Federation of South African Trade Unions
FP	Freedom Party
FRELIMO	*Frente da Libertacão de Moçambique* (Mozambican Liberation Front)
FSAW	Federation of South African Women
FVB	*Federale Volksbeleggings Korporasie Beperk* (Peoples' Federal Investment Corporation Limited)
GAWU	General and Allied Workers' Union
GDP	Gross domestic product
GK	*Gereformeerde Kerk* (Reformed Church)
GWU	General Workers' Union
GWUSA	General Workers' Union of South Africa
HNP	*Herstigte Nasionale Party* (reconstituted Nationalist Party*)
HNP/V	*Herenigde Nasionale of Volksparty* (Reunited Nationalist or Peoples' Party*)
IAS	Industrial Aid Society
IC	Industrial Council
IC Act	Industrial Conciliation Act
ICFTU	International Confederation of Free Trade Unions
ICS	The Imperial Cold Storage and Supply Company Limited
ICU	Industrial and Commercial Workers' Union of Africa
IDAF	International Defence and Aid Fund
IDC	Industrial Development Corporation
IIE	Institute for Industrial Education
I & J	Irving and Johnson Limited
ILO	International Labour Organization
INM	*Inyandza* (United) National Movement
ISCOR	Iron and Steel Corporation
ISL	International Socialist League
IUEF	International University Exchange Fund
JCI	Johannesburg Consolidated Investment Company Limited

*A strictly correct translation of *Nasionale Party* should be rendered as 'National Party'. However common English South African usage refers to the 'Nationalist Party' which rendering we have retained.

KDC	KwaZulu Development Corporation
KP	*Konsewatiewe Party* (Conservative Party of South Africa)
LLA	Lesotho Liberation Army
LPP	Lebowa Peoples' Party
MACWUSA	Motor Assembly and Component Workers' Union of South Africa
MAGWU	Municipal and General Workers' Union of South Africa
MAWU	Metal and Allied Workers' Union
MINORCO	Minerals and Resources Corporation Limited
MK	*uMkhonto we Sizwe* (the Spear of the Nation)
MNR	Mozambique National Resistance Movement
MPLA	*Movimento Popular da Libertacão de Angola* (Popular Movement for the Liberation of Angola)
M-Plan	Mandela Plan
MP	Member of Parliament
MWASA	Media Workers' Association of South Africa
MWU	Mine Workers' Union
Nacoc	National African Chambers of Commerce
Nafcoc	National African Federated Chambers of Commerce
NCP	National Conservative Party
NEUM	Non-European Unity Movement
NFBW	National Federation of Black Workers
NGK	*Nededuitse Gereformeerde Kerk* (Dutch Reformed Church)
NHK	*Nederduitsche Hervormde Kerk* (Dutch Reconstituted Church)
NIC	Natal Indian Congress
NIS	National Intelligence Service
NP	Nationalist Party
NPU	Newspaper Press Union
NRC	Natives' Representative Council
NRP	New Republic Party
NUMARWOSA	National Union of Motor and Rubber Workers of South Africa
NUTW	National Union of Textile Workers
OAU	Organization of African Unity
OB	*Ossewa Brandwag* (Oxwagon Sentinels)
OFS	Orange Free State
PAC	Pan Africanist Congress of Azania
PAIGC	*Partido Africano de Independencia de Guiné e Cabo Verde* (African Party for the Independence of Guiné and Cape Verde)

PC	President's Council
PEBCO	Port Elizabeth Black Civic Association
PFP	Progressive Federal Party
POLSTU	Political Students' Organisation
PRP	Progressive Reform Party
PWV	Pretoria-Witwatersrand-Vereniging
Recces	Reconnaissance Commandos
RI	Republican Intelligence
RP	Republican Party
RTZ	Rio-Tinto Zinc Corporation
SAAF	South African Air Force
SAAN	South African Associated Newspapers Limited
SAAWU	South African Allied Workers' Union
SAB	South African Breweries Limited
SABA	South African Black Alliance
SABC	South African Broadcasting Corporation
SABCTV	South Africa, Bophuthatswana, Ciskei, Transkei and Venda
SABRA	South African Bureau for Racial Affairs
SACC	South African Council of Churches
SACLA	South African Confederation of Labour
SACP	South African Communist Party
SACTU	South African Congress of Trade Unions
SADCC	Southern African Development Coordination Conference
SADF	South African Defence Force
SAFEMA	South African Federation of Engineering and Metallurgic Associations
Safmarine	South African Marine Corporation Limited
SAFTU	South African Federation of Trade Unions
SAIC	South African Indian Council
SAIF	South African Industrial Federation
SAIRR	South African Institute of Race Relations
SANLAM	South African National Life Assurance Company
SANTAM	South African National Trust and Insurance Company
SAP	South African Police
SAPPI	South African Paper and Pulp Industries Limited
SAR & H	South African Railways and Harbours Administration
SASM	South African Students' Movement
SASO	South African Students' Organization
SASOL	*Suid Afrikaanse Steenkool, Olie en Gaskorporasie* (South African Coal, Oil and Gas Corporation)
SASPU	South African Students' Press Union
SATLC	South African Trades and Labour Council
SATS	South African Transport Services

SAYRC	South African Youth Revolutionary Council
SBDC	Small Business Development Corporation
SCA	Soweto Civic Association
SEIFSA	Steel and Engineering Industries Federation of South Africa
Soweto	South Western Townships
SP	Security Police
SSC	State Security Council
SWAPO	South West African People's Organization
TC Lands	Transvaal Consolidated Land and Exploration Company Limited
TDC	Transkei Development Corporation
TEBA	The Employment Bureau of Africa
TLC	Trades and Labour Council
TNIP	Transkei National Independence Party
TUACC	Trade Union Advisory Coordinating Council
TUCSA	Trade Union Council of South Africa
UAW	United Automobile and Rubber Workers' Union
UBJ	Union of Black Journalists
UF	Urban Foundation
UK	United Kingdom
UKSATA	United Kingdom South Africa Trade Association
UMSA	Unity Movement of South Africa
UNITA	*União para a Independencia Total de Angola* (Union for the Total Independence of Angola)
UP	United Party
URC	Umbrella Rentals Committee
USA	United States of America
UTP	Urban Training Project
UWO	United Women's Organisation
VIPP	Venda Independence Peoples' Party
VNP	Venda National Party
WASA	Writers' Association of South Africa
Wenela	Witwatersrand Native Labour Association
WFTU	World Federation of Trades Unions
WPF	Western Province Federation (of trade unions)
WPGWU	Western Province General Workers' Union
WPWAB	Western Province Workers' Advice Bureau
ZAPU	Zimbabwe African Peoples' Union

Preface

For us in Mozambique the struggle for South Africa is much more than an academic question.

Along with the South African masses, the people of Mozambique and indeed all of Southern Africa have been victims of the vicious system of exploitation and oppression which the world knows as apartheid. For decades, thousands of our people were compelled to work as low paid migrant labourers in the mines, farms and industries of apartheid South Africa. Our ports and transport system were geared to the needs of South African capitalism, and we served as a market for the commodities of South African industry. Today, with the apartheid system in deep crisis, the states of Southern Africa are subjected to repeated acts of aggression and an ongoing process of destabilisation by Pretória. Both our struggle to build socialism in Mozambique and the collective efforts of the independent states in the region to forge peaceful cooperation between them, represent a profound threat to South African hegemony over Southern Africa. Apartheid South Africa is a fundamental part of the daily reality of our region. All the people of Southern Africa therefore have a direct interest in the outcome of the struggle for South Africa.

The Centro de Estudos Africanos is to be congratulated on producing this clear and comprehensive guide to that struggle. We are proud that despite our limited resources and our difficulties in obtaining the reference material which most universities take for granted, our Eduardo Mondlane University has been able to produce a work of this calibre. This book is free from academic jargon yet firmly based on scientific analytical method.

To my knowledge, no equivalent reference work exists, and I believe that this book will be of use to a wide audience. It is a reflection of the creativity unleashed by our revolution that such a work was produced in the People's Republic of Mozambique.

Jose Luis Cabaço
Minister of Information

Acknowledgements

These two books grew out of the ongoing engagement of the Centre of African Studies with issues relating to South Africa and its place in the struggle for liberation in the region. The first full-scale research project carried out by the Centre dealt with the flow of Mozambican labour to South Africa. Over the years a body of material on South and Southern Africa has been produced. It was felt, however, that within Mozambique there was a pressing need for a more structured and coherent guide to the various organisations involved at all levels of the struggle in South Africa. This guide was originally intended for use by party and state officials, as well as journalists within Mozambique. It was later realised that it might also be of use to solidarity organisations, students, academics and all of those outside Mozambique concerned with South Africa. Both volumes will thus appear in both the Portuguese and English languages.

The idea of a reference manual was first proposed by the Director of the Centre, Aquino de Bragança; the planning of its structure was carried out by a collective of specialists in South African Studies within the Centre, in consultation with the then Director of Research, Ruth First. The actual writing of all material was done by Robert H. Davies, Dan O'Meara and Sipho Dlamini.

The final draft was read and commented upon by the Centre's academic staff. We also wish to thank John Saul, Harold Wolpe and Thozamile Botha for their useful comments and criticisms.

Various drafts of a lengthy manuscript were typed by Vibeke Giagheddu, Luz Klingler, Adelina Lucas, Adelaide Tojais, Luisa Cipriano and Christine Littlejohn.

Introduction:
How to Use this Book

OBJECTIVES

This book is intended to be used as a reference guide to the organisations, movements and institutions involved in the struggle for South Africa in the 1980s. It consists of a collection of analytical essays and entries on various individual organisations. Together, these seek to provide, from a Marxist perspective, both an overview of the issues and processes of this struggle, and more detailed information on the myriad organisations involved. As such, the book is fundamentally concerned with the interlinked processes of, and contradictions around, capital accumulation, class struggle and national liberation in South Africa.

STRUCTURE

The book is structured in such a way as to attempt to cater for the needs of a number of different types of reader.

It contains ten chapters. The first of these comprises four essays. These are intended to provide an overview of the historical development and current functioning of the apartheid system, the trajectory of struggles in contemporary South Africa, and the policies of the South African state in the Southern African region. These essays situate in general terms the more specific chapters which follow.

The remaining nine chapters cover the spectrum of the major organisations involved in the struggle for South Africa. Most chapters contain both an introductory essay and a number of individual entries. The introductory essays provide the historical background and general overview to the theme of the chapter. They link the entries to the wider historical and contemporary context. Thus, for example, Chapter 2 deals with the major forces and economic organisations of the ruling capitalist class. The introductory essays analyse firstly the current structure of the South African economy, and secondly the historical development and current extent of monopoly capitalism in South Africa. The individual entries which follow deal with the various enterprises and organisations which collectively make up the major economic organisations of the capitalist class.

Most of the individual entries within each chapter begin with a portion in a boxed border, followed by a longer text. The boxed portion of the entry provides a resumé of the organisation in question, summarises its class nature and position and role in the current phase of the struggle. These boxed portions are intended for use by those readers who require only the broadest outline of each organisation. For those interested in a more detailed perspective, the complete entry provides a more extensive analysis of the history and current position of the organisation.

Each chapter concludes with a bibliographical note. This indicates the major sources used and includes a brief guide to further reading; it is not an exhaustive bibliography.

Throughout the text, whenever reference is made to events or an organisation discussed elsewhere in the book, this is indicated by a bracketed reference '(see pp.0–00)'. This method of cross referencing has been used in an attempt to reduce to the minimum the repetition unavoidable in a book of this sort.

PROBLEMS OF CLASSIFICATION

Overall, this book is concerned with the question of *power*. It deals with the numerous organisations and forms through which the struggle for and maintenance of power in South Africa takes place; this has been our fundamental perspective and all entries are written around it. This means that, for instance, the entries on individual capitalist organisations are concerned primarily with the power they represent and their place in the struggle for that power. The reader who is looking for more conventional economic information on these organisations — such as earnings ratio per share — will not find it here.

At the outset, because we wished to analyse the struggle for power in South Africa, it was decided that the book should be more than a simple alphabetical catalogue of organisations. Instead we have sought to identify a number of crucial themes and areas of struggle. These are broadly grouped around the capitalist class, its allies, policies and state structures on the one hand, and the forces making up and supporting the national liberation struggle and organised opposition to the regime on the other. These themes provide the basis for individual chapters. The entries in each chapter then examine the principal organisations in these groupings.

The major divisions of the book and its organisation, and a breakdown of the entries within each chapter is provided in the detailed Table of Contents (p.v).

Clearly, the actual process of struggle in South Africa is not as cut and dried as our classification suggests. Inevitably there are omissions in the book and we have had to make choices. Certain organisations have been excluded because it was felt that they were not overtly concerned with the immediate issues of struggle and did not therefore justify extensive research.

This is the case, for example, with some churches and sporting bodies which nevertheless play an important role in the cultural life and political organisation of the oppressed population in South Africa. This is also the case with organisations such as the Rotary Club and the Jewish Board of Deputies, both of which are a significant medium for the organisation of specific interests of the capitalist class.

Other organisations were difficult to classify. Where an organisation did not fit easily into the groupings identified in the chapters, either because it crossed our thematic boundaries, or because of its contradictory character and demands, it has been included in Chapter 10, under 'Other Political and Miscellaneous Organisations'. Examples of such organisations are the South African Institute of Race Relations, the Labour Party, the media etc.

A book which deals with current struggles in South Africa is bound to date rather rapidly. This reference manual has been more than two years in preparation. During that time a number of important changes and shifts have occurred. While we have tried to include such changes in the text, it was impossible to remain constantly up to date and complete the book at the same time. The final editing of the manuscript was made in April-May 1983. While in some cases developments of early 1983 are referred to, in general the book covers the period up to mid-1982 — except for the entries in Chapter 2, where we have only been able to include data from the 1981 reports of these undertakings.

HOW TO READ THIS BOOK

The book can be used in two ways. Firstly, it can be used as a reference manual to provide information on specific organisations. For example: if a reader wants information on an organisation called the Port Elizabeth Black Civic Organisation (PEBCO), he or she should refer first to the alphabetical index of organisations at the back of the book. The first reference to the organisation in this index appears in bold type and indicates the page on which the specific entry on the organisation is to be found. Additional references indicate other places in the book where reference is made to PEBCO. In cases such as PEBCO, where an organisation is also commonly known by its abbreviation, the abbreviation also appears in the index and the reader is referred to the full title of the organisation. A list of abbreviations is also provided on p.xiii.

Secondly, the book is intended to provide a coherent analysis of the current struggle in South Africa. The reader interested in a more general analysis of the situation, rather than the detailed account of its component parts, is advised to consult the essays in Chapter 1. These provide an overall view of the historical development and current operation of the system and forms of struggle in South Africa. He or she should then read the introductory essays at the beginning of the subsequent chapters. This type of reading will, however, necessarily involve some repetition.

1. Setting the Scene

INTRODUCTION: UNDERSTANDING APARTHEID

Apartheid in South Africa is internationally notorious as a system of national oppression, racial discrimination, and extreme repression. Black people in South Africa are classified into three distinct 'racial groups' — Africans, the so-called Coloureds (i.e. people of mixed racial descent) and Asians (predominantly of Indian origin). Although the particular forms of racial discrimination to which these groups are subject differ slightly, the racist system has for many years placed them all in conditions of brutal oppression. Black people in South Africa have no effective political rights and no freedom of movement. The official state policy denies that Africans are even South Africans. The state machinery is totally dominated by whites. Blacks may not own land in the 87% of the country deemed to be 'white South Africa'. They may not choose freely where to live, where to work, or where to send their children to school. On grounds of their 'race', blacks are denied access to a wide range of facilities and amenities available to whites. Taken together, all the oppressive measures of apartheid have produced a situation in which most of the wealth of South Africa is in the hands of four-and-a-half million whites, while the overwhelming majority of the 25 million blacks in South Africa live in poverty.

All this is well known: it has been exhaustively catalogued in numerous publications, and we shall not dwell on it here. Rather, our concern is how to understand the development and operation of this racist system, the easier to do away with it and transform South Africa from an international pariah into a democratic country in which all South Africans enjoy full political rights and live free and prosperous lives.

The four essays which follow attempt to provide an understanding of the historical development and current functioning of the apartheid system. They seek to furnish a historical and contemporary perspective in which to locate and situate the rest of this book. They deal with:

The Historical Development of Racial Capitalism 1652–1948;

The Apartheid Onslaught 1948–1973;

South Africa in the 1980s: An Overview of the Present Phase of the
    Struggle;

The Apartheid State in the Southern African Region.
It is intended that, taken together, these essays will provide the background for an understanding of the contemporary struggle for South Africa, and the myriad local, regional and national organisational forms through which it is now being fought out.

One final introductory point about our approach to explaining these processes and struggles remains to be made. Given the all-pervading nature of national oppression and racial discrimination in South Africa, apartheid and the forms of segregation which preceded it, have often been explained simply in terms of racial prejudice. Whites, or more especially the Afrikaans-speaking section of the white population, popularly known as the Boers, are presumed to suffer from intense racial prejudice, and this system of racial discrimination is the result. It is certainly true that most whites are highly racially prejudiced, but this explains little. In our view, explanations which stress only the racial component of the apartheid system and fail to explain the historical development and current functioning of the system, are positively misleading. Such types of explanation actually conceal the most important elements of the system.

The approach on which this book is based assumes from the outset that the various changing historical forms of national oppression and racism in South Africa are organically linked with, and have provided the fundamental basis for, the development of a capitalist economy in that country. In other words, the various complex and intersecting class struggles through which capitalist forms of production and relations of production were developed and consolidated under colonialism in South Africa, themselves generated racist ideologies and a racially structured hierarchy of economic and political power. The national oppression of black people in South Africa is a product of, and was indeed the necessary historical condition for, the development of capitalism in that country.

Apartheid, then, is much more than a system of intense racial discrimination. Fundamentally it, like the segregationist policies which preceded it, is a system of economic, social and political relations designed to produce cheap and controlled black labour, and so generate high rates of profit. As such, it serves both the dominant capitalist class — which benefits directly from the high levels of exploitation and rates of accumulation made possible by a cheap and controlled labour force — and certain other privileged classes in white society. While these latter are not themselves capitalists, for reasons explained in the following four essays, they came to form a supporting alliance in the exercise of the white monopoly of power. Thus both the historical development and contemporary functioning of the apartheid system can only be properly understood through an analysis of, the contradictions around and the interlinked processes of capital accumulation, class struggle and national liberation.

Whilst in the late 1970s and the early 1980s the apartheid system has been and is being modified in various minor ways (see essay p.32), it has always operated to secure cheap black labour through the following mechanisms:

1) a white monopoly of land ownership;
2) a comprehensive system of control over the movement of the black population in general and black workers in particular;
3) a political system which excludes all blacks and
4) a repressive state dominated by the military, police, and security services.

These have themselves thrown up their own particular forms of class struggle. The first three of the four essays which follow analyse the struggles and processes by which apartheid capitalism was consolidated. The first sketches the development of racial capitalism between the establishment of the first colonial settlement in 1652 and the coming to power of the ruling Nationalist Party with its apartheid policies in 1948. The second examines the development of the apartheid system of capitalist exploitation and the struggles around it in its so-called 'classic' period, 1948-73. The third essay analyses the continuing crisis of this apartheid system from 1973 to the present, and the strengths of the major contending forces. Finally, given the longstanding integration of the other states in the region into a regional economic system dominated by South African capitalism, the fourth essay examines the evolving strategy of the apartheid state in southern Africa in response to the advancing liberation struggles in the region. The rest of the book provides more specific and detailed information on these forces involved in the struggle for South Africa.

THE HISTORICAL DEVELOPMENT OF RACIAL CAPITALISM, 1652-1948

The present day social conflict in South Africa is derived from the way in which the country was colonised, and from the social pressures initiated by colonialism. The colonial occupation of South Africa began with the establishment of a refreshment station at the Cape of Good Hope by the Dutch East India Company in April 1652. However, the colonial conquest of what is now South Africa was a lengthy process. It encountered fierce, armed resistance from all of the indigenous inhabitants and was only completed in the 1880s. The final wars of colonial conquest were in fact the direct result of the development of forms of capitalist production after 1870, and ushered in a new phase of South African history. The years 1652-1948 can be divided into two very broad eras — the period of mercantile colonialism 1652-1870, and the age of imperialism and the segregation phase of capitalist development *circa* 1880-1948.

The Period of Mercantile Colonialism

Dutch Colonialism, 1652-1806
Dutch colonialism held sway over large parts of what is now the Cape Province (see map) from 1652-1806 (with an interruption 1795-1803). Between

1806 and 1910, all of present day South Africa came under British colonial rule.

The Dutch East India Company came to the Cape to secure the conditions of accumulation in its mercantile plunder of the East Indies. Dutch colonialism was always structured by the needs of this primitive form of capitalist accumulation. Thus from the very outset the colonial policies in South Africa and developing colonial society were shaped by the needs of metropolitan accumulation.

Dutch colonialism was notable for three things: firstly the rapid dispossession of the indigenous colonised population; secondly, the largely corrupt and inefficient rule of the Dutch East India Company officials; and thirdly, the establishment of a stratified settler population. Contradictions soon emerged between settler colonists and the colonial state; towards the end of the period, the white settlers became involved in strenuous conflict with the Dutch colonial state, and sought forms of local self-government (strictly reserved for whites).

The Cape colony was primarily intended to replenish the passing ships of the Dutch East India Company, thereby reducing the costs of its trade with the East Indies; Dutch colonial authorities constantly sought to reduce their administrative costs at the Cape. One of the most important measures in this regard was the early abandonment of the initial policy of using Company employees to produce supplies, in favour of encouraging the permanent settlement of white agriculturalists on land seized from the Khoisan inhabitants of the Western Cape. These white *vryboers* (free farmers) received no salary and produced on their own account, making extensive use of Khoisan slave labour. They were nevertheless subject to numerous restrictions and were obliged to sell their produce to the Company at fixed prices. Resistance to these conditions drove many of these colonists to seek to escape the jurisdiction of the rule of the Company. Over the 150 years of Dutch colonialism a significant differentiation developed amongst the settler population (which gradually came to speak a new, Dutch-derived language, later termed Afrikaans). Roughly speaking, in the areas around the Western Cape and present Boland districts, there developed a group of relatively large-scale landowners producing wheat, wine and other crops for sale to the Dutch East India Company's monopoly. They farmed almost exclusively with slave labour.

On the other hand, relatively large numbers of settlers trekked beyond the jurisdiction of the Company and established themselves as largely subsistence stock farmers in outlying areas on land expropriated from the Khoi pastoralists. By the mid 1700s, however, this form of settler colonial expansion became increasingly difficult as the settlers encountered the militarily powerful Xhosa people in the region of the Fish River. For 50 years a series of inconclusive wars for control of the grazing lands of the Zuurveld region were fought between Boer colonists and the Xhosa, with neither side able to impose itself finally on the other.

Thus the slow expansion of Dutch colonialism rested on the twin props of the expropriation of the land of the indigenous inhabitants, and their enslavement as farm and other types of labourers for their white colonial masters. Accompanying these oppressive processes was the development of a strong racism justifying expropriation and enslavement in biblical terms. Extended discussions on the status in 'the Divine Hierarchy of Being' of the enslaved Khoi, concluded that they were *skepsels* — i.e. creations of God, higher than animals but lower than 'men' (whites). By the end of Dutch colonialism in 1806, colonial production at the Cape remained based on slave labour which performed both skilled and unskilled tasks; no forms of capitalist production had emerged. While large numbers of the indigenous pastoralists were driven off their land, this colonial exploitation did not produce a proletariat selling its labour in a free market; wage labour was virtually unknown. Rather, colonial expropriation led to the enslavement of some and the flight of others to parts of South Africa not yet colonised. However, by 1806 only a small part of what is today South Africa was controlled by European colonialism. The majority of the inhabitants of the region lived in various forms of pre-capitalist societies which had shown the military capacity to resist colonial exploitation and settlement.

Strong contradictions had emerged between the interests of the metropolitan Dutch state and its always weak colonial administration on the one hand, and the settler colonists on the other. The latter controlled colonial production. They often resented what they saw as the limitations imposed on their freedom to exploit the colonised inhabitants of the Cape by the Dutch state — particularly in the period of the short-lived rule of the Batavian Republic (1803–6). Political separatism was a growing force among them when the British seized the Cape in 1806. It was strengthened by the policies of British imperialism.

British Colonialism after 1806

The British seized the Cape from the Dutch in 1806 to guarantee the security of British imperialism's vital sea-going trade with India. Thus, while initially at least, British colonialism at the Cape was not principally geared around the exploitation of the resources of the Cape colony as such, nevertheless colonial policy was always shaped by the needs of British imperialism and its imperatives of capital accumulation on a world scale. The social structure of the colony began to change with the advent of British colonialism. Two interlinked processes set in motion a transformation of the political and social map of the region. Britain was in the process of the Industrial Revolution and emerging as the world's foremost capitalist power. Through its free trade policies, British imperialism sought to open the world market to its industrial goods. In the Cape colony this policy saw the gradual abolition of slavery (the slaves were only finally freed in 1838) and the relaxation of other measures of control over the labour market. The aim of this policy was not only to create a market for British industrial goods, but also to foster the development of commercial farming which would pay the costs of maintaining the colony. Commercial agriculture began to develop slowly under British rule. By the end of the 1860s, capitalist farming was established in parts of the Cape and Natal colonies; the black labour force, however, remained tightly controlled.

This British policy of relaxing controls over the labour and other markets increased the economic pressures on the Boer pastoralist colonists and led to increasing antagonism between them and the British authorities. The end result was the large-scale exodus from the Cape colony in the mid to late 1830s of the so-called *Voortrekkers*. These Boers now sought to colonise areas outside British control. However, the forms of production they engaged in were in no sense capitalist, but relied on the extraction of surplus from a rent-paying peasantry. The British followed the Boers erratically, annexing at times their conquered 'republics', further exacerbating the Boer antipathy to British imperialism.

The second crucial social process under way at the end of the 18th Century was the consolidation of numbers of small African chiefdoms into powerful kingdoms. The vast social disruptions this gave rise to — known as the *Mfecane* — completely reorganised the political map of southern Africa. By the mid-1830s, five powerful African kingdoms straddled much of the central and eastern areas of present day South Africa (the Zulu, Ndebele, Swazi, Basotho and Bapedi kingdoms). The expansion of Boer and British colonialism into the hinterland of South Africa after 1830 brought them into conflict with these various pre-capitalist societies. Again, whilst rifles and artillery generally proved superior to the assegai, the majority of these societies remained politically and economically independent throughout the period, and retained large and powerful armies. Yet they were increasingly incorporated in widespread trading networks with colonial capitalists and thus became increasingly dependent on British commodities.

Thus, by the end of the 1860s, British colonialism had overseen the emergence of significant capitalist farming by white settlers in the Western and Eastern Cape and Natal. There also existed pockets of commercial capitalism around the ports of Cape Town, Port Elizabeth and Durban. A network of migrant merchants were slowly insinuating commodity relations into all the societies of the region. However, there still existed no proletariat worth speaking of. The Afrikaans-speaking Boer colonialists who had set up republics in the Transvaal and Orange Free State in the 1850s were engaged mainly in rentier forms of exploitation. They lived mainly off the rents in labour and in kind from the various squatters on their extensive landholdings. They justified this pre-capitalist form of colonial exploitation in terms of rigid racist ideologies which forbade any 'equality in church or state' between white master and black servant.

In the British colony of the Cape, men of property (regardless of colour) had been given a form of local self-government. Nevertheless, social relations in the Cape were also marked by a strong racism and racial patterns of power and privilege. However, under British rule, class position — the ownership or non-ownership of the means of production — rather than outright racial discrimination, determined the patterns of economic and political power. A significant liberal ideology developed, which stressed class rather than race in determining social and political relations. It also regarded British imperialism as the great progressive force in the world, and the necessary bulwark against the more brutal exploitation of the colonised by 'primitive' Boers.

Within the various African pre-capitalist societies, more than a century of trade with capitalism was slowly transforming social relations. However, the vast majority of South Africa's indigenous inhabitants remained in control of their own means of production, producing a surplus to be expropriated by their chiefs and/or white landlords. These societies remained militarily powerful and retained large measures of political, economic and cultural autonomy. All this was transformed in the last 30 years of the 19th Century.

The Age of Imperialism and the 'Segregation' Period of Capitalist Development

In the mid-1860s and mid-1880s, the world's largest deposits of first diamonds, and then gold, were discovered at Kimberley and Johannesburg respectively. Diamond mining began in 1867 and gold mining in 1886. The interest of the British metropolitan state in South Africa were transformed virtually overnight. South Africa was no longer an expensive unproductive burden on the British treasury, sustained to protect Britain's vital interests in India. Rather, South Africa was transformed from a colonial backwater into a central prop of British imperialism — itself now scrambling for colonies all over Africa.

The mineral discoveries shattered the existing social systems in what is today South Africa, hurling men and women into new types of social relations, forging new cultures and modes of living; it also transformed the political map of the region. The colonial conquest of the independent African societies was hastily completed between 1868 and 1881. All were now subject to some or other form of colonial rule. The British also sought to smash the independence of the Boer republics they had recognised in the 1850s. Following the Anglo-Boer war of 1899–1902, all of present day South Africa was incorporated into four British colonies. These were finally united as the existing four provinces of South Africa in 1910, and the white colonists were given internal self-rule (the vast majority of the black population remained without political rights). Finally, in 1931 the complete legal 'sovereignty' of the white power-holders over South Africa was conceded by British imperialism. The emergence of the particular form of state and political relations characteristic of South African racial capitalism is discussed pp.131-7. Here the developing economic or social relations on which this form of state rested — the consolidation of capitalist exploitation through new forms of national oppression — is examined.

The development of the mining industry marked a fundamental turning point in South African history. Here first emerged capitalist production on a large scale; three aspects of this are significant. Firstly, it was in the mining industry that the *wage labour system of exploitation*, which distinguishes the capitalist mode of production from others, was first introduced into South Africa on a significant scale. Whilst the various forms of production established under colonialism between 1652 and 1870 had produced the large-scale exploitation and often brutal oppression of the colonised, they were not exploited (nor oppressed) *as wage labourers*. However, with the establishment of the mining industry, very large numbers of black workers were rapidly drawn into the wage labour system. Within three years of the opening of the Witwatersrand gold-fields in 1886, over 17,000 African workers were employed in the mines, together with 11,000 whites. Twenty years later the figure had reached 200,000 black workers and 23,000 whites.

The mining industry was significant secondly because it created the conditions for the early development of capitalist production in agriculture and manufacturing. The huge market created by the mine labour force stimulated the development of commercial production in agriculture and, unevenly, the growth of industrial production. The years 1870–1920 mark the development on a large scale of capitalist production in agriculture, whilst the period 1910–40 saw the industrialisation of South Africa.

Thirdly and finally, it was in the mining industry that many of the institutions or forms of exploitation and consequent national oppression specific to South Africa were first developed in their modern form — the migrant labour system, pass laws, job colour bars, the racial division of labour, compounds etc. These were later adapted and used in agriculture and industry. Thus it may be said that the forms of exploitation and relations which developed in the gold mining industry largely shaped the development of labour practices and social relations in other sectors for a long period.

The Mining Industry

The Witwatersrand gold-fields were the largest hitherto discovered, but the ore was of a low grade, was very deep underground and widely scattered — and hence difficult and expensive to mine. To produce one ounce of gold, something like four tons of rock had to be brought to the surface. Moreover, for most of this period, the price of gold was fixed, whilst the price of mining machinery, stores and equipment rose steadily. These constraints meant that from the very beginning of gold-mining, capital accumulation in the industry critically depended on the capacity of the mining capitalist to do two things: firstly, to obtain the large amounts of advanced capital necessary to establish a producing gold-mine under difficult technical conditions; and secondly, to minimise the costs of production to make profitable the mining of low-grade ore under the constraints of a fixed price and difficult technical conditions.

These imperatives of capital accumulation resulted in firstly, the *rapid centralisation and concentration of capital* in the mining industry — the early emergence of monopoly capital. With the commencement of deep-level mining in 1897, a rapid process of financial concentration and amalgamation began. This brought all mines under the control of six large groups of mining houses by about 1910. These great mining monopolies were the most power - ful political force in South Africa; they fought for state policies which would speed up their own accumulation under these difficult constraints.

Secondly, the specific conditions in the mining industry led to the *establishment of highly exploitative and coercive social relations of production*. Measures were taken to compel African peasants to leave their land and enter mine labour (see pp.169-70). A pass law system was instituted to control the influx of African labour to the towns. The mineowners grouped themselves together in the Chamber of Mines (see p.105) and set about monopolising the recruitment of mine labour and reducing competition between them for labour. This finally resulted in the formation of two recruiting organisations, the Native Recruiting Corporation (NRC, which functioned inside South Africa) and the Witwatersrand Native Labour Association (WNLA or Wenela, which operated in the other countries of southern Africa). Through these monopolies, the Chamber was able to slash African mine wages in 1897 and hold them at these levels in real terms until the early 1970s. A highly restrictive contract system was also introduced together with the notorious compound system which barricaded tribally divided workers into enclosed and guarded compounds under very tightly policed conditions. All of this was based on a system of migrant labour.

Migrant labour was the key to the cheap labour policies of the mining industry. It presumed that African workers still had access to land in the rural areas and on completion of their contracts would return to these plots of land. Their families would be housed and fed in the rural areas through production on this land, and not out of the wages of the migrant worker. Thus wages could be kept very low. As an official spokesman of the mining industry explained to the Lansdown Commission on Mine Wages in 1944:

> It is clearly to the advantage of the mines that native labourers should
> be encouraged to return to their homes after the completion of the
> ordinary period of service. The maintenance of the system under which
> the mines are able to obtain unskilled labour at a rate less than
> ordinarily paid in industry depends on this, for otherwise the
> subsidiary means of subsistence would disappear and the labourer
> would tend to become a permanent resident upon the Witwatersrand
> with increased requirements.

These cheap labour policies were justified by a racist ideology directed exclusively against blacks. The measures facilitated a high rate of accumulation in the mining industry, and the migrant labour system enabled mining capitalists to overcome profitably the difficult technical conditions of the extraction of gold-bearing ore on the Witwatersrand.

The third product of the specific technical and price constraints of gold-mining was the emergence of a rigid *racial division of labour*. When mining first commenced, the skilled work necessary for the extraction of ore was performed by labour imported from Europe or America for the purpose, generally assisted by gangs of unskilled black migrant workers. The wages of these white skilled workers were often dependent on the amount of gold-bearing rock mined, and they thus had a direct interest in intensifying and speeding up the labour process of the black work-gangs which they controlled. From the outset then, the formation of a proletariat in the mining industry was marked by a racial division. White workers were relatively highly paid and tended to be organised into trade unions; they also engaged in often militant struggles against capital to protect their interests.

With the introduction of deep-level mining in 1897, mining capitalists began a protracted attempt to 'de-skill' the tasks performed by these relatively expensive white skilled workers. Through reorganising labour processes, capital sought to replace more expensive whites with cheaper black workers, or at least push whites into the role of supervisors of ever larger gangs of black workers. These processes were fiercely resisted by white miners for 25 years, culminating in the great 'Rand Revolt' of 1922. Under the slogan 'Workers of the World Unite for a White South Africa', a general strike by white labour against such de-skilling measures by the Chamber of Mines led to a three month strike and armed revolt which was suppressed with great violence by the state.

These struggles of white labour against the bosses were not fought by organising all mineworkers, but by demanding job colour bars which would compel the mine owners to reserve certain skilled and supervisory categories of work exclusively for whites. These job colour bars were slowly introduced after 1897. The 1911 Mines and Works Act gave them statutory force, and they were extended and consolidated in the years which followed (see pp. 174). When the Nationalist/Labour Party coalition came into office in 1924, this so-called 'Pact' government entrenched the Act and extended this racial division of labour into other sectors under its 'Civilised labour' policy.

Thus the imperatives of capital accumulation produced a division of labour within the working class in which whites did skilled, highly-paid tasks, and black migrant workers performed unskilled or semi-skilled jobs for starvation wages. This division of labour within production created extreme social and ideological divisions within the emerging South African proletariat. Moreover, to protect the rule of capital, white workers were encouraged by the colonial state to see themselves as part of the 'civilised' colonising population, some-how innately superior to the 'raw tribal natives' who constituted the bulk of the mine labour-force. Indeed, even when confronted with a shortage of unskilled labour after the Anglo-Boer war, mining capitalists refused to employ 'poor whites' in unskilled jobs, partly on the grounds that the political impact of seeing part of the colonising population doing 'native work' would encourage disaffection among the 'natives'. Under such conditions, in order to protect their precarious position against exploitation from the capitalist class, white workers developed highly racist ideologies and a demand for rigid job colour bars reserving 'skilled' work for whites (see p.241). However, at least until 1922 they also engaged in militant struggles against capital under the banner of socialist ideologies.

Thus from the beginnings of large-scale capitalist production in the mining industry, the national oppression of black workers and the African population generally, racism and racial discrimination, were actively fostered by both capital and white labour in pursuit of specific class and/or sectional interests. Through a complex process of struggle and concession, such racial discrimination also served as the ideological basis on which alliances were eventually forged between components of the capitalist ruling class and white labour after 1924.

Finally, it should be noted that the state policies required by 'expatriate' monopoly mineowners in the Transvaal in order to secure what they saw as the necessary conditions for their own accumulation, were not identical to those of the Boer rentier landlords who controlled the colonial state of the 'South African Republic'. To protect themselves from the overwhelming economic power of the mining monopolists, and to guarantee their independence from British imperialism (which had briefly colonised the Boer Transvaal republic 1877-81), the Boer colonists denied political rights in their state to such *Uitlanders* (foreigners — as they termed the largely British mine owners and white mineworkers). This, and the tardiness of the Boer state in pursuing the policies wanted by the mining capitalists, led the mine owners to attempt to overthrow the Boer Republic in 1895, and ally with British imperialism in a three year war to colonise both the Transvaal and its sister Boer republic of the Orange Free State, 1899-1902. The destruction of Boer independence, and the death of over 20,000 Boer women and children in British concentration camps during the Anglo-Boer war, led to a hatred of 'British imperialism and its *alter ego*, monopoly capitalism' which stimulated the growth of Afrikaner nationalism and an Afrikaner separatism over the next 60 years.

The Road to Capitalism in Agriculture

Capitalist agriculture in South Africa developed 'from above'. Pre-capitalist forms of production, in which white colonist landlords extracted various forms of rent from a surplus producing peasantry, were transformed into capitalist production based on the large landholdings of such rentier land-lords. This process of transformation was extremely uneven across the four provinces. But in every case, the intervention of the state was fundamental; in the process, the economic independence of the African peasantry was destroyed. They were chained to the land first as labour tenants (roughly 1913-60) and then as contract wage labourers compelled by the apartheid system to continue working for white farmers. This transformation of colonial-ist landlords into local capitalist farmers was also possible only through an intensification and consolidation of the national dispossession and oppression of the entire African population. Here the uneven character of capitalist development in South Africa is most visible. In agriculture, these conditions of capital accumulation through national oppression were only finally and conclusively secured through the apartheid state after 1948 (see p.24).

This process of transformation developed only through protracted class struggles. Immediately after the beginnings of diamond-mining, it was in fact African peasants rather than the white landlords who first began supplying surplus produce for the large market created by the mines. For almost 50 years after 1865 there was a fierce struggle between these surplus-producing peasants who marketed their crops, and the white landlords. Once again the process was extremely uneven between the four provinces of South Africa. However, in all areas the colonial state finally acted to consolidate the interests of white landlords against the African peasantry. Eventually, in 1913 was enacted the key piece of legislation which finally shattered the remaining economic independence of the African peasantry and intensified the process which was transforming them into landless wage labourers or labour tenants. The 1913 Land Act demarcated 8% of the total land area of South Africa as the only areas in which Africans could own land (extended to 13% in 1936). The rest was reserved for whites (see pp.169–70). Moreover, the Land Act also limited the number of African families which could live on one white farm, thereby breaking the back of the surplus-producing squatter peasants who had occupied so many 'white' farms, particularly in the Transvaal and Orange Free State. These were now transformed into labour tenants, obliged to supply labour for newly emerging capitalist farmers. This Land Act not only secured labour for newly emerging capitalist agriculture, but by finally destroying the economic independence of the African peasantry, it also made their labour available to the mining industry. It is one of the fundamental pieces of legislation in the so-called segregation period of development of South African capitalism.

Other forms of state intervention were also central to the development of capitalism in agriculture: the first was the provision of large-scale credit. Various measures were adopted here, the most important being the establishment of the Land Bank in 1912. At another level, the state intervened to regulate conditions in the market for agricultural produce. These measures tended to be *ad hoc* until the political reorganisation of the capitalist class into the United Party in 1934 (see p.157) finally made possible the passage of the Agricultural Marketing Act of 1937. This provided for a single-channel marketing system with prices determined by control boards on which white farmers were heavily represented; the intention was to establish stable profitability for capitalist agriculture.

These various forms of state intervention to secure the conditions of accumulation for agriculture were the product of protracted political struggles within the ruling class during the first 50 years of this century. The mining capitalists in particular opposed the various state subsidies to agriculture and the marketing measures, as, in effect, they were paid for in higher taxation of, and costs to, the mining industry. As is shown below, these struggles within the capitalist class had important effects for the development of industry.

One final point must, however, be noted: an important side-effect of this particular path of development of capitalism in agriculture was that very large numbers of smaller Boer landlords lost their land and were driven into penury in the cities. The emergence of the so-called 'poor white problem' after 1890 was nothing less than the proletarianisation of small white farmers (almost exclusively Afrikaans-speaking). By 1933 it was 'conservatively' estimated that one-sixth of the white population of 1.8 million had been made 'very poor' by the development of capitalist agriculture, whilst a further 30% were 'poor' enough not to be able 'adequately to feed or house their children'.

The development of capitalism in agriculture thus proletarianised both black and white producers, but it did so unevenly. White, predominantly Afrikaans-speaking, proletarians could move freely to the cities whilst blacks were subject to forms of influx control and the hated pass system. However, among the urban poor, social segregation was not very strong and a number of sprawling slums sprang up in which both black and white lived. This tended to undermine the ideology of white supremacy so essential to capitalist exploitation in South Africa. It also raised the spectre of joint struggle by the white and black urban poor. Moreover, the newly proletarianised whites had the vote and were thus a potential political force (one which, after 1933, the petty bourgeois militants of organised Afrikaner nationalism sought to mobilise for their own purposes). For these reasons, successive regimes fostered measures to 'uplift' the poor whites.

The Development of Industrial Production
The development of the mining industry also stimulated the emergence of a manufacturing sector, producing various inputs for the mines such as dynamite, and on a larger scale, consumer wage goods. The tiny manufacturing sector received a further stimulus when the shortage of imported products during World War I resulted in increased demand for locally produced goods. The years between 1910 and 1920 saw the rapid expansion of local manufacturing.

However, this sector still remained fairly small; in the period before 1924 it was in the phase of manufacture as distinct from machinofacture. That is to say it was based on artisanal rather than mechanised production. Its labour-force consisted of skilled artisans (mainly whites, but with a few so-called coloureds in the Cape) supported by unskilled workers (mainly Africans, but in that period also with large number of coloureds and mainly Afrikaans-speaking whites). African workers in manufacturing were, at this stage, pre-dominantly migrants housed in compounds and paid wages roughly equivalent to those in the mines.

This situation began to change following the election of the Nationalist/Labour Pact government in 1924. The Pact came to power on a platform pledged, *inter alia*, to protect fledgling South African industries and a programme of state provision of various infrastructural requirements for industry. Under the Pact, the state steel producer, ISCOR (see pp.101-104) was established and protective tariffs were instituted for a wide range of local products. Equally importantly, through its Wage Act and state controlled systems of national collective bargaining for industry, set up under the Industrial Conciliation Act, the wage policies of the regime favoured the emergence of more efficient — that is more mechanised — producers. Thus, particularly in the 1930s, the old artisan/unskilled division of labour characteristic of manufacture began to break down; machinofacture began to emerge on a significant scale. This led to a rapid rise in the size of the African proletariat. By 1939, over 800,000 Africans were employed in manufacturing and mining.

White skilled workers began to resist the process of de-skilling these transformations implied. During this period, the white trade unions remained essentially craft based. They did not attempt to recruit new industrial workers (white or black) into their ranks, but strongly resisted attempts to introduce less skilled black or Afrikaner workers into what these unions considered skilled jobs. Their defence of the threatened position of white artisans and skilled workers produced strongly anti-black and anti-Afrikaner worker policies — and so provided fertile soil for the later mobilisation of the latter into so-called 'Christian national' trade unions by the petty bourgeois *Afrikaner Broederbond* (see pp.266–70).

Contradictions and Class Struggles

Thus by the outbreak of the Second World War in 1939, capitalist production had taken hold in mining, agriculture and industry. Capital accumulation in each of these sectors was based on the exploitation of a low wage, highly controlled African migrant labour force. This migrant labour system was itself dependent upon the state enforced system in which Africans were still deemed to have access to land in the reserve areas. The state also attempted to regulate the flow of African labour to the cities under the various influx control measures and through the many laws in operation. This was based on the 'Stallard principle' that blacks were to be admitted to the cities only to 'minister to the needs' of whites, and to leave the cities when they 'ceased so to minister'. In each of the three major sectors of capitalist production, the state had intervened decisively to foster the conditions of accumulation of capital, and control where necessary the struggles of African workers and peasants. This was the basic thrust of the gamut of 'segregation' policies during this period.

There nevertheless remained important contradictions within the capitalist class which affected both its political organisation and the thrust of state policies. Thus, whereas mining capital was monopoly capital virtually from the outset, and was based on high levels of investment (mainly from British and other external sources) and employed very large conglomerations of wage labour under fairly mechanised conditions of production, the situation in both industry and agriculture was very different. Unlike the 'foreign capital' which still controlled the mining industry, agricultural and industrial capital were essentially local. Both sectors were characterised not by monopoly, but by a high level of production units owned largely by individual proprietors. Thus there were 9,999 industrial undertakings in 1939. Their total contribution to the gross domestic product in this year was significantly lower than that of the 40 producing gold-mines (37 of these mines were owned by the seven major mining finance houses and together produced 96.7% of the gold mined in South Africa). Moreover, both industry and agriculture were relatively 'cost efficient' in international terms. This meant that the bulk of the small undertakings which made up these sectors were profitable only behind barriers of state protective tariffs and subsidies — which were paid for out of increased taxation of the monopoly and 'imperialist oriented' mining industry.

These and other contradictions between various capitals gave rise to severe conflict between them. It centered on questions such as the supply of labour and prices/protection — not to mention the wider question of the relationship between the South African settler state and British imperialism, which subsumed these questions. The political organisation of these class forces changed during the period 1910–40 (see chart, 'White politics' pp.159–65). However, for much of this period industrial and agricultural capitalists were allied against mining capital on a protectionist and interventionist platform. Mining capital, on the other hand, tended to favour 'free trade' policies. This alliance took its most open form in the 1924–33 'Pact' government. It continued in a modified form in the 'fusion' government of the United Party, 1934–9, (though mining capital was also represented in the United Party).

The development of capitalist production in all sectors of the economy was uneven in other senses as well. Leaving aside for the moment its differential impact on the white and black populations, within the white population it affected English and Afrikaans-speakers differentially. The only sector in which a significant group of Afrikaner capitalists emerged was within agriculture — where it has been estimated that in 1939 Afrikaner capitalist farmers controlled 85% of the turnover of all marketed produce. However, by 1939 agriculture was the least significant productive sector in terms of contribution to GDP. The share of Afrikaner-owned concerns in the turnover of other sectors ranged from 1% in mining, 3% in manufacturing, 5% in finance to 8% in commerce. The language of the urban economy was English, and Afrikaans-speakers were strongly discriminated against. Moreover, Afrikaans-speakers were clustered in the worst off positions amongst whites in the capitalist economy. Leaving aside the massive poor white population (which consisted almost exclusively of Afrikaans-speakers), Afrikaner workers occupied the lowest categories of wage labour reserved for whites. In 1939, for example, almost 40% of adult white male Afrikaans-speakers occupied the categories of unskilled labourer, railway worker, mineworker and bricklayer — compared with 10% of other whites. This relatively disadvantaged position of Afrikaner capitalists, petty bourgeoisie and labourers provided a fertile base for their mobilisation in terms of an anti-monopoly and racist Afrikaner nationalist ideology in the 1940s. Such an ideology was able to argue that 'foreign' [i.e. British] capitalism' had dispossessed and 'exploited' all Afrikaners. Its answer was an 'Afrikaner republic' which would be 'free of the golden chains of British imperialism'. The interests of all Afrikaners could then be advanced under a system of 'state controlled private enterprise' through more intensive exploitation of the black population.

By the end of the 1930s, the vast majority of rural Africans were rapidly being proletarianised while the urban African population almost doubled from 1921 to 1939. Significantly, subsistence production in the rural areas upon which the entire structure of the migrant labour system was based, and which nourished the accumulation of capital in South Africa, was rapidly collapsing. Beginning in the 1930s, a series of government commissions warned of acute landlessness, overcrowding, severe soil erosion, the creation of 'desert conditions' and the 'spectre of mass starvation' in the reserves.

This period too had witnessed sharp class struggles and various forms of resistance against proletarianisation were undertaken. By 1920 the first embryonic African trade unions were developing. The formation of the Industrial and Commercial Workers' Union of Africa (ICU) for a while mobilised together both African urban workers and the peasantry on a militant platform. By 1927 the ICU was a powerful political force claiming some 100,000 members. It was destroyed, however, by a combination of repression, internal contradictions and the impact of the depression. Yet out of the ICU emerged new industrial unions which were to mushroom into a strong trade union movement in the 1940s.

During this period, the relatively small African petty bourgeoisie (estimated at just over 60,000 in 1939) was subject to increasing economic and political pressures. In 1936 the old Cape Franchise was abolished — this had reserved the vote for persons of property, irrespective of race. Its extension to the other provinces had long been the thrust of the political demands of the African petty bourgeoisie. Now the social, economic and political position of this class force was increasingly ordered in the same terms as those of African workers. Both were part of a nationally and politically rightless population; both were subject to the intense and brutal forms of oppression and racism generated by South African capitalism. The hitherto cautious and conservative political organisations of the African petty bourgeoisie — and in particular the African National Congress — slowly began to revive after 1936. In the 1940s they began the long process of transforming themselves into mass movements.

The Crisis of Segregation 1940–1948 and the Coming to Power of the Nationalist Party

The Second World War produced a period of very rapid economic growth in South Africa: in particular it saw the massive expansion of industrial production. The gross value of manufacturing output rose by 141% during the period 1940-6. By 1943 the contribution of manufacturing to national income surpassed for the first time that of mining (it had overtaken agriculture in 1930). Increasingly, more mechanised forms of industrial production were encouraged by state industrial policy, and the industrial group consisting of metal products, machinery and equipment emerged as the most important subsector within manufacturing.

These changes also led to a very rapid expansion of the African proletariat. Migrant workers were increasingly cut off from a productive base in the Reserves. This is best seen in census figures: in 1936, 51% of the economically active African population were classified as peasants; by 1946 this had fallen to 17%, declining to 8% in 1951. This reflected the collapse of production in the reserves upon which the migrant labour system was based. Given the rapid expansion of industry, African workers began to enter into semi-skilled and even skilled positions in industry (and to a lesser extent, mining) on a large scale. This development was actively fostered by the United Party government which sought to create a low wage, skilled African workforce whilst simultaneously retraining white workers and shifting them upwards into supervisory positions.

The growth of the African proletariat during the war saw the rapid rise of a militant African trade union movement: by 1945 almost 40% of African industrial workers were unionised. The biggest union group, the Council of Non-European Trade Unions, claimed a membership of 158,000 workers in 119 affiliated unions. The collapse of the ability of reserve production to 'subsidise' the pathetic wages of migrant labour led to fierce wage struggles in all sectors. The militant action of these unions and the rapid rise in strikes produced a steady rise in African industrial wages. The real earnings of African industrial workers rose by almost 50% in the period 1939–48, and the earnings gap between white and black workers closed slightly for the first time.

These continuing struggles by an increasingly organised working class were supplemented by an intensification of class struggle in all areas. In the rural areas of the Transvaal in particular, fierce conflicts erupted over attempts by capitalist farmers to intensify the exploitation of their labour tenants. There were reports of armed clashes, and the South African Air Force was used to quell disturbances in the northern Transvaal. So strong was the resistance of labour tenants that the government was forced to suspend the application of Chapter IV of the 1936 Natives' Land and Trust Act designed to restrict the access to land of labour tenants and so increase their exploitation. Among the urban African petty bourgeoisie a new militancy also developed. The African National Congress adopted for the first time a demand for universal franchise, and slowly began to involve itself in mass organisation and active co-operation with the political organisations of other oppressed groups. Its militant Youth League developed an 'Africanist' ideology which stressed active mass resistance. Following the brutal suppression of the 1946 African mineworkers' strike, even conservative bodies which represented the African petty bourgeoisie, such as the Natives' Representative Council, adopted policies of confrontation with the state.

In this context of heightened class struggle, deep divisions emerged within the capitalist class; these fatally weakened the capacity of the ruling United Party to organise together all elements of capital, and so enabled the Nationalist Party to build against it a new alliance of class forces, and to take power with a narrow parliamentary majority — on a minority of votes cast — in May 1948.

Capitalists were divided primarily over the question of what to do about the disintegrating base of the migrant labour system, and hence the militant trade union struggles which erupted out of this. Industrial capital favoured a policy of labour stabilisation and controlled recognition of African trade unions – positions strongly rejected by mining and agricultural capital. Both these latter sections of the capitalist class experienced intense labour shortages during the war as workers flocked to the cities seeking the higher wages paid in industry. They both favoured a policy of intensified influx control and the continuation of the migrant labour system.

Pricing policy further divided the capitalist class; questions related to the price of agricultural commodities in particular created severe conflicts. The 1937 Marketing Act had instituted a system of single-channel marketing with the aim of guaranteeing relatively high prices to agricultural capitalists. During the war, however, the Smuts government used its powers under this act to keep down the price of food. At the end of the war, mining, industrial, and commercial capitalists favoured the continuation of this policy. Some even agitated for the repeal of the Act. Agricultural capital, on the other hand, demanded state regulations to ensure high prices for its crops.

The unity of the capitalist class was further strained by a range of other issues such as housing, taxation policy etc. Significantly strong differences also emerged over the appropriate response to the organised political demands of the oppressed class forces. Whilst no section of the capitalist class advocated an end to segregation and the introduction of non-racial democracy, or even a move in this direction, within influential intellectual circles of the bourgeoisie, pressure began to mount for the easing of some of the restrictions imposed on the black petty bourgeoisie by segregation. This carried the germ of a political strategy which sought to win political allies for the capitalist class amongst the black petty bourgeoisie, and which divided them from the workers. On the other hand, other sections of the capitalist class favoured an intensification of repression and further segregation of the various race groups.

In this context of heightened class struggle, division within the capitalist class on all the vital issues of the day, and growing international pressure on South Africa through the United Nations (which first condemned segregation practices in 1947), the ruling United Party was unable to maintain its political cohesion. Originally formed in 1934 to organise together all sections of capital (see UP entry p.157), it now tried to appease all conflicting demands and adopted vacillating and extremely contradictory politics. The Nationalist Party was able to seize on this and organise, for the first time, a new political alliance under the banner of a militant Afrikaner nationalist ideology.

In the 1948 elections, the Nationalist Party won support from four central groups, and welded these into a cohesive class alliance. In response to its severe labour shortage and acute pricing problems, and confronted with the vacillating policies of the UP, agricultural capital finally deserted the UP. The Nationalist Party promised farmers rigid influx control measures to stem the efflux of labour from white farms and general control over African workers. The NP also promised a pricing policy which would guarantee a higher rate of profit to agriculture. Whereas the NP had always been the party of agriculture in the Cape Province, following the formation of the United Party in 1934, it was the UP which was the primary agricultural party in the

Transvaal and the Orange Free State. In 1948 these elements finally went over to the NP.

A second new element in the Afrikaner nationalist alliance in 1948, was specific strata of white workers, particularly in the mining, metal and building industries. The rapid influx of African workers into industry, their increasing incorporation in skilled and semi-skilled positions, the rapid rise in African industrial wages and the militancy of the African trade union movement in the period 1942-6, all appeared to threaten the carefully carved out niche of privilege of white labour – particularly the Afrikaner workers who were clustered at the lower end of the job categories reserved for white labour. For much of this period the Labour Party was formally allied to the major party of capital, the ruling United Party. The Labour Party effectively abandoned the fight for the interests of white workers. Dominated by the officials of the highly corrupt and autocratic Mine Workers' Union, the party did nothing to take up the complaints of white workers against the authoritarian and corrupt management of this union. The period 1936-47 saw a major struggle for control of key unions between the craft-dominated established labour movement and petty bourgeois elements of the *Afrikaner Broederbond*. The latter sought to win Afrikaans-speaking workers into support for the Nationalist Party. Following 12 years of bitter and often violent struggle, given the inability of the Labour Party to advance the interests of white labour, these Afrikaner nationalist groups finally won control of certain key unions. By 1948 they had brought crucial strata of white labour into the Afrikaner nationalist alliance on the dual promise of rigid job colour bars to protect their position against the entry of black semi-skilled and skilled labour, and increased welfare measures financed through an attack on monopoly profits. In 1948 the Nationalist Party committed itself to the nationalisation of the gold-mining industry.

The Afrikaner petty bourgeoisie comprised the third element of this 1948 Afrikaner nationalist alliance. This class force had been the principal base of the Nationalist Party since its 'purification' in 1934 (see NP entry, p.138). Threatened by rising mass struggles, the economic advances of the African proletariat, the political demand for integration etc., this petty bourgeoisie gave its support to ever more exclusivist racist policies. It was the moving organisational force in the NP and in the formulation of its apartheid policies for the 1948 election.

Also out of this petty bourgeoisie, emerged the fourth class force organised in the nationalist alliance – small Afrikaner finance, commercial and manufacturing capital. Following the 1934 split in, and reorganisation of, the Nationalist Party, the secret *Afrikaner Broederbond* (see entry p.266), which operated as the political vanguard of the Afrikaner petty bourgeoisie, consciously decided to advance a programme of developing Afrikaner financial commercial and industrial capital. As this so-called 'Economic Movement' developed, particularly after 1939, its strategy of accumulation likewise consciously rested on the welding together of the united forces of all classes of Afrikaans-speakers. The capital for the development of new concerns was to come initially from the surplus profits of agricultural capital (dominated by Afrikaners in all provinces except Natal). The savings and purchasing power of Afrikaner labour and the petty bourgeoisie were likewise to be mobilised to benefit emerging Afrikaner capital. However, the key to the successful consolidation of Afrikaner capital rested on two things: a high rate of profit in agriculture (and hence support for policies which would ensure a stable labour supply and high prices for agriculture) and, secondly, Afrikaner nationalist control over the economic apparatuses of the state. In the 1940s, state economic policy was dominated by the concerns of, and state economic boards etc. virtually controlled by, monopoly capital. The Nationalist Party programme promised this group of aspiring Afrikaner capitalists a far greater measure of state intervention and control to ensure access to key resources and the conditions of accumulation for this capital.

This Afrikaner nationalist alliance thus consolidated under an Afrikaner nationalist ideology which had two major elements. The first was a strongly anti-monopoly rhetoric; and since these monopolies were conceived of in the ideology as 'British', this also took the form of a strong rhetoric against 'imperialism' and a pledge to transform South Africa into a republic. The second element was the policy of apartheid: this drew together the interests of each of these class forces and held out the promise of state policies to resolve their problems. It is, however, important to realise that while apartheid clearly promised to stem what it called 'the flood of natives to the cities', and, more concretely, to push the unemployed back into the reserves and barricade them there behind the pass laws and tighter influx control measures, at no stage did it threaten the labour supply of any section of capital. It held out a scheme for the 'efficient' channeling of labour to sectors where it was needed in the labour market through a system of state labour bureaux; and it promised to deal very firmly with any sign of resistance by the oppressed class forces. As such, it promised to resolve the crisis of segregation and raise the rate of exploitation and profit for all capitals. This is explored in the next essay.

THE APARTHEID ONSLAUGHT 1948–1973

The previous essay analysed how the Nationalist Party came to power through organising an alliance of those forces among the dominant classes and their allies most threatened by the crisis of the 1940s — sections of non-monopoly finance and industrial capital, capitalist agriculture, the Afrikaner petty bourgeoisie and sections of white labour. These class forces were organised in the Nationalist Party under the banner of the anti-monopolist ideology of Afrikaner nationalism (which was, however, differently interpreted by the various class forces). The other critical component of Nationalist Party ideology was the doctrine of apartheid. This held that the solution to the 'racial problems' of South Africa lay in the complete separation of the races in all spheres of life — economic, political and social — and the maintenance of white supremacy.

This essay considers the major state interventions and social transformations during the phases of the apartheid period prior to the crisis of the 1970s. At the outset it is necessary to stress that these cannot be 'explained', as they are in liberal interpretations, as being exclusively or even principally the result of attempts to 'apply' the doctrine of race separation of the ruling party. Equally, they cannot be reduced to attempts to promote the material interests only of those class forces directly represented in the Nationalist Party.

Early Apartheid Measures

Above all, what characterised the apartheid period, was a change in the relationship between the dominant classes as a whole and the dominated classes, a change which permitted an increase in the rate of exploitation and profitability of all capitals. This was brought about by an assault, organised through the state, on the organisations and living standards of the masses. In the first phase of the apartheid period (1948 until the 1960 Sharpeville crisis), the major measures deployed in this offensive (the full range of apartheid laws is discussed on pp.169-78) were:

1) the Suppression of Communism Act of 1950. This Act both outlawed the Communist Party and empowered the Minister of Justice to place restrictions on any person he considered to be engaged in 'communist activities' (extremely broadly defined). Such persons could be confined to a particular magisterial district and/or prevented from carrying out any office or functions and/or prevented from attending meetings. This law was used over the years to attack militants and leaders within both the national liberation movement and workers' and other progressive organisations;

2) a policy described by the Minister of Labour as 'bleeding the black trade unions to death'. Whilst not formally outlawed (so as to avoid international repercussions), every attempt was made to ensure that there was no recognition of, or negotiation with, African unions. Under the Native Labour (Settlement of Disputes) Act of 1953, African unions were specifically excluded from the formal system of industrial relations. The only form of 'consultation' between employers and African workers provided for was through Works and Liaison Committees — bodies wholly under the control of employers. At the same time, strikes by African workers were outlawed and many union officials and militants were restricted under the Suppression of Communism Act;

3) an intensification of controls through the pass laws. Although this had a number of objectives, one effect was to pressurise African proletarians into making themselves available as wage labourers on terms set by employers. (See p. 171).

These and similar measures drove down African wages. The average wages for Africans in secondary industry (the highest paying sector), which had risen under pressure of working-class action by more than 50% in real terms between 1939/40 and 1947/8, actually declined for some years after 1948 and were still stagnating around the 1947/8 level at the end of first phase of the apartheid period.

Table 1.1
Average Annual African Wage Rates in Secondary Industry

	At Current Prices	At Constant (1959/60) Prices
1939/40	96	212
1947/8	210	329
1948/9	220	324
1949/50	222	319
1950/51	234	317
1951/2	252	316
1952/3	266	313
1953/4	278	320
1954/5	292	327
1955/6	300	328
1956/7	308	331
1957/8	316	326
1958/59	330	333

Source: W.F.J. Steenkamp, 'Bantu Wages in South Africa', *South African Journal of Economics* Vol.30, 1962. D. Hobart Houghton, *The South African Economy* (Cape Town, 1976).

This assault on the organisations and living standards of the masses clearly permitted a number of smaller, weaker capitals threatened by the crisis of the 1940s to survive; but it also had other effects. Most importantly it increased the rate of exploitation and general level of profitability of all capitals. This created the conditions for a number of important changes in the patterns of accumulation and class structure.

The generalised increase in profitability led to a large and sustained inflow of foreign investment capital, particularly following the devaluation of British and South African currency in 1949, and consequent increase in the price of gold. In accordance with the general trend in a number of 'more developed' peripheral economies following the Second World War, a substantial part of this foreign investment went into the manufacturing sector. This accelerated the process of transition to monopoly capitalist relations of production, a process which had already begun in a limited way during the war years (see pp.56–7).

It is important to note here that despite the programme of the Nationalist Party, which presented itself as defending 'national interests' against foreign monopolies, the state did not in fact act against the development of monopoly capitalism. The Nationalist regime never implemented any significant anti-monopoly measures, even of the normally ineffective type found in other capitalist countries. The sole piece of monopoly legislation — the Regulation of Monopolistic Conditions Act — was only introduced in 1955. However, this weak act was not intended to curtail monopoly. As the minister responsible explained:

> This is not anti-monopolistic legislation. It is just a bill to regulate monopolistic conditions, and it appears very clearly from this Bill that even though a monopoly exists and even though combines exist they can still be justified in South Africa if they do not have a deleterious effect on the public.

The Act provoked major criticisms from sections of capitalist agriculture and the petty bourgeoisie within the Nationalist Party and a major row within its parliamentary caucus.

The state's role in the transition to monopoly capitalism was not limited to refraining from impeding the process; it also acted positively to encourage it in a number of ways. This was seen, *inter alia*, through the establishment of state bodies such as the Industrial Finance Corporation in the 1950s, and the fostering of a merchant banking sector and 'money market'. Here the state promoted the centralisation of credit and a financial system favourable to monopoly capitalism. More directly, state corporations such as the Industrial Development Corporation encouraged the 'rationalisation' (i.e. amalgamation and merger of firms) in a number of industries. Tariff protection policies (made dependent on a certain level of 'efficiency') and fiscal and taxation policies favourable to efficient firms, all encouraged the trend towards monopoly capitalism.

This did not, however, imply that the Nationalist Party had abandoned its still largely anti-monopoly class base. In addition to the measures which benefitted all capitals and facilitated the transition to monopoly capitalism, a number of specific measures were introduced to advance the particular interests of the class forces represented within the NP.

With respect to Afrikaner capital, a number of interventions were made both to protect Afrikaner firms and to integrate them on favourable terms into the emerging relations of monopoly capitalism. These included handing over 'plum' government contracts to Afrikaner firms, transferring the bank accounts of government departments, local authorities and state corporations to Afrikaner financial institutions, and appointing leading Afrikaner businessmen to a range of official boards where they were able to influence administrative decisions in ways favourable to their interests.

The effects of these measures are well illustrated by a consideration of NP assistance in this early apartheid period to SANLAM, Rembrandt and Volkskas — today respectively the second, fourth and fifth largest conglomerates in South Africa. SANLAM controlled assets in 1981 of over R19,000 million.

In 1948 it was a medium size life assurance and banking group with a small number of industrial subsidiaries and assets of R60 million. It benefited by having pension schemes transferred to it; one of its subsidiaries was able to break into the mining sector through being awarded the contract to supply coal to the state-owned Iron and Steel Corporation.

Rembrandt, in 1981 controlled assets of over R6,000 million. In 1948 it was a modest tobacco and liquor company with assets of only R6 million. It was 'assisted' by the blatant bending of liquor licensing regulations in its favour and against its competitors.

Volkskas controlled assets valued at over R5,000 million in 1981. In 1948 it was a small banking concern dependent on deposits from Afrikaner farmers, workers and petty bourgeoisie, and its assets stood at only R30 million. It was 'assisted' by the transfer to it of bank accounts of government departments, state corporations and Nationalist Party controlled local authorities.

To assist capitalist agriculture a number of steps were taken to resolve the labour crisis which this sector had experienced since the war years. This crisis arose as a consequence of the migration of a large number of former farm labourers from the white-owned farms (where wages and conditions were very poor) to the expanding industrial sector (where wages and conditions were somewhat better).

The Nationalist regime resolved this problem by placing further controls on the movement of black workers from farms to towns. 'Influx control' regulations governing the entry of Africans into towns were tightened up and applied in such a way as to 'redirect' part of the reserve army of labour, which had built up in the cities, to farms. At the same time a labour bureau system was established in the 'white' rural areas to control all movement of black labour out of these zones. Before any African resident in these areas was permitted to leave to seek employment elsewhere, the local labour bureau had to be satisfied that the labour situation in the area was satisfactory from the point of view of local capitalist farmers. After 1954, prison labour was also made available to capitalist farmers at a minimal cost.

Capitalist agriculture was further assisted by a series of measures establishing a controlled agricultural marketing system guaranteeing favourable prices for agricultural commodities. Amendments to the Agricultural Marketing Act set up a number of control boards and capitalist farmers were encouraged to form marketing co-operatives. In sharp contrast to the pattern under the wartime United Party regime, where the Marketing Act was used to hold down the prices of agricultural commodities, in the first years of NP rule the Act was applied so as to enable capitalist farmers to reap the full benefit of rocketing world prices of raw materials during the Korean War. Taking 1947/8 prices as a base of 100, by 1953/4 the index of producers' prices for farm products had risen to 146. In addition the NP implemented taxation and fiscal policies which were extremely favourable to capitalist farmers.

For the benefit of white labour steps were taken to respond to demands which arose in the late 1940s and 1950s from less skilled white industrial workers, for further 'protection' against 'displacement' by cheap black labour.

These demands arose from the fact that the process then underway of drawing more African workers into industry, although generally one in which whites were also being promoted, had in some cases been uneven, with blacks entering particular jobs at a faster rate than whites were promoted. Precisely these demands for 'protective colour bars' had been encouraged by the Nationalist Party in its struggle to build up a mass base. Under the 1951 Native Building Workers Act, a statutory colour bar was applied to the building industry. Section 77 of the 1956 Industrial Conciliation Act, set up an industrial tribunal with powers to recommend the application of legally enforceable job colour bars in any industry or sector (with the exception of agriculture). The Department of Labour, moreover, encouraged the negotiation of racially exclusive closed shop agreements and generally adopted a stance more favourable to the demands of racist trade unions.

However, despite the fears of certain industrial capitalists, the regime did not act to block the employment of blacks in industry, nor to freeze the existing racial division of labour. It continued to encourage the process in which, as monopoly capitalist relations of production were emerging, whites were promoted to supervisory technical and clerical positions. As the Minister of Labour put it in 1951:

> We have a reservoir of unskilled European labour, and my contention is that we should not create a permanent stratum of unskilled European labour. We should lift them out of it. . . . we should take out those unskilled Europeans who are adaptable, who have the necessary aptitude . . . [and] give them training. That is how we get the movement from the unskilled right up to the skilled.

In effect, therefore, the state acted to encourage a process in which the colour bar was constantly floated upwards, whilst at the same time ensuring that due account was taken in the process of the demands of white labour. Thus throughout the period, large numbers of white wage earners were promoted from manual tasks to supervisory, technical and clerical posts.

A number of steps were taken to advance the material and ideological interests of the Afrikaner petty bourgeoisie. Immediately, on taking office for example, the Nationalist regime used existing regulations to remove Asian traders from a number of areas where they were competing with Afrikaner shopkeepers. The 1950 Group Areas Act then provided for the progressive implementation of a comprehensive system of racial zoning with the objective of 'protecting' white business and residential areas against 'incursion' by other racial groups. Another measure to benefit the Afrikaner petty bourgeoisie was their large-scale integration into a range of positions in state departments. In some cases this followed purges of officials associated with the previous United Party regime. Petty bourgeois influence was also evident in a number of other measures intended to 'protect the white race' e.g. the Immorality Amendment Act of 1950 prohibiting sexual relations between whites and members of other population groups.

Finally, a number of steps were taken to ensure that the Nationalist Party regime remained in power: such measures included the removal of so-called coloured voters from the common voters roll, the inclusion of six parliamentary representatives from Namibia's white population, the frequent redrawing of constituency boundaries so as to favour the Nationalist Party, and a virtual purge of the top military commanders, judges and other key state officials — who were replaced by Nationalist Party loyalists.

Response of the Masses: The Crisis of Sharpeville 1960–1963

The apartheid assault on the oppressed masses after 1948 and consequent increased exploitation and oppression was not simply accepted with passivity: it was met by defensive action on a number of fronts, and indeed new forms of mass struggle emerged during this period. In 1949 the African National Congress (ANC) adopted a new radical 'Programme of Action' which set out a policy of mass action, boycotts, strikes and civil disobedience. This was followed in 1952 by the Defiance Campaign: volunteers defied apartheid laws with the objective of clogging up the jails and bringing the enforcement of these laws to a halt.

Although the Defiance Campaign was eventually broken, it did have a number of positive political effects. The ANC itself experienced a massive influx of new members, with total membership rising from 7,000 to over 100,000. The experience of the Defiance Campaign also led to closer co-operation between the ANC and other organisations of the oppressed. The mass movement, in short, emerged from the Defiance Campaign stronger than it went into it. This created the conditions for the establishment of the Congress Alliance and the series of mass mobilising activities culminating in the adoption of the Freedom Charter in 1955 (see ANC entry, p.283).

At the same time, the formation of the South African Congress of Trade Unions (SACTU) in 1955 brought a greater level of unity to the struggle of militant trade unions against attempts to 'bleed them to death' (see SACTU entry, p.329). Protracted women's campaigns against the extension of pass laws (culminating in the famous 1956 march on the Union Buildings in Pretoria) laid the basis for the mass anti-pass campaigns which characterised the last part of the period.

The turning point of this period of struggle and the event which marked the end of the first phase of the apartheid period, was the Sharpeville massacre of 21 March 1960. The police opened fire on a crowd of demonstrators, killing 69 of them. Sharpeville marked a crisis point for the apartheid system. It showed to the world that apartheid was clearly not based on any ideological consent from the oppressed masses and that it was furthermore characterised by generalised 'unrest'.

The massacre itself was followed by the declaration of a state of emergency and the banning of the ANC and Pan Africanist Congress (PAC). This in turn was followed by the formation of *Umkhonto we Sizwe* in 1961 by the ANC and Communist Party underground, and the launching of a sabotage campaign. The regime, in short, was being challenged by armed action and to many, its capacity to survive appeared in doubt.

During the same period — on 31 May 1961 — South Africa became a republic outside the British Commonwealth. This development both appeared to isolate the country within the imperialist chain and, since it was met by the calling of a nation-wide three-day strike, emphasised the general state of 'unrest'. These developments together had the effect of creating a crisis of confidence among foreign investors. Thus, between 1960 and 1963, South Africa experienced a net outflow of foreign capital of between 60% and 134% of the levels of the net inflow recorded in 1958 (smaller net outflows were also recorded in 1959 and 1964, representing respectively the pre-emptive actions of those investors who 'saw the writing on the wall', and the 'lag' following the restoration of 'confidence' in 1963). This had the effect of sharply reducing growth rates and of creating a crisis of capital accumulation in the economy as a whole.

Table 1.2
Net Capital Movements 1958–1972 (R millions)

1958	+	134
1959	–	61
1960	–	180
1961	–	129
1962	–	88
1963	–	80
1964	–	41
1965	–	255
1968	+	459
1971	+	764
1972	+	415

Source: D. Hobart Houghton, *The South African Economy* (Cape Town, 1976, p.292).

The Response of the State and the Dominant Classes: The Second Phase of Apartheid 1963–1973

The resolution of the Sharpeville crisis and the passage into the next phase of the apartheid period (a ten year uninterrupted boom) came about through the combined effects of an intensified assault by the state on the masses and of various activities aimed at 'restoring confidence' by leading elements of the capitalist class.

The Nationalist regime responded to the Sharpeville crisis and the events which followed it by launching a reign of state terror. This aimed both at subduing the masses and at convincing foreign investors that the highly profitable apartheid system was not about to collapse. A range of new 'security' laws provided for increased penalties for 'offences against the state' and detention without trial. Increased powers of banning and restriction were directed against large numbers of militants and activists at all levels of the mass struggle.

The real turning point for the regime and the dominant classes was the arrest of much of the ANC underground leadership at Rivonia in 1963: this practically put an end to the sabotage campaigns. Together with the continuing use of state terror against any incipient sign of popular struggle in the years that followed, it had the effect of considerably dampening down mass action for nearly a decade.

While the apartheid state succeeded in 'restoring order', important forces within the capitalist class acted in other ways to 'rebuild confidence' in South Africa capitalism. One event of decisive importance was the negotiation of an agreement between the Anglo American Corporation and the Engelhard Corporation of the United States. This much publicised deal in which Engelhard made a large investment in Anglo, had the effect of encouraging other foreign investors, and is often seen as the event which marked the restoration of foreign confidence in apartheid capitalism. A further significant action of Anglo American at this time was its practically giving the General Mining and Finance Corporation (later renamed Gencor) to *Federale Mynbou*, the mining subsidiary of Sanlam. This move was intended to bring Afrikaner capital into the gold-mining industry in the hope that this might have a 'moderating' effect on some of the 'extremist' policies of the Nationalist Party.

Through these measures, and in particular the success in subduing the challenge of the oppressed masses, the ruling class created the conditions for nearly a decade of uninterrupted boom from 1963 to 1972. This period was the real golden age of apartheid for those class forces which benefitted from the system. It saw real growth rates of between 6% and 8% per annum. Based on the maintenance of a consistently high level of repression, which kept the wage levels of black workers at a constant low level, the period also saw record profit rates well above the world average. Figures produced by British government sources, for example, show average annual returns on British capital invested in South Africa of between 11% and 12% in the period between 1968 and 1971, compared to average returns on British foreign investments throughout the world of between 9% and 10%.

These conditions of boom and spectacular capital accumulation facilitated a number of further changes in the patterns of accumulation and class structure of South African capitalism. First was the consolidation of monopoly capitalism in all sectors, with the partial exception of agriculture. This was a period of frantic centralisation of capital: through mergers and take-overs, large numbers of individual companies became absorbed into a small number of giant conglomerates. Secondly, this was accompanied by a process of interpenetration of monopoly capital between sectors and across South African/foreign, Afrikaner/non-Afrikaner barriers. Monopolies which had previously been largely confined to the mining sector began acquiring industrial, financial, property and even agricultural interests. Industrial monopolies began buying into mining, finance etc, and a number of banking and insurance giants acquired substantial industrial, mining and agricultural holdings. South African based corporations began entering into joint ventures and agency deals with foreign multinationals and Afrikaner and non-Afrikaner monopolies began making substantial investments in each other.

Through these processes the eight corporations listed below emerged as the dominant forces in the non-state sector of South African capitalism.

Assets controlled in 1981 (R millions):

Anglo American Corporation	27,000
SANLAM	19,000
Barlow Rand	7,000
Rembrandt	6,000
Volkskas	5,536
South African Mutual	5,140
Anglovaal	2,847
South African Breweries	2,600

Together with a small number of foreign multinationals and state corporations such as Iscor and the South African Transport Services, these monopolies today control the vast bulk of all capitalist production, with the partial exception of agriculture and related sectors.

This period, moreover, saw some important changes within capitalist agriculture; most important was a process of considerable mechanisation accompanied by the rapid replacement of the 'labour tenant' system (in which whole families resided on the white farmer's land) by the 'contract labour' system (in which individual workers came from the reserves for a certain period of service). The combined effect of these two processes was to render large numbers of former farm labourers and their families surplus to the requirements of capitalist agriculture. It is estimated that over the decade almost one and a half million such farm labourers were forcibly removed by the state to the Bantustan areas. (See pp.208-99).

A further important consequence of the process of mechanisation of agriculture was a growing differentiation among capitalist farmers. A minority emerged with highly mechanised, profitable agri-businesses with links to major monopolies. This minority increasingly dominated the organisations of capitalist agriculture. By the late 1970s it began to see marketing control measures as a brake on its profitability, and thus to have differences with less mechanised, smaller farmers for whom 'featherbedding' by the state still remained essential.

A further major change which had an impact on the class structure was that of the role of the Bantustans over the period. This is covered in detail in Chapter 4 and an outline only will be given here. In socio-economic terms the role of the Bantustans or reserves began to change after the Second World War. Prior to this their principal role had been to serve as areas for the reproduction of a migrant labour force. After World War II their role increasingly became that of a dumping ground for the 'surplus population' expelled from capitalist production.

This role of the Bantustan areas was particularly consolidated during the decade 1963–73 which saw massive population expulsions to these areas as industry and agriculture underwent rapid mechanisation. It was during this period that South Africa's structural unemployment (currently estimated at nearly three million) began to assume its present proportions.

In addition to this new socio-economic role, the Bantustans also began to assume a political role: this emerged at the end of the 1950s and corresponded with the strategic vision of the Verwoerd regime. In response to the demand for political rights for all, the Bantustans, or 'Homelands' as they were styled, were to be prepared for 'self-government' and eventual 'independence'. The African masses were to be told that political rights would be granted to them but only on a tribal basis in one of the ten so-called ethnic 'homelands'.

Much work to advance this project was done during the 1960s and 1970s: the administrative structures of these areas were remodelled in such a way as to incorporate a small collaborationist petty bourgeoisie. In addition, steps were taken to provide these with some (very limited) opportunities for accumulation. As a result there began to emerge within these areas during this period a small stratum of collaborators tied to, and dependent on, the apartheid regime for their privileges.

The Class Structure and Pattern of Class Relations on the Eve of the Crisis of Apartheid
By the end of the 'golden age' of apartheid when the system stood on the eve of a crisis (1973 onwards), the combined effect of all the processes described was a class structure characterised by the following main features – on the side of the dominant classes and their allies:
1) monopoly capital had been consolidated as the preponderant force within the capitalist class;
2) included among the leading monopolies were a number of Afrikaner con-glomerates – as a class force Afrikaner monopoly capital continued to form part of the Afrikaner nationalist class alliance, but one with increasing strategic differences with other class forces in that alliance, i.e. agricultural capital, the Afrikaner petty bourgeoisie and white labour. These differences were manifested in an intense ideological struggle between *'verligtes'* (moderates) and *'verkramptes'* (reactionaries) in the Nationalist Party;
3) while capitalist agriculture remained characterised by a level of competitive capitalism, divisions had nevertheless emerged between a minority of 'more efficient' capitalist farmers and the others. The former were now beginning to link themselves with some of the positions of monopoly capital;
4) among the Afrikaner petty bourgeoisie, large numbers were integrated into the state bureaucracy; they were highly dependent for their positions on maintaining in power a political organisation committed to a strong state

bureaucracy and to favouring Afrikaners.

5) white wage-earners were overwhelmingly incorporated into clerical super-visory, administrative and technical positions. By 1970, 65% of the white 'economically active' population filled such posts, compared with 45% in 1946. By contrast the number filling manual working-class posts had dropped to 14% compared to 28% in 1946. At the same time the wage gap between white and black workers had steadily widened. In 1970 for example, the average wage paid to white wage-earners in manufacturing was 5.5 times that paid to Africans, whilst in mining the ratio stood at 16.3:1. The overwhelming majority of white wage-earners were clearly identified with capitalism; a considerable number, however, also saw their position as dependent on the rigid maintenance of the existing political-social system, with no concessions to the demands of the oppressed masses.

On the side of the exploited and oppressed masses:

1) the period since the Second World War produced considerable expansion in the size of the urban black proletariat (despite 'influx control' measures). Although figures for the number of proletarians as such are not available, some indication of this emerges from figures for the total recorded urban African population, which rose from 1,794,212 or 23.2% of the total African population in 1946 to 4,368,920 or 29% in 1970. Of the remainder of the recorded African population, 3,664,280 or 24.4% were resident in 'white' rural areas at the time of the 1970 census, whilst 7,003,160 or 46.6% were resident in the Bantustans. The overwhelming majority of the latter were unemployed proletarians, forced by apartheid to live there, rather than peasants reproducing themselves in rural production. In terms of income, black workers in all sectors experienced static or even declining living standards. The average monthly wage paid to African workers in mining was R24 in 1970 — a figure lower in real terms than the wage paid in 1889. In industry, the highest paying sector, monthly wages paid to African workers stood at R70 — or well below the various estimates of the minimum necessary to support a family at minimal nutritional levels.

Moreover, as indicated above, as a consequence of mechanisation, consider-able numbers of African proletarians were facing unemployment;

2) all classes among the black population had been subjected to increased national oppression, with an intensification of discriminatory measures;

3) the black petty bourgeoisie, with the exception of a tiny handful of collaborators in the Bantustans, had great limitations imposed on their prospects of socio-economic 'advance' by apartheid measures (particularly those intended to benefit the white petty bourgeoisie and white labour).

In summary then, South Africa was characterised on the eve of the crisis of apartheid, by a polarisation of class forces along broadly racial lines as well as by acute structural contradictions between the exploiting and oppressing classes on the one hand and the exploited and oppressed masses on the other. At the same time, secondary contradictions were beginning to emerge between the most important sections of the capitalist ruling class and their historic allies. While the boom lasted and repression could still maintain 'social peace', these contradictions remained largely latent. But when the log jam was broken by mass action in the 1970s, an organic crisis erupted which shows little sign of abating. This is discussed in the next essay.

SOUTH AFRICA IN THE 1980s: AN OVERVIEW OF THE PRESENT PHASE OF STRUGGLE

In order to grasp the complexities of the struggle for South Africa in the 1980s, it is important to recognise at the outset that the society is characterised by a dramatically different balance of forces between oppressor and oppressed, to that which existed ten years or so ago. A superficial glance will show a number of things apparently unaltered — for example apartheid still in force, the Nationalist Party still in power. Nonetheless, even only a slightly more thorough examination reveals that the state of the struggle today is vastly different to that at the beginning of the 1970s.

The Mid-1970s Crisis

The apparent political tranquility and the economic boom of the years 1963–73 were discussed in the previous essay. These rested on a balance of forces between oppressor and oppressed established in previous struggles. In this period the initiative lay with the ruling class and its allies whilst the masses had been placed on the defensive.

In the wider southern Africa region, the situation in the early 1970s also favoured the South African ruling class. South Africa was surrounded by a number of so-called 'buffer' states. To the west were the Portuguese colony of Angola and the South African-occupied territory of Namibia. In the centre was the settler ruled British colony of Rhodesia (Zimbabwe), and to the east the Portuguese colony of Mozambique. The economies of all these territories were linked and subordinated to South African capitalism — as suppliers of labour power, raw materials and/or services (e.g. transport), as well as being markets for South African commodities. Moreover, they were all ruled by colonial regimes in close alliance with the South African ruling class. Although these regimes were coming under increasing pressure from liberation struggles in the early 1970s, they were still definitely in power. Other independent territories in the area (particularly Botswana, Lesotho and Swaziland) were virtual economic hostages of South Africa; they were in any case ruled by conservative regimes anxious not to disturb their good relations with South Africa. When the 1970 elections in Lesotho threatened to remove one of these regimes, the South Africans engineered a coup to maintain it in power. The net effect of this balance of forces in the region was that all these territories remained at the disposal of South African capitalism and their ruling groups would not challenge South African hegemony. The South African liberation movement was denied any operational base in the region.

An armed struggle was raging in the region (particularly in the two Portuguese-ruled territories) but it remained hundreds of kilometres from South Africa's borders.

This internal and regional balance of forces began to change dramatically in the following decade through the combined effects of mass action on a number of fronts. Within South Africa itself, the first clear indication that the tide was turning came in the wave of mass strikes which began in Durban at the end of 1972/beginning of 1973 and subsequently spread throughout the country. The immediate cause of these strikes was the sharp rise in the price of wage goods from the late 1960s onwards, caused by the onset of the crisis in the world capitalist economy. Wages for black workers were maintained at extremely low levels and the rising prices put intense pressure on working-class living standards. The Durban strikes, which were largely spontaneous in character, were on such a large scale that the ruling class could not respond to them in its customary manner of arresting the strikers and replacing them with new recruits. Although the police used tear-gas to break up gatherings of strikers, in the event, the state backed away from attempting mass arrests and a number of employers began offering concessions in order to enable production to resume.

The lessons of the Durban strikes — that gains would be made through mass action — were not lost on workers in other areas; the Durban strikes were followed by similar actions elsewhere. Moreover, the need for organisation was soon realised, and it thus was not long before trade union organisations began to emerge. By 1975, black workers were putting forward the demand for the right to organise as well as demands over wages and conditions. A sustained high level of strike action has been maintained ever since (with cyclical fluctuations), whilst the number of black workers organised in trades unions has grown steadily. Both these points are clearly indicated by the statistics shown in Table 1.3.

The advance in popular struggles in the 1970s was not confined to the trade union front: during the late 1960s and early 1970s, other forces among the oppressed — particularly students and sections of the petty bourgeoisie — began to organise and engage in various forms of struggle. In the phase up to and including the Soweto uprising of 1976, the dominant ideological form within which these struggles were conducted was that of Black Consciousness. Black Consciousness was initially developed by, and confined to, university students and student organisations. By 1972, however, its leaders had realised the need to turn to the oppressed communities and develop a mass base. A number of different community and cultural organisations broadly based on Black Consciousness sprang up, and its influence spread rapidly particularly among the youth. (see p.302).

The high point of this phase came in 1976, with the uprisings which began in Soweto and rapidly spread throughout the country. The immediate causes of the 1976 uprising were the pressure being put on black school students by a 'Bantu education' system, itself increasingly in crisis. At one level, the relatively large influx of students into secondary schools since the mid-1960s

Table 1.3
Strikes and Trade Unionism of African Workers 1971–81

	Number of strikes by black workers	*Estimated number of workers involved*	*Estimated Number of black workers organised in trade unions*
1971	69	4,067	
1972	71	8,711	
1973	370	90,000	
1974	384	58,000	
1975	274	22,000	40,000
1976	245	26,000	
1977	90	14,000	
1978	106	13,578	
1979	104	15,000	
1980	207	42,000	100,000
1981	342	85,000	247,000

Source: South Africa Institute of Race Relations, *Survey of Race Relations in South Africa 1981* (Johannesburg, 1982, annual)

coupled with the notorious under-funding of black schools, resulted in students being subjected to more and more overcrowding and worsening conditions of study. At the same time, apartheid ideology (built into the curriculum of Bantu education) was pushed with ever more vigour onto the increasingly assertive and militant black student community. The breaking point was a decree by the Department of Bantu Education that Afrikaans should be the medium of instruction for half the subjects taught in all African secondary schools; the rest is well known. When the students of Soweto responded with a peaceful mass demonstration on 16 June 1976, they were met with a hail of bullets. This provoked further sustained demonstrations and boycotts which spread rapidly to other areas and brought the system of Bantu education to a halt for several months.

The 1976 uprisings had profound effects both on the future course of mass struggles and on the eventual response of the dominant classes. One of the most immediate effects was that large numbers of participants in the 1976 struggles realised that the existing methods of struggle were inadequate. After Soweto, thousands of young people left the country to seek military training. Most of these joined the ANC and its military wing *Umkhonto we Sizwe*. This, plus the changed situation in the region after 1975 (see below), permitted a resurgence of armed struggle within the country on a much greater scale than hitherto. Since the new wave of armed action was launched in 1977, the armed struggle of the ANC has advanced steadily and sometimes spectacularly. In 1977, 11 incidents were reported by the South African media; this rose to 15 in 1978 and by mid-1981 the total number of incidents in the previous four and a half years had reached 62. Between January and

October 1981, 40 actions were reported in the urban areas alone, whilst a study carried out by the 'Terrorism Research Centre' (run by a former member of the Security Police) concluded that in the second half of 1981 an incident occurred on average once every 53.2 hours. Such has been the scale of these operations in recent years that, as a US Central Intelligence Agency report confirmed in 1982, the regime, concerned at the possible impact on the morale of its supporters, adopted a policy of either deliberately not reporting or else playing down a number of incidents. Following the December 1982 ANC attack on the Koeberg nuclear power station, the head of the regime's security police was forced to retract earlier claims that ANC attacks had fallen off in 1982. He now declared that during 1982 there had been more instances of ANC armed action than in any previous year.

These attacks have largely been directed at key economic and strategic installations (mostly in the transport and energy sectors); at military bases and police stations and at symbols of repression (Administration Board offices, courts, the chamber of the President's Council, etc.). They have included some spectacular operations such as the attacks on two SASOL oil-from-coal plants in June 1980 and the Koeberg nuclear power station in December 1982.

In an interview with a Kenyan newspaper in 1982, ANC President, Oliver Tambo, declared that the movement was preparing for more concentrated military engagement with the security forces of the apartheid regime.

Advances in the post-Soweto period were not confined to the armed struggle. The period has also seen important changes in the class character of, and forms and levels of, struggle being waged through legal and semi-legal organisations. Apart from the trade unions, a large number of new community organisations and civic associations, women's, students' and campaign organisations have sprung up since about 1978, whilst many of those existing before have undergone important qualitative changes. Most importantly there has been a definite turn towards the working class; this is not to say that all such organisations are led by the working class; clearly many are not. However, even in the case of those led by other class forces, there is a growing realisation of the need for community-based organisations to address themselves in some way to the concerns of the working class, if they are to mobilise or retain the mass base necessary to advance (see pp.356–66).

The post-Soweto period has also seen an increasing link and growing unity between the different forms and levels of mass struggle. In numerous cases, community organisations have engaged in boycott campaigns in support of striking workers. Armed action has also been directly related to other forms of struggle; perhaps the most notable example was the use of armed action in direct support of a community struggle in the Durban area against increased electricity charges. When the municipal authorities responded to a campaign of withholding payments by cutting off supplies, electricity substations supplying industrial zones and white residential areas were sabotaged by ANC units.

The growing unity has also been evident at another level; the period has –

35

seen a notable decline in the influence of Black Consciousness ideology. While many militants acknowledge its positive mobilising role in the past, they now argue that the time has come to move on. In its place, mass organisations have increasingly adopted a non-racial perspective emphasising unity within a broad-based struggle for democracy, and combining this with class analysis and a critique of capitalist exploitation. This growing unity in action was perhaps most clearly demonstrated in two campaigns in 1981 – one against the Republic Day celebrations and the other against the Indian Council elections. A large number of diverse organisations declared themselves to be struggling for a society based on the principles of the Freedom Charter (the document adopted at the Congress of the People in 1955 and the basic programatic document of the African National Congress (see p.314).

It is also evident in the widespread adoption of ANC slogans and symbols – which led the Minister of Law and Order to lament in 1982, 'the ANC is everywhere'.

To sum up: ten years on from 1972 has seen a heightening of mass struggle on a number of fronts – armed struggle, the trade unions, struggle by community, women's, students', and other organisations. A growing link and greater unity between the different levels and forms of struggle has been forged. Within the country, the balance of forces between oppressor and oppressed has changed dramatically. The Nationalist regime is still in power, apartheid is still in force, more state repression is being mobilised than ever before, but the situation is very different to the early 1970s. The initiative no longer lies exclusively with the dominant classes, and the masses are no longer entirely on the defensive.

Moreover, this change in the internal balance of forces has been accompanied by (and partly been facilitated by) a fundamental change in the regional situation. The advances made by the liberation struggle in the Portuguese colonies provoked a major crisis in Portugal, resulting in the popular coup of 25 April 1974. This was followed by the independence of Mozambique and Angola (under governments formed by the liberation movements) the following year and the humiliating withdrawal of the South African intervention force from Angola. This in turn created a situation in which the settler regime in Zimbabwe (Rhodesia) was placed under increasing pressure until it, too, collapsed in 1980, whilst the struggle in Namibia was able to break out of the Caprivi area to which it was previously confined and advance throughout the northern area.

- In short, apartheid South Africa is no longer surrounded by buffer states and impotent 'economic hostages'. Its neighbours now include states that have committed themselves to socialism and to supporting the liberation struggle both in South Africa itself and in Namibia. Furthermore, it now has to contend with two regional alliances – the Front Line States, which seek to co-ordinate support for liberation struggles, and the Southern African Development Coordination Conference (SADCC) grouping nine independent southern states, whose objective is to reduce South African capitalism's economic stranglehold on the region. All of this together has created a vastly different balance of forces at the regional level.

Response of the State and Dominant Classes

How then have the dominant classes and the apartheid state responded to these changes in the balance of forces at both the internal and regional level? The first point to note is that this changing balance of forces, taking place in the context of, and intimately linked to, an acute economic recession (only partially alleviated by the sharp rise in the gold price in 1979 and 1980), have created a profound crisis for the ruling class. This crisis can broadly be characterised as the collapse of the economic, political and ideological conditions which had hitherto sustained a form of capital accumulation based predominantly on cheap, unskilled black labour. The current crisis for South Africa's ruling class is 'organic' in the sense that structural contradictions have revealed themselves.

The emergence of this organic crisis in the 1970s raised major strategic questions for the ruling class and its historic allies. In general terms the issue was: given the persistent and deep nature of the crisis, should it be responded to by intensified repression and defensive action alone, or should it also be met by formative action? — that is to say, by a strategic shift aiming at the creation of a new balance of forces based on a new historic bloc, through the *restructuring* within limits, of state policies and the terms of ideological discourse.

This issue has divided the capitalist ruling class and its historic allies. Broadly speaking, monopoly capitalist class forces have favoured a strategy aimed at combining increased repression with some attempt to restructure (or in their terms 'reform') some of the institutions of apartheid. Large sections of the white petty bourgeoisie and white labour have been opposed to all attempts to modify 'traditional apartheid', fearing that this is the first step in a process of sacrificing their privileges. These divisions have, moreover, penetrated right into the heart of the governing Nationalist Party.

The character of the Afrikaner nationalist alliance and the numerous measures taken to consolidate the interests of its constituent class forces, were analysed in preceding essays (see pp.23-6). Here it is sufficient to note that with the emergence of this organic crisis in the mid-1970s, the Afrikaner monopolies in effect loosened their links with their traditional class allies in Afrikaner nationalism and began to organise together with non-Afrikaner monopoly capital to effect specific forms of economic and political restructuring. They sought the relaxation of controls on the vertical and horizontal mobility of labour and on the training of labour to permit its more productive utilisation in more capital intensive forms of production. In terms of wider policies aimed at securing the conditions of capitalist rule, the monopolies began to advocate the abolition of certain overt forms of racial discrimination. Neither white labour nor the white petty bourgeoisie supported the initiatives of monopoly capital, and in fact opposed them as a threat to 'the interests of the white man'. The old nationalist class alliance was split; it was unable to sustain its old policies and unable to implement the

37

'reforms' required by the monopolies. The result was a two-year paralysis within the Nationalist Party government under Vorster, 1976–78.

Monopoly capital was not the sole important political force within the power-bloc pushing for reform. The top echelons of the military — well-schooled in current theories of national security and alarmed at the collapse of social and ideological controls over the oppressed masses — also came to see some of these changes as necessary to secure a 'militarily defensible state'. The period after 1976 saw growing political co-operation between monopoly capital and the military: these forces coalesced in a campaign to eliminate the strongest opponent of such 'reform' in the government, the Minister of Information and leader of the Transvaal Nationalist Party, Dr Connie Mulder, in the so-called Information Scandal or Muldergate. This made possible the election of the Minister of Defence, P.W. Botha, as national leader of the Nationalist Party, and hence Prime Minister, in September 1978. The election of Botha marked the consolidation of a new political alliance of monopoly capital and the military as the dominant force within the state. It also created the conditions for the emergence of a series of new initiatives and state policies, both at the internal and regional level. These measures and policies are described together in the ideology of the regime, as its 'Total Strategy'.

Strategic Shifts Embodied in the Total Strategy

As enunciated by the military strategists who first formulated it, the Total Strategy aims to protect 'free enterprise' in South Africa from the 'Marxist threat' and 'total onslaught'. It involves the mobilisation by the military-monopoly alliance of the full range of economic, political, ideological and social-psychological, as well as military, resources of South African capitalism against its perceived enemies. Shorn of its jargon, it puts forward a new constellation of economic, political and ideological policies; these seek to reconstruct the basis for stable capitalist rule in South Africa in such a way as to defuse mass struggles and incorporate specific strata of the oppressed masses into a new 'historical bloc', but within clear limits. The strategic shifts embodied in the Total Strategy have both an internal and regional dimension.

At the internal level, these strategic shifts are seen firstly in state policy towards the black working class. In response to the demands of monopoly capital, specific controls over the vertical and horizontal mobility of black labour have been relaxed. This was concretised in legislation following the 1979 reports of two crucial commissions of enquiry, Wiehahn and Riekert, which changed certain aspects of job reservation and the pass laws. Moreover, the struggles of the independent trade unions for the right to organise forced a concession from the state. New industrial legislation has conceded this right, but in a manner which attempts to incorporate African trade unions into an industrial relations system, which would isolate and contain the work-place struggles of black workers to levels and forms which would not threaten the basic structure of the capitalist system. These policies have been marketed by the regime and its apologists as a 'new dispensation' for black labour. Embodied in this is the assumption that all the 'reasonable' demands of black labour have been met, and that racial discrimination within the industrial relations system has been abolished.

This points to a further significant strategic shift: under the rubric of 'doing away with discrimination' and 'hurtful legislation', the Total Strategy → has sought to make economic and ideological concessions aimed at winning support for capitalism from the burgeoning black petty bourgeoisie, and so to reverse the prevalent tendency in South Africa for this class force to become increasingly hostile not only to the structures of national oppression, but also to capitalism itself. In the words of the influential Johannesburg *Financial Mail*: 'If South Africa is to enter an era of (relative) stability and prosperity, government must ensure that as many people as possible share in that prosperity and find their interests best served by an alliance with capitalism'. Such 'reforms' as have been implemented in this area hold out the possibility of real, though limited, social mobility to the black petty bourgeoisie, and an ideology which stresses movement towards equality of opportunity under the 'free enterprise' system, in opposition to the prospect of 'Marxist tyranny'.

This policy is nevertheless ambiguous: it appears to seek to weaken the national liberation alliance by dividing the nationally oppressed black petty bourgeoisie from the working class; however, it also seeks to utilise the ideological leadership role of the petty bourgeoisie with respect to the working class in order to further limit and contain workers' struggles within the parameters of 'acceptable' trade unionism, and so create broad support amongst all oppressed classes for an ideology of 'free enterprise' and its rigid separation of economic from political struggles.

This ideological offensive around 'the movement away from racial discrimination' contains another crucial aspect: the Botha regime has sought, not very successfully, to win over the historic mass base of Afrikaner nationalism — white labour, the Afrikaner petty bourgeoisie, and smaller farmers — for the necessary 'reforms'. This has involved an insistence that the days of unbridled white domination are over and that 'healthy power-sharing' is necessary if 'the white man' (i.e. capitalism) is to survive. This has involved something of a tightrope act: the regime has sought to persuade groups whose relative privilege has historically rested on intense forms of discrimination and particularly vicious racist ideologies, that the only way in which these privileges can be protected against 'the Marxist threat' is through timely (and minor) concessions. However the 'adapt or die' slogan has not won wide support amongst these class forces.

The consolidation of 'free enterprises' has likewise seen the first moves to reduce state ownership in key productive sectors of the economy. Thus far, this has been limited to the sale of shares in the state-owned oil-from-coal undertaking SASOL (see entry, p.102), but the Botha regime remains pledged to extending this process. This forms part of the aggressive promotion of an ideology of 'free enterprise', which clearly separates the (allegedly positive) economic structures and bases of South African capitalism from the (not so healthy) political apartheid forms, and promises slow reform of the latter.

These 'reforms' further extend to the 'new political dispensation'. In effect, the implementation of the Total Strategy since 1978 has seen a gradual but far-reaching reorganisation of the form of the state. It first involved a reorganisation of the machinery of government, and a slow shift away from a cabinet form of government responsible to a (whites only) elected legislature, to a State Security Council appointed by the Prime Minister. The period 1978–82 saw a marked centralisation of powers in the office of the Prime Minister and a striking militarisation of the administration of the state. Hand in hand with this went the appointment of the President's Council, a body of appointed whites, Indians and coloureds to 'advise' on all matters.

The 1982 report of the President's Council was broadly endorsed by the government and Nationalist Party Congress. It proposed the appointment of an executive president and the establishment of three separate legislatures — white, coloured, and Indian. In effect the president would have dictatorial powers and would not be accountable to the legislatures (see pp.136–7).

This so-called 'de Gaulle option' is explicitly designed to achieve two objectives: firstly, to enable the ruling class to push through reforms, even against strong opposition from class forces in the previous nationalist alliance; secondly, it has the explicit objective of dividing the nationally oppressed groups by incorporating some elements into emasculated representative state apparatuses. This would give the appearance of conceding political rights whilst in reality not providing for the possibility of challenging the existing structure of power.

The growing militarisation of the South African state, points to a further central aspect of the Total Strategy. The 'reforms' introduced have all rested on new forms of intensified repression in response to growing mass struggle — and in particular the development of the armed struggle after 1976. The result has been an insidious escalation of state terror. One significant development here has been the use of the puppet regimes of the Bantustans, and the Ciskei and Venda in particular, to implement crudely vicious attacks on opponents of the apartheid regime. At the same time, however, the growing strength of internal opposition and a strong revulsion in some ruling-class quarters against the more sanguinary aspects of state terror — such as unexplained deaths in detention and the widespread use of torture — has led to a recognition of the need to gain a wider consensus within monopoly capital for its use. This has resulted in an attempt to restructure repressive laws to bring them more into line with the 'norms' in other countries, and to modify some of the practices which have drawn severe international criticism. Changes at this level are distinctly limited, but have been adopted in legislation enacted following the report of the Rabie Commission in 1982 (see p.177).

Finally, the Total Strategy has also involved the development of a number of new policies at the regional level. These are discussed in some detail in the next essay. Here it is sufficient to note that the ultimate objective of regional policy has now been defined as the creation of a 'constellation' of anti-Marxist states politically allied to, and economically tied to, South Africa. A more immediate objective has been to attempt to reduce support among political forces in the region for the liberation struggle.

Perspectives in the Early 1980s

The Total Strategy of the Botha regime has not succeeded in overcoming the organic crisis created for the apartheid system by the growing mass challenge. Above all, it has patently failed in its key objective: to win sufficient black middle class allies with enough influence among the masses to create a new historical bloc capable of stabilising South African capitalism. There are a number of reasons for this. Firstly, the fundamental dependence of the capitalist class on a cheap and highly controlled black labour force plus its need to maintain some level of support from its historic white allies, has meant that concessions offered (particularly at the political level) have been derisory. Secondly, the black middle class which the Total Strategy seeks to draw into a new historical bloc remains subject to the full range of apartheid oppression, whose daily brutality, humiliations and negative effects far outweigh the impact of the meagre concessions thus far offered to the black middle class. Thirdly, the state of the mass struggle is such that the acceptance of incorporation on the terms of the Total Strategy would imply rejection by the masses, or in other words, would require the petty bourgeoisie to abandon its political trump card — its real and potential leadership role with respect to the masses and its ability to use mass struggles to advance its own position.

On the other hand, despite the advances made by mass struggles, few would argue that the oppressed masses now stand poised for an imminent capture of state power. The capitalist ruling class still has substantial resources at its disposal and retains powerful allies. Furthermore, it would be a mistake to conclude that the failure of the Total Strategy to resolve the organic crisis facing the ruling class means that it has had no impact whatsoever on mass struggles.

At one level, organisations of the popular masses are confronted with direct concrete questions of how to respond to particular measures introduced as part of the Total Strategy. For example, the new labour legislation which conceded the right of recognition to trade unions including African members, but which simultaneously sought to impose various controls, has raised a whole series of tactical questions for trade unions. (see p.328). More generally, the greater material concessions being made available to sections of the black petty bourgeoisie have thus far failed to produce the allies necessary to stabilise the rule of the capitalist class. However, they can be expected to produce a greater level of general support for 'free enterprise' among the black petty bourgeoisie.

The conjuncture of the early 1980s thus poses a number of key strategic and tactical questions for the struggles of the oppressed masses. How can this struggle be advanced on all the different fronts, and how can the counter-moves of the ruling class be thwarted? In particular, attempts to divide the oppressed masses and win support for capitalism raises one of the key issues in the liberation struggle: how to ensure forms of organisation, practice and programmes which will on the one hand mobilise all oppressed classes while on the other hand ensuring working class leadership.

On the side of the capitalist ruling class and its historic allies (white petty bourgeoisie and white labour), the conjuncture of the early 1980s likewise poses a series of key strategic and tactical questions. Given their failure to resolve the organic crisis, what further moves should they make? How can they prevent the mass struggle from advancing further? Should they, as some sections of monopoly capital are arguing, offer further concessions (but still within clear limits)? Should they roll back the 'reforms' already made and return to 'traditional' apartheid as advocated by certain petty bourgeois forces? Or should they (as increasingly seems to be the position of the Botha regime) attempt to hold the present ground in the expectation that if no more 'reforms' are granted and the mass struggles can be stalled, a sufficient number of petty bourgeois forces among the oppressed population can be persuaded to settle for what is on offer? This issue can be expected to loom particularly large in the near future as the original package of 'reforms' envisaged in the Total Strategy is rapidly running its course. 1982 saw the last major 'reform' programme – the 'new constitutional dispensation' – being proposed. According to the timetable, 1983 should see legislation to set up the three-chamber parliament and executive presidency, to come into force in 1984.

To conclude: the current situation is one of the intensifying struggle between oppressor and oppressed with key strategic and tactical questions being posed for major class forces on all sides. The objective of this book is to provide the reader with an accessible guide to the major organisations, movements and institutions of the principal class forces engaged in the struggle for South Africa. It hopes to make clear how these different organisations fit into the overall pattern of the struggle and what strategic and tactical positions they are following and/or advocating at the present time. This chapter concludes with an analysis of South African policy at the regional level.

THE APARTHEID STATE IN THE SOUTHERN AFRICAN REGION

The interventions by the apartheid state in the southern African region – in the form of military incursions, assassinations, economic destabilisation, offers of economic 'co-operation' through a 'constellation of states', and proposed land cessions – are a large part of the daily news of the region. Yet they should all also be seen as particular tactics in a relatively coherent regional strategy developed under the Botha regime. In part, this should be understood as an aspect of the Total Strategy of the regime, and in part in the context of the history and specific dynamic of regional policy.

South African Regional Policy from the End of the Second World War to 1978

Historically, all of the countries of the region were subordinated to South African capitalism as labour reserves and/or suppliers of particular raw materials or services (such as transport) as well as providing markets for South African commodities. One long-standing objective of South African regional policy has accordingly been to ensure that these countries continue to fulfill these roles. However, in the era of heightening liberation struggles both in the region and in South Africa itself, the regime has also sought to prevent these countries from providing effective support to liberation movements.

Until the mid-1970s, the fundamental bedrock upon which South Africa's entire regional strategy was constructed, was to reinforce the surrounding 'buffer states' as a protective layer for South Africa itself (see p.32). This involved forging alliances with and supporting neighbouring colonial regimes. After the onset of armed struggle in these countries in the mid-1960s, various forms of military assistance were rendered to their rulers by South Africa.

With respect to other countries in the region, until the mid-1960s South African policy sought the direct incorporation of Botswana, Lesotho and Swaziland (the BLS countries). These so-called High Commission Territories were administered from South Africa by the British High Commissioner (ambassador). Over the years, successive South African regimes called on Britain to transfer the administration of these territories to them, placing these territories under its own direct control. This would also have had the additional ideological advantage of enabling the apartheid regime to present the land division in a 'greater South Africa' as a 'fair' 50:50 instead of the existing 87% white/13% black division. When it became clear with the era of decolonisation that Britain would not accede to these demands, the Verwoerd regime floated a new proposal in 1963 to create a 'commonwealth' of white- and black-ruled southern African States. This was to consist of South Africa as the 'mother country', the 'white-ruled' buffer states and the 'black-ruled' BLS countries plus other states to the north such as Malawi and Zambia.

Although this proposal never succeeded in attracting any of the independent states of the region, economic links continued to be maintained and even deepened over the following decade. Moreover, despite growing international isolation, apartheid South Africa scored a number of important political-diplomatic successes in the region in this period. Perhaps the most important of these was the building up of links with the Banda regime in Malawi, culminating in the establishment of full diplomatic relations and Banda's state visit to South Africa in 1971.

The Mid-1970s Crisis of South African Regional Policy
Such gains gave the illusion that South Africa's fortunes in the region were

advancing throughout the 1960s and early 1970s; in reality, however, the tide was turning. The position of the colonial ruling classes in key buffer states was being undermined by the advancing liberation struggles. This became dramatically evident when the fascist regime in Portugal was overthrown in April 1974 as a direct consequence of the heightening of contradictions within Portugal by the pressures of the colonial wars. This was followed by the independence of Mozambique and Angola in 1975, under governments formed by the liberation movements, Frelimo and the MPLA. Thus, by the end of 1975, the South African ruling class confronted a situation in which two of its key 'buffers' had fallen. The South African invasion of Angola to forestall an MPLA victory had been humiliatingly defeated. Furthermore, at the same time, the Smith regime in Zimbabwe had clearly been forced on to the defensive in large measure due to the facilities made available to Zimbabwean freedom fighters by Frelimo, whilst South Africa's own forces in Namibia were placed under increasing pressure from SWAPO guerrillas now able to operate along the entire 1,000 km. northern border.

The collapse of Portuguese colonialism gave rise to a hasty reformulation of regional strategy by the Vorster regime in 1974; one aspect of this involved a further expansion of military forces (see p.182). Another was the launching of a new diplomatic political initiative known as detente. Orchestrated and conceived by BOSS (see p.193), 'detente' had as its objectives a search for influential allies within the Organization of African Unity. Bribery, secret diplomatic contacts (often arranged through BOSS's contacts in western intelligence services), a visit by Vorster to a number of West African countries, and a meeting with President Kaunda of Zambia, were all used to achieve this end. At the same time some minor internal changes, such as the scrapping of some forms of 'petty apartheid' sought to give credence to 'dialogue' as a viable alternative to 'confrontation'.

Despite some important initial successes, however, the detente initiative began to crumble in the debacle of the South African invasion of Angola in 1975 and its eventual expulsion by MPLA and Cuban forces by March 1976. While there still remained some impetus from Zambia and some other southern African states to maintain dialogue with South Africa, this was finally destroyed by the brutal repression of the Soweto uprising. Not even the most moderate African regime could now afford to be seen to be collaborating with a regime which slaughtered schoolchildren in the streets.

By the end of 1976, then, in addition to its internal crisis, the apartheid regime faced a collapse of its regional policies. Senior military strategists had become more stridently critical of the bases on which regional, as well as other aspects of state security policy, had hitherto been conducted. These criticisms covered both important aspects of the organisation of military interventions in the region and the existing approach towards winning regional allies, which relied on influencing individual 'decision makers' rather than the objective environment within which decisions were made. In the 1977 Defence White Paper — the document in which these generals first publicly laid out and called for the adoption of their Total Strategy — it was argued that mobilisation of economic, political and ideological (psychological) as well as military, resources was necessary to defend and advance the interests of the apartheid state both at the internal and regional levels. More specifically, it identified the need 'to maintain a solid military balance relative to neighbouring states in Southern Africa'. It also called for 'economic action' and 'action in relation to transport services, distribution and telecommunications' to promote 'political and economic collaboration among the states of Southern Africa'.

Total Strategy at the Regional Level

The Botha regime has taken a number of steps to restructure regional policy in important respects. Firstly, the objectives of regional policy have been reformulated: the ultimate objective is now defined as the creation of a 'constellation' of anti-Marxist states, informally allied to, and tied through, a range of joint economic projects to South Africa. More immediately, regional policy seeks to reduce support in the region for the liberation struggle. Secondly, a greater range of resources has been mobilised. This has involved the further build-up of military forces and the development of new types of military capabilities directed at neighbouring states. (See p.184). It has also involved the mobilisation of non-military state departments and 'private' corporations to act in various ways in support of regional policy objectives. The particular co-ordinating mechanism here has been the State Security Council (see p.136).

At the level of the utilisation of economic and other non-military resources, two tactics can be identified. On the one hand certain economic incentives, particularly in the areas of trade, infrastructure and transport services, but more recently also including the offer of land transfers and finance for 'development' projects, have been held out to those states prepared to collaborate with the Pretoria regime. On the other hand, South Africa has used its position of control over existing economic linkages to create economic problems for neighbouring states acting against its perceived interests. The application of these policies has gone through three phases:

The first covers the period from early 1979 until the Zimbabwean elections of February 1980. Economic incentives were offered in the hope of persuading neighbouring states to join a pro-South African 'Constellation of Southern African States' (CONSAS). Although this 'Constellation' was potentially seen as embracing 11 African states 'stretching to the Equator', particular attention was focused on Zimbabwe, Malawi and BLS countries as the essential core members. This first phase came to an end with the defeat of the Muzorewa forces in the Zimbabwe elections, and hopes that a 'blackruled' Zimbabwe would become a key member of the 'Constellation', thus attracting other 'moderate' states.

The second phase ran roughly from February 1980 until mid-1981: it saw the formation of the Southern African Development Coordination Conference (SADCC) on the initiative of the Frontline States and the adhesion of all states in the region to SADCC. These developments confined the field of operation of the various 'constellation' related state apparatuses to the so-called 'inner constellation' embracing South Africa and the 'independent' Bantustans. They also provoked a new set of South African tactics, most importantly, the initiation of destabilisation measures on a fairly generalised level, drawing on both economic and military resources. Such tactics were applied to neighbouring states which were seen to be supporting the liberation struggle or having alliances with the socialist countries. Their application was also partly assisted by the growing support for South African intransigence by the new Reagan regime in the US.

The third phase ran from mid-1981 to the time of writing (December 1982); this phase has seen the selective use of both economic incentives and threats. Specific economic concessions, including land cessions, support for key 'development' projects and the offer of allegedly more efficient transport services have been dangled before the BLS countries, Zambia, and, at times, Zimbabwe, with the threat of economic destabilisation always in the background. These tactics appeared to have the specific, more limited objectives of weakening SADCC alternative strategies and undermining support for the ANC. At the same time they attempted to isolate Mozambique and Angola, both of which are subject to an intensified military and economic onslaught. By the end of 1982, the regime again threatened military intervention against a number of states and attacked ANC residences in Lesotho, killing a number of Lesotho citizens as well.

In addition to general questions of regional strategy there is also the particular question of Namibia. For many years, South Africa stalled negotiations and played for time. However, following the inauguration of the Reagan administration, indications began to emerge that the Botha regime was seriously considering a 'settlement' along the lines of a formula which would ensure that even if a SWAPO government came to power, it would not be able to act in ways which threatened vital South African interests. One key element in such a formula was to be a voting procedure which would guarantee the internal puppet parties at least one third of the seats in the Constituent Assembly – sufficient to block any major constitutional changes. During the first part of 1981, the Botha regime was under strong pressure from domestic monopoly capital and the Reagan administration to 'settle' on these terms. However, strong resistance also emerged from far right forces both within Namibia and South Africa itself, which had a paralysing effect on the regime.

In February 1982 a central prop of any such settlement strategy collapsed when the former president of the puppet Democratic Turnhalle Alliance withdrew from the DTA taking his Ovambo party with him. This reduced the DTA to an alliance of minority parties with no potential mass base. Following this crisis in the internal puppet parties, South Africa's strategy again appears to be to stall; hoping to draw in American support by linking the question of a Namibian settlement to the demands that Cuban troops be withdrawn from Angola, and that Unita be recognised as a party to any ceasefire agreement. Desperate attempts also seem to be being made to try to weld the internal puppet parties into a more coherent bloc. By the end of 1982 the regime appeared to be seeking a military solution to the Namibian question — in line with its even more militaristic stance in the southern African region as a whole.

BIBLIOGRAPHICAL NOTE

a) Dutch and British Colonialism, 1652–1870

Elphick, R., *Kraal and Castle*, New Haven and London, Yale University Press, 1977.

Elphick, R. and Giliomee, H. (eds.), *The Shaping of South African Society 1652–1820*, Cape Town and London, Longman, 1979.

Marks, S. and Atmore, A. (eds.), *Economy and Society in Pre-Industrial South Africa*, London, Longman, 1980.

Parsons, N., *A New History of Southern Africa*, London, Macmillan, 1982.

Wilson, M. and Thompson, L. (eds.), *The Oxford History of South Africa Vol.I*, London, Oxford University Press, 1969.

b) The Segregation Period of Capitalist Development, 1870–1948

Bozolli, B., *The Political Nature of a Ruling Class: Capital and Ideology in South Africa, 1890–1933*, London, Routledge and Kegan Paul, 1981.

Bundy, C., *The Rise and Fall of the South African Peasantry*, London, Heinemann, 1979.

Callinicos, L., *Gold and the Workers*, Johannesburg, Ravan, 1980.

Davies, R., 'The 1922 Strike on the Rand: White Labor and the Political Economy of South Africa', in P. Gutkind, R. Cohen and J. Copans (eds.), *African Labor History Vol.II*, Beverly Hills, Sage, 1978.

Davies, R., *Capital, State and White Labour in South Africa*, Brighton, Harvester, 1979.

Johnstone, F.A., *Class, Race and Gold*, London, Routledge & Kegan Paul, 1976.

Kaplan, D., *Class Conflict, Capital Accumulation and the State: An Historical Analysis of the State in Twentieth Century South Africa*, D. Phil. dissertation, Sussex University, 1977.

Legassick, M., 'The Making of South African "Native Policy" 1903–1923: The Origins of "Segregation" ', Institute of Commonwealth Studies seminar paper, London, 1973.

Legassick, M., 'The Rise of Modern South African Liberalism: Its Assumptions and its Social Base', seminar paper, Afras, Sussex University, 1974.

Legassick, M., 'South Africa: Capital Accumulation and Violence', *Economy and Society*, 3, 3, 1974.

Legassick, M., 'The Analysis of Racism in South Africa: The Case of the Mining Industry', IDEP/UN seminar paper, Dar es Salaam, 1975.

Lerumo, A., *Fifty Fighting Years*, London, Inkululeko Publications, 1972.

Marks, S. and Trapido, S., 'Lord Milner and the South African State', *History Workshop*, 8, 1979.

Morris, M., *The State and the Development of Capitalist Relations in the South African Countryside: A Process of Class Struggle*, D. Phil, Sussex

University, 1979.

Morris, M., 'The Development of Capitalism in South African Agriculture', *Economy & Society*, 5, 3, 1976.

O'Meara, D., 'The 1946 African Mine Workers' Strike and the Political Economy of South Africa', *Journal of Commonwealth and Comparative Politics*, XIII, 2, 1975.

O'Meara, D., *Volkskapitalisme: Class, Capital and Ideology in the Development of Afrikaner Nationalism, 1934-1948*, Cambridge, Cambridge University Press, 1983.

Simons, H.J. and Simons, R.E., *Class and Colour in South Africa, 1850-1950*, Harmondsworth, Penguin, 1969.

van Onselen, C., *Studies in the Social and Economic History of the Witwatersrand, Vols. 1 & 2*, London, Longmans, 1982.

Walshe, P., *The Rise of African Nationalism in South Africa*, London, Hurst, 1970.

Webster, E. (ed.), *Essays in Southern African Labour History*, Johannesburg, Ravan, 1978.

Wolpe, H., 'Capitalism and Cheap Labour Power: From Segregation to Apartheid', *Economy & Society*, 1, 4, 1972.

c) The Consolidation of Apartheid

Greenberg, S., *Race and State in Capitalist Development*, New Haven, Yale University Press, 1980.

Hindson, D., 'The Role of the Labour Bureaux in the South African State's Urban Policy', African Studies Institute, University of the Witwatersrand, 1980.

Kaplan, D., op. cit.

Legassick, M., 'Legislation, Ideology and Economy in Post-1948 South Africa', *Journal of Southern African Studies*, 1, 1, 1974.

Lodge, T., *Black Politics in S.A. since 1945*, Johannesburg, Ravan Press, 1983.

Lewis, D., 'The South African State and African Trade Unions, 1947-1953', mimeo, 1976.

Luckhardt, K. and Wall, B., *Organise . . . or Starve! The History of SACTU*, London, Lawrence & Wishart, 1980.

Morris, M., op. cit., 1979.

Rogers, B., *Divide and Rule: South Africa's Bantustans*, London, IDAF, 1980.

Sachs, A., *Justice in South Africa*, London, Sussex University Press, 1973.

Slovo, J., 'No Middle Road' in B. Davidson, J. Slovo and A. Wilkinson, *Southern Africa: The New Politics of Revolution*, Harmondsworth, Penguin, 1976.

South African Institute of Race Relations, *Survey of Race Relations in South Africa* (annual), Johannesburg, SAIRR.

South African Institute of Race Relations, *Laws Affecting Race Relations in South Africa*, Johannesburg, SAIRR, 1978.

d) The Crisis of the 1970s and the Struggle in the 1980s

CEA, *The Enemy: The S.A. Apartheid State*, Maputo, 1981.

CEA/CEDIMO, 'Is Botha's Total Strategy a Programme of Reform?', *Review of African Political Economy*, 19, 1980.

Davies, R., 'Capital Restructuring and the Modification of the Racial Division of Labour', *Journal of Southern African Studies*, 5, 2, 1979.

Davies, R. and O'Meara, D., 'Issues Raised by South African Strategy', *Review of African Political Economy*, 29, 1983;

Hemson, D., 'Trade Unionism and the Struggle for Liberation in South Africa', *Capital and Class*, 6, 1978.

Institute for Industrial Education, *The Durban Strikes*, Durban, 1974.

Moss, G. 'Total Strategy', *Work in Progress*, 11, 1980.

O'Meara, D., 'Muldergate and the Politics of Afrikaner Nationalism', *Work in Progress*, 22, 1982.

Saul, J. and Gelb, S., *The Crisis in South Africa*, New York, Monthly Review Press, 1981.

Seidman, J., *Facelift Apartheid*, London, IDAF, 1980.

South African Communist Party, 'Forward to Peoples Power – the Challenge Ahead', *African Communist*, 80, 1980.

South African Research Service, *The South African Review*, Johannesburg, Ravan, 1983.

'Focus on Wiehahn', *South African Labour Bulletin*, 5, 2, 1979.

'Focus on Riekart', ibid., 5, 4, 1979.

Wolpe, H., 'Apartheid's Deepening Crisis', *Marxism Today*, 23, 1, 1983.

e) South Africa's Regional Policy

Adam, Y., Davies, R. and Dlamini, S., 'The Struggle for the Future of Southern Africa: The Strategies of CONSAS and SADCC', *Mozambican Studies*, 3, 1981.

Centre of African Studies, 'CONSAS: A New Strategic Offensive by South Africa', *Review of African Political Economy*, 18, 1980.

' "Carrot and Stick" Policy', *Sechaba*, April 1982.

Leys, R. and Tostensen, A., 'Regional Cooperation in Southern Africa', *Review of African Political Economy*, 23, 1982.

Nolutshungu, S., *South Africa in Africa*, Manchester, Manchester University Press, 1975.

Vale, P., 'Pretoria and Southern Africa', in *South African Review*, Ravan Press, 1983.

2. The Capitalist Ruling Class: Major Forces and Economic Organisations

INTRODUCTION

This chapter seeks to identify the major monopoly powers and other significant forces within the contemporary capitalist class in South Africa. The individual entries indicate the power represented by particular corporations or capitalist organisations, the influence they wield in the state and the policies they favour – in short, the role they play in the contemporary struggle for South Africa.

These corporations have, however, emerged from a specific historical process of capitalist accumulation. Moreover, they operate today within a capitalist economy with certain basic structural characteristics forged through the specific historical processes by which South Africa was incorporated into the world capitalist economy. Before focusing on the individual capitalist organisations, it is necessary to understand something of the overall character of the contemporary South African capitalist economy.

The major features of the historical process of accumulation and incorporation of South Africa into the world capitalist economy were outlined in the essays of Chapter 1. Building on these, this introduction consists of two essays. The first presents a brief sectoral analysis of the contemporary South African economy, indicating something of its performance in the last decade. The second deals with the extent of monopolisation of this economy.

South Africa's Capitalist Economy: A Brief Sectoral Analysis[1]

Production per Sector
As a result of the historical processes discussed in Chapter 1, South Africa currently has a capitalist economy characterised by a number of 'advanced' features.

Firstly, its manufacturing sector is large compared with that of other Third World countries. Table 2.1 shows the contribution to the gross domestic product made by the three main productive sectors.

After 1960, the manufacturing sector contributed more than agriculture and mining combined. Put another way, by 1977 manufacturing output constituted 22% of the GDP – compared with 25% in South Korea, 16% in

Table 2.1
Contribution to GDP of Main Productive Sectors for Selected Years
(R millions)

	Agriculture	Mining	Manufacturing
1912	46	72	18
1925	102	80	56
1935	81	126	91
1945	164	192	265
1955	578	470	972
1960	601	684	1,298
1965	760	947	2,225
1970	973	1,207	3,644
1974	1,894	3,193	6,191

Source: D. Hobart Houghton, *The South African Economy* (Cape Town,
1976, p.273)

India, 25% in Britain and 38% in the Federal Republic of Germany. In addition,
it is clear from this table that the manufacturing sector has historically been
the 'dynamic' sector of the economy, with an average annual growth rate in
the 1960–74 boom period of 11.8% at current prices, compared with 11.6% in
mining (on a smaller base) and 8.5% in agriculture.

However, the South African manufacturing sector also displays a number
of 'backward' features; these reflect South Africa's incorporation into the
world capitalist economy as essentially a primary producer. Most important
for present purposes are the following: firstly, the capital goods sector (heavy
machinery and equipment) is small by comparison with that in developed
countries. It does not meet the domestic demand for capital goods, the vast
majority of which have to be imported. Secondly, the manufacturing sector
as a whole does not make a major contribution to export earnings. These two
points emerge clearly from Tables 2.2 and 2.3.

On the side of imports, the most significant point is the increase from 20%
to 53% in a (rising) total of imports, of machinery and transport equipment.
These figures reflect principally the large and growing dependence of the
manufacturing sector on imported capital goods.

On the side of exports, South Africa's balance of payments figures show
the critical importance of gold exports as the major foreign exchange earner,
notwithstanding the growth of other merchandise exports (Table 2.3).

Moreover, within non-gold merchandise exports, manufacturing contributed
only a modest 26% of the total in 1975 (compared with 23% in 1946), whilst
machinery and equipment accounted for less than 6% (compared with less
than 2% in 1946). Amongst these non-gold merchandise exports, by far the
most important are products of the agricultural sector and other mining sectors
Thus the categories of food, beverages, crude materials and animal and
vegetable products accounted for just under 56% of such exports in 1975

Table 2.2
Proportions of Total Imports of Various Categories 1946–1975 (percentages)

Imports	1946	1955	1960	1965	1970	1975
Food, beverages, crude materials, animal and vegetable products	21.5	13.5	12.9	12.4	11.1	10.0
Chemicals and mineral fuels	8.2	14.9	13.8	13.2	12.8	10.5
Manufactured goods	35.1	31.5	28.6	24.3	19.5	18.7
Machinery and transport equipment	19.7	31.8	36.9	42.1	46.7	53.1
Miscellaneous	15.5	8.3	7.8	8.0	9.9	7.7

Source: M. Fransman, *The South African Manufacturing Sector and Economic Sanctions* (Geneva, 1980, p.11).

Table 2.3
Current Account of South African Balance of Payments (R millions)

	1974	1975	1976	1977
Merchandise exports (excluding gold)	3,164	3,653	4,889	6,332
Net gold output	2,565	2,540	2,346	2,795
Service receipts	1,114	1,400	1,505	1,615
Sub-total:	6,843	7,593	8,740	10,742
Merchandise imports	−5,768	−6,742	−7,443	−6,893
Service payments	−2,157	−2,802	−3,023	−3,145
Sub-total:	−7,925	−9,544	−10,466	−10,038
Transfers (net receipts)	84	138	96	47
Balance current account	*−998*	*−1,813*	*−1,660*	*751*

Source: South African Reserve Bank, *Quarterly Bulletin(s)*

(compared with 57% in 1946). If gold exports are included, the products of the primary industries of agriculture and mining accounted for 75% of total merchandise exports in 1975 — a pattern not unlike other Third World countries.

This analysis highlights one critical point: given that the manufacturing sector is fundamentally dependent on imported capital goods, and is not a major earner of foreign exchange, but on the contrary, *a net user of foreign exchange earned by other sectors*, expansion and/or contraction of South Africa's capitalist economy depends on its capacity to import large quantities of capital goods from the developed capitalist world. This, in turn, depends on its receipts of foreign exchange, firstly through the sales of its exports — particularly of minerals, and above all, gold — and secondly the influx of foreign capital.

Thus, apart from the effects of its own internal cycle of upswing and downswing, the South African economy is also critically affected by two externally controlled variables — the gold price, and the level of foreign investment. These operate both positively and negatively. They may ameliorate internally generated downswings or stimulate upswings on the one hand, or act as a brake on accumulation on the other.

The Crisis of the 1970s and the Effects of the Gold Price Rise

With the collapse of the Bretton Woods international financial system in 1971, the price of gold rose rapidly in the 1970s. However, this was an uneven process with dramatic speculative increases followed by sudden slumps. By mid-1980, the gold price reached 15 times its 1970 level in real terms. More recently, it has fallen to about half that 1980 level.

In the period 1973/4 to 1979, the South African economy underwent acute recession with serious balance of payments problems; this was partly precipitated by the world recession. More centrally, however, the recession grew out of contradictions inherent in apartheid capitalism, particularly the political and ideological crisis brought on by growing mass resistance.

The South African boom of the 1960s had been partially financed by large inflows of foreign capital; much of this investment was speculative — made in expectation of future growth. Under conditions of boom, such levels of foreign capital inflow could be sustained; but in terms of the growing post-1973 recession, South Africa had in effect massively overborrowed. This foreign debt was further aggravated by state policy 1974-6 to cover the balance of payments deficit through heavy borrowing abroad.

From 1974 onwards, as the economy plunged into recession and profit rates fell, speculative capital inflows began to dry up and then leave the country. In 1974 there was a net outflow of short-term capital; by 1975 the previous net inflows of long-term capital had also collapsed; by the second quarter of 1976 — i.e. *before* the Soweto uprising — a balance of payments crisis could no longer be averted. The loss of over a quarter of the foreign exchange reserves in three months was then followed by the Soweto uprisings which precipitated a further flight of foreign capital. The financial year 1976/7 saw a total net foreign capital outflow of some R 121 million, compared with a net inflow of R 1,635 million in 1974/5.

By the end of 1977, South African capitalism confronted both a serious financial and balance of payments crisis and an acute political and ideological crisis. A more serious economic collapse was averted only by a combination of severely deflationary economic policies 1976-9 (which lowered real living standards) on the one hand, and firm repression on the other (both of which partially restored 'foreign confidence'). Also significant was the negotiation of loans on extremely unfavourable terms on the Euro-dollar market.

At this point, the rising gold price temporarily rescued South African capitalism. Between 1979 and 1980, the price of gold rose from around $350 an ounce to a high point of over $800 an ounce. This had a number of important effects:

1) it relieved the balance of payments pressures. The sharp deficits of 1973–7 were eliminated despite a large increase in imports. In the first seven months of 1980, South Africa's trade surplus stood at R3,786 million. This was entirely attributable to gold export earnings, as the non-gold account balance was consistently negative;

2) it enabled South Africa to withstand the effects of the sharp rise in the price it had to pay for oil following the overthrow of the Pahlevi regime in Iran, which had left South Africa dependent on the spot market where prices are substantially higher;

3) it led to a sharp rise in revenue: government revenue from gold rose from R114 million in 1970 to R745 million in 1975 to reach R1,703 million in 1979 and R3,838 million in 1980. This had fuelled further large-scale state expenditure in projects such as the Richards Bay port and Sasol 2 and 3. It also permitted a massive acceleration of production by the state armaments producer, Armscor;

4) the additional revenue realised permitted a growth of consumer demand, mainly by wealthier whites, which stimulated productive activity in some sectors;

5) all of these above factors stimulated renewed inflows of foreign capital. The resultant new investment inflow permitted a 'restructuring' of the economy on a more productive (and thus more profitable) basis, primarily in the mining and manufacturing sectors;

6) all of this led to a rise in real GDP from 3.75% in 1979 to 8.5% in 1980 and 4.5% in 1981. In 1980, direct value added by gold-mining accounted for 17% of the GDP. Allowing for the indirect effects of mining spending on other sectors, the *Financial Mail* estimated that in 1980, 26% of expenditure on GDP was generated by the gold-mining industry.

The gold price rise did not, however, resolve the growing unemployment facing the African working class, which stood at over 3 million by the end of 1982. Unemployment in South Africa is caused fundamentally by the structural characteristics of the economy, not by cyclical downswings. In fact the restructuring which took place during the 1980–1 upswing is likely to increase structural unemployment. The 'modernising' of the mining and manufacturing sectors is essentially a process of mechanisation which implied reducing the number of jobs per unit of invested capital.

Neither did the increase in gold revenues result in significant wage increases for the mass of African workers. The state followed very conservative monetary policies. Those wage increases which did occur were largely the result of struggle by an increasingly militant and organised trade union movement (see p.323).

Thus the gold price rise temporarily cushioned the South African capitalist economy from its own contradictions. By the end of 1981, however, speculative increases in the gold price seemed to have receded and it fell sharply to below $400 an ounce. Coupled with the virtual collapse of the world diamond market, increasing profitability problems in industry and agriculture and the worst drought of the century, this has pushed South Africa back into serious recession. A negative growth rate was recorded in 1982 and a further decline is expected in 1983.

Monopoly Capitalism in South Africa[2]

South African capitalism today is monopoly capitalism. Ownership and control of the major means of production in the mining, manufacturing, transport, trade and finance sectors is largely in the hands of a small number of *locally-based* conglomerates (often with vast interests in other countries in the region and further afield), the state corporations, and relatively few foreign-based multinationals. Only the agricultural sector still remains characterised by a significant level of competitive relations — mainly due to the high level of state subsidies and other forms of support to sustain uncompetitive white farmers. However, even here the last ten years have seen a significant penetration by monopolies. Those forms of agriculture based mainly on plantation production were first affected (today 80% of the sugar industry, for example, is controlled by Barlow Rand and Anglo American). A number of monopolies, or their subsidiaries, have extensive cattle ranching interests (Anglo American, SANLAM). Others, such as Rembrandt and South African Breweries, have now integrated direct control over wine production through the mechanism of control of liquor outlets. Moreover, four of the monopolies listed below have very large food divisions. These subsidiaries are beginning to move into agri-business on a significant scale.

The Growth of Monopoly Capitalism in South Africa: A Periodisation
The following phases can be identified:
i) 1896-1920: monopolisation in the mining industry
Monopoly capitalist relations of production first developed in the mining industry. The conditions giving rise to the centralisation of mining capital into six mining houses in the period 1896-1910 are discussed pp.8-9.

ii) 1945-1960: monopoly capitalism in manufacturing
Until the end of the Second World War, the mining industry remained the only sector dominated by monopolies. This situation began to change after 1945 largely as a result of the more general change in centre-periphery relations which took place in the imperialist world economy. Very briefly, prior to World War II, imperialist capital — with few exceptions — had not invested in manufacturing industry outside the advanced capitalist countries. After the war however, it began to invest primarily in consumer goods and import-substitution industries in the periphery. In the case of

South Africa, monopoly capitalist relations of production began to appear in the manufacturing sector through the investments of mainly British multi-nationals in consumer goods industries. Moreover, during the late 1940s and the 1950s, a number of mining companies (with Anglo American in the lead) began either to diversify into industrial production or develop large investments in industrial companies. The coming to power of the Nationalist regime in 1948 did not fundamentally alter these processes (see p.23). However, through giving a large measure of support to 'Afrikaner' capitalist enterprises, the NP government did facilitate their integration into the relations of monopoly capitalism on favourable terms. It also supported the establishment or consolidation of a number of state corporations, thus reinforcing another crucial component of present day South African monopoly capitalism — the state sector.

iii) Post-1960: the consolidation and interpenetration of monopoly capital
The period of the post-Sharpeville 'boom' (1963-73) saw the consolidation of monopoly capitalist relations of production in manufacturing. Some currently important monopolies, such as Barlow Rand, only emerged as such through a process of centralisation and concentration of capital which took place during this period. The other feature of this period was that of inter-penetration; mining monopolies extended their industrial interest to emerge as major industrial producers; finance houses began to move into mining and manufacturing, and manufacturing monopolies into mining, finance and trade. Sectoral differences between capitals accordingly became decreasingly important. Moreover, non-Afrikaner monopolies, Afrikaner monopolies and foreign multinationals all began buying into one another, thus reducing the importance of the different 'national origins' of monopoly capitals. Finally, the more recent period has seen interpenetration between 'private' mono-polies and state corporations.

Current Indices of the Extent of Monopolisation
In 1976 the regime appointed a Commission to inquire into the largely ineffective 1955 Regulation of Monopolistic Conditions Act. The Commission reported in 1977, and its recommendations form the basis of the regime's current 'competition policy'. The Report did not condemn the existence of monopoly *per se*; it argued that the state should intervene to limit the centralisation of capital only where and when this was considered to have 'harmful effects'. In practice, the Competition Board set up after the Commission's report has made few interventions, none of which have altered the trend towards ever greater centralisation of capital in South Africa.

Nevertheless, the Commission concluded that there was 'an exceptionally high degree of concentration of economic power in the major divisions of the South African economy' — a greater degree of concentration in fact than in many other capitalist countries. The basis for reaching this conclusion had many limitations: the Commission made a purely empiricist computation on the basis of industrial census data of the percentage share of total turnover of

differing numbers of firms. The results nevertheless provide a first approxima-
tion of the extent of monopolisation of sectors other than mining (itself
highly monopolised), and agriculture (still relatively competitive). Table 2.4
shows that in all four sectors, 10% of the firms controlled 75% or more of
the market, whilst 25% of the firms controlled approximately 90% in 1972.
Since 1972 the centralisation of capital has progressed enormously.

The data in Table 2.4 does not, however, highlight the fact that the
majority of the largest producing companies in the mining, manufacturing,
trade and transport sectors are controlled by a small number of conglomerates.
Most of these hold shares in one another and are linked through many
interlocking directorships (see Figure 1). Thus, to take just the manufacturing
sector: at first sight the 628 firms (or 5% of the total) or 1,257 firms (10%
of the total) listed in Table 2.4 appear to be a relatively large number.
However, when it is borne in mind that in 1979 the Anglo American Industrial
Corporation had 109 operating industrial subsidiaries and associates, the
Barlow Rand Group 300, *Federale Volksbeleggings* (a SANLAM subsidiary)
323, the Anglovaal Group 72, and South African Breweries 6, a different
picture begins to emerge. In 1979 these five conglomerates together had over
800 operating subsidiaries and associates, and investments in nearly 200
other companies. Along with the Volkskas Bank, the South African Mutual,
the Rembrandt groups (none of which publish data on the full extent of their
holdings), a few multinationals — such as, among others, Ford, General
Motors, Unilever, Shell-BP, British Associated Foods and Lonrho — and
state corporations such as ISCOR (iron and steel), SASOL (oil from coal),
and ARMSCOR (armaments), these monopolies control the vast bulk of the
South African manufacturing sector.

Another way of showing the extent of the economic power of the major
conglomerates is to consider the assets that they control. Table 2.5 shows the
assets in 1981 of mining, manufacturing, construction, trade, transport and
finance companies listed in the *Financial Mail*'s 'Giants League' and 'Top
100', by major conglomerate groups. In 1981, over 70% of the total assets
of the top 138 companies in South Africa were controlled by state
corporations and eight 'private' conglomerates. Together, these eight private
conglomerates controlled assets of R70,895.4 million. The largest, Anglo
American, individually controlled assets in 1981 worth more than the combined
1979 GDPs of the nine member countries of the Southern African Development Coordination Conference (R27,098.5 million as opposed to $17,679
million). It is also worth noting that three of these conglomerates —
SANLAM, Volkskas and Rembrandt — are 'Afrikaner' capital, showing the
degree to which 'Afrikaner' capital became integrated into monopoly capital
after 1948.

Figure 1 shows another important characteristic of present day South
African monopoly capitalism — the high level of interpenetration between
different conglomerates. Each of the eight conglomerates shown in Table 2.4
have shares and/or directorships in at least one other; five have shares and/or
directorships in two or more; three in three or more; while SANLAM has

Table 2.4
Distribution of Turnover in Four Sectors of the South African Economy, 1972

Percentage of firms	Manufacturing		Construction		Wholesale & Retail Trade		Transport	
	Number of firms	% of turnover	Number of firms	% of turnover	Number of firms	% of turnover	Number of firms	% of turnover
5.00	628	63.1	392	63.2	2,679	68.5	465	72.6
10.00	1,257	78.7	785	74.6	5,360	77.0	931	81.5
25.00	3,142	90.3	1,961	87.9	13,404	87.8	1,327	91.0
100.00	12,568	100.00	7,845	100.00	53,623	100.00	9,307	100.00

Source: *Report of the Commission of Inquiry into the Regulation of Monopolistic Conditions Act, 1955* (March 1977).

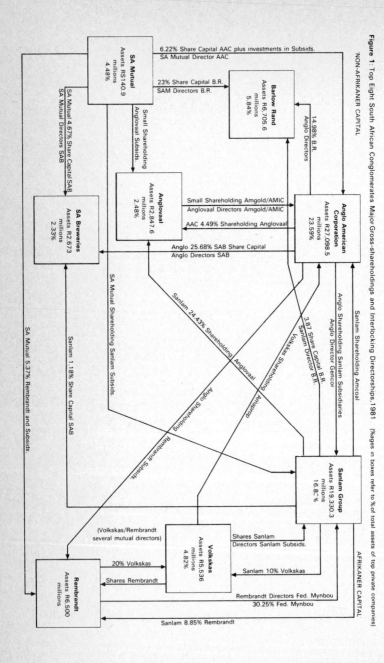

Figure 1: Top Eight South African Conglomerates Major Gross-shareholdings and Interlocking Directorships, 1981. (%ages in boxes refer to % of total assets of top private companies)

shares and/or directorships in six other conglomerates. Furthermore, the pattern of cross-shareholdings and interlocking directorships also extends to foreign-based multinationals and state corporations. For example, Anglo American has shares and/or directorships in the British-owned Barclays Bank and Goldfields; SANLAM in the West German Siemens group, the American Firestone tyre company and the SASOL state corporation; and Anglovaal in Barclays Bank.

Finally, it should be noted that the centralisation and interpenetration of capital in South Africa is a generalised process which extends beyond the consolidation of the eight major conglomerates. As part of this process, a number of powerful, and growing, medium-sized conglomerates have also emerged. Probably the most important of these are the Liberty Life Group and the Kirsch group. These are themselves following aggressive policies of acquisition and consolidation in all sectors of the economy.

In the process, individual operations are effectively being eliminated from the South African economy as conglomerate control is extended over the vast majority of undertakings; this is a continuing process and any analysis of it is bound to date rapidly. Unless otherwise indicated, the figures cited in the entries which follow are based on the 1981 financial year.

Table 2.5
The Centralisation of Capital as Reflected in the *Financial Mail*'s 'Giants League' and 'Top 100' for 1981[a]

Group (i)	Group's total assets (R millions)[b] (ii)	% of total assets of top 138 (iii)	% of total assets of non-state corporations[c] (iv)
1. State corporations:			
SATS	10,186.0		
ESCOM	8,972.8		
SA Reserve Bank	7,692.6		
ISCOR	3,457.0		
SA Post Office	3,190.6		
Landbank	2,691.7		
Industrial Development Corp.	2,006.8		
SASOL	1,232.5		
ARMSCOR	1,156.9		
Safmarine	618.6		
Dorbyl	354.0		
Metkor	116.2		
Sub-total:	41,675.7	26.61	

2. Anglo American group:

Anglo	9,802.0		
De Beers	5,603.8		
AMGOLD	2,537.0		
JCI	1,241.9		
AMIC	1,168.2		
AECI	1,103.6		
Vaal Reefs	968.4		
Driefontein Cons.	672.9		
De Beers Indus.	590.8		
AMCOAL	555.4		
Hullets	552.4		
Western Deep	552.1		
Tongaat	526.1		
Hiveld	475.4		
LTA	214.3		
Toncoro	166.9		
Argus	133.4		
McCarthy	131.5		
Cullinan	102.4		
Group total:	27,098.5	17.30	23.57

3. SANLAM group:

Bankorp	4,622.4		
Gencor	4,091.8		
Sanlam	3,073.0		
Trustbank	2,575.7		
Saambou	967.2		
FVB	812.3		
Sentrachem	745.5		
Boland Bank	578.1		
Sappi	455.9		
Greatermans[d]	279.7		
Fedfood	225.2		
Abercom	174.0		
Kanhym	155.7		
D & H	154.7		
SA Druggists	129.3		
Karoo	115.2		
Kohler	94.9		
Trek	79.7		
Group total	19,330.3	12.34	16.82

4. Barlow Rand:

Barlow's	3,668.6
C.G. Smith	940.1

TC Lands	704.8		
P.P. Cement	338.8		
Nampak	306.1		
Plate Glass	273.8		
Romatex	222.1		
Reunet	128.9		
Plevans	102.4		
Group total:	6,685.6	4.27	5.82
5. Volkskas group:			
Volkskas	4,770.0		
L & G Volkskas	632.3		
Bonuskor	133.7		
Group total:	5,536.0	3.53	4.82
6. SA Mutual:			
SA Mutual	4,298.5		
Tiger Oats }[e]	601.1		
ICS	241.3		
Group total:	5,140.9	3.28	4.47
7. Rembrandt group:[b]			
Remgro	1,221.9		
Kaapwyn	341.6		
Group total:	1,563.5	1.00	1.36
8. Anglovaal group:			
Anglovaal	1,249.8		
ATI	666.6		
Anglo Alpha	366.1		
South Atlantic	199.8		
Grinaker	158.0		
I & J	111.9		
Consol	95.4		
Group total:	2,847.6	1.82	2.48
9. South African Breweries:			
SAB	1,507.6		
OK Bazaars	464.0		
Southern Suns	205.4		
Edgars	204.7		
Afcol	168.6		
Amrel	122.7		
Group total:	2,673.0	1.71	2.32

Sub-total: Top eight private conglomerates	70,875.4	45.25	61.66
10. Other Building Societies:			
United	3,769.7		
SA Perm	2,961.3		
Allied	2,189.5		
Natal	1,189.2		
Sub-total:	10,109.7	6.45	8.79
11. British-controlled multinationals (listed companies only):			
Barclays Bank	8,694.8		
Standard Bank	6,459.0		
Goldfields South Africa	1,649.1		
Prudential	727.5		
Premier Milling	510.7		
Stewart and Lloyds	276.7		
Afrox	264.1		
Blue Circle Cement	212.1		
Metal Box	189.5		
Sub-total:	18,983.5	12.13	16.52
12. Others (46 companies)	14,974.5	9.56	13.03
Grand total:	*156,618.8*	*100.00*	*100.00*

Notes:

a As reported in *Financial Mail* (annual) Special Survey on Top Companies, 30 April 1982. This includes 138 top state, and listed and unlisted companies in all sectors. Total assets shown in this Survey = R 156,618.8 million. The groups and companies listed in this table each calculate their assets according to different criteria, and employ various accounting methods. It is therefore impossible to apply a standard procedure to each. To arrive at the total assets of each group we have added the total listed assets for each component company. Inevitably this has involved a degree of double counting.

b The total assets listed in column (ii) include *only* assets of companies listed in the *Financial Mail*'s 'Top 100' and 'Giants League' tables, and not other assets controlled by the groups. Thus, we have ranked Rembrandt at number 7 among the monopolies, although according to assets shown in column (ii) it should appear as number 9 For various reasons to do with the mode of classification adopted by the *Financial Mail*, a very substantial part of the assets of the Rembrant group are not included in these tables (see Rembrandt entry).

c Total assets of non-state corporations: R 114,963.1 million.

ᵈDuring 1982, Greatermans was taken over by the Kirsch group, and its name changed to Checkers.

ᵉDuring 1982, Tiger Oats and ICS were acquired by Barlow Rand. In return, SA Mutual substantially increased its stake in Barlow Rand (see p.76).

THE MAJOR DOMESTIC PRIVATE MONOPOLIES

The Anglo American Corporation[3]

The largest and most powerful South African-based conglomerate and multinational, Anglo owns 69% of the total capital invested in the South African mining industry. It has vast industrial holdings and is a prime monopoly force in agriculture. The Corporation also has a major presence in the South African insurance, finance, property, press and service sectors. It has extensive interests in all SADCC countries. In 1981 Anglo became the single largest foreign investor in the United States, and it has substantial interests in many European and 'Third World' countries.

Anglo American and its immediate past chairman, Harry Oppenheimer, have long been regarded as the leading liberal monopoly force in South African politics. The group plays a key role in the 'reform' initiatives of monopoly capital, embodied in the Total Strategy.

In 1981 Anglo controlled total assets of some R 27 billion in South Africa alone. This represents almost one quarter of the total assets controlled by South Africa's 'Top 100' non-state corporations. The Anglo group has some 831 South African-based subsidiaries and associates, and 186 subsidiary and associated companies outside South Africa. It also has investments in a further 505 companies; these include substantial investments in other South African monopolies. Thus, Anglo owns 12.7% of the share capital of Barlow Rand; 18.55% of South African Breweries; 17.8% of Barclays National Bank; 8.55% of Gencor (SANLAM's mining subsidiary and the second biggest mining finance house); 1.84% of Nedbank and 28% of the Goldfields mining house (which Anglo is rumoured to be trying to take over).

Historical Development

The origins of the Anglo American Corporation date back to the beginning of the century when the Oppenheimer family took over a small diamond trading company, Dukelsbuhler. The company's phenomenal growth was largely due to its strategy of buying into particularly profitable ventures before their potential was generally recognised. In 1905 Dukelsbuhler bought into and eventually took over two companies holding mineral rights in the far East Rand; by 1914, the far East Rand mines were the most profitable in South Africa. In 1917, in order to expand its operations in the area, the company established itself as the Anglo American Corporation under the chairmanship of Ernest Oppenheimer.

The First World War provided a further opportunity for expansion. At the end of the war the large German diamond interests in Namibia were put up for sale to British companies. With diamond connections via Dukelsbuhler and investment funds available from its lucrative gold-mining operations, Anglo bought up most of the German fields in 1920. It then set out to acquire all diamond interests not controlled by De Beers and eventually took over De Beers itself in 1929. Its control of the diamond industry gave Anglo a unique support and liquidity during downswings in the gold-mining industry. This enabled it to stay ahead of the other mining houses.

In the 1930s Anglo opened up the rich gold-field on the far West Rand. It also made large investments in the Zambian copper mines and in various Zimbabwean mines. After South Africa abandoned the gold standard in 1933, the prices of gold, diamonds and copper all rose rapidly. This provided the Corporation with a base to secure control of half the mines (including six of the seven most profitable) on the new and very rich Orange Free State gold-fields after World War II. When these mines came into operation, Anglo's dominant position in the mining industry was beyond doubt. Today it owns 69% of the total invested capital in South African mining; it controls one other mining house (JCI), owns 29% of Goldfields and 8.55% of Gencor. Through its substantial holdings in Barlow Rand, it also shares in the profits of Rand Mines.

Until 1945, Anglo remained a mining and finance concern operating almost entirely in southern Africa. Its diversification into other activities and out of the southern African region began after the Second World War. The Corporation's industrial subsidiary, AMIC, currently has 109 South African subsidiaries and associates and 61 such subsidiary and associated companies outside South Africa. During the 1960s, Anglo moved into the insurance sector; it now controls the large Eagle Star group (renamed Anglo American Life in 1981) as well as a large number of property and service activities. In conformity with the general trend towards interpenetration, during this period Anglo began to invest in, and enter into, joint ventures with both foreign multinationals and 'Afrikaner' capital. The most important of the latter was Anglo's assistance in 1963 to the SANLAM subsidiary (*Federale Mynbou*) to buy up, at a discount, the ailing General Mining and Finance Corporation (now renamed Gencor, and the second biggest mining house). This was one of the several actions taken by the Corporation to arrest the 'crisis of confidence' confronting South African capitalism following the Sharpeville massacre.

Anglo's movement outside the southern African region began in a major way in the late 1960s. Until then, its links with capital outside the region were mainly in the form of external investments in Anglo activities in the region. One such link was with the Englehard Corporation of the United States — one of the world's largest refiners and fabricators of precious metals. In fact, Oppenheimer's successful negotiation of an investment deal with Englehard in 1963 heralded the 'restoration of foreign confidence' in South African capitalism after the Sharpeville crisis. Between 1969 and 1972, a complicated share deal in fact gave Anglo control of Englehards: from this base it began moving into American mining, oil and manufacturing industries. In 1970 it set up an offshore holding company (MINORCO) based in Bermuda. This corporation now serves as the principal vehicle for Anglo's investments in the US. By 1981, through MINORCO, Anglo had become the largest single foreign investor in the United States. Its sales of approximately $15 billion in that year beat into second place Royal Dutch Shell (in which Anglo retains an interest). A further important acquisition in the late 1960s was Anglo's take over of Charter Consolidated, with interests in Australia, Canada and a number of African countries. As a British registered company, Charter gave Anglo a convenient entrée into parts of the world where, as a South African company, Anglo might have faced difficulties.

Political Role

The Anglo American Corporation and its recently retired chairman, Harry Oppenheimer, are perhaps the best known exponents within the capitalist class of liberal 'reformist' politics. With its exceptional profitability, Anglo is more able than most to afford concessions. In the late 1940s and early 1950s, Oppenheimer was himself a United Party MP. When the Progressive Party split from the United Party in 1959 (see p.146), Oppenheimer supported the 'Progs' and became the party's chief financial backer. Links between Anglo and the PFP remain close. Oppenheimer's former son-in-law, Gordon Waddell, a key Anglo director, was a 'Prog' MP, 1974–7, and National Treasurer of the party, 1978–9. As such he played a key role in rebuilding its financial links with big business. Zac de Beer, a long time 'Prog' official and MP, is now Anglo's executive director. Alex Borraine, now a PFP MP, was labour consultant to the Corporation, whilst the current holder of that post, Bobby Godsell, is a former chairman of the 'Young Progressives'.

Given the political weakness of the 'Progs', Anglo and Oppenheimer have also been prominent in extra-parliamentary political activities. After the 1976 Soweto uprising, and together with Anton Rupert of Rembrandt (see p.82), Oppenheimer set up the Urban Foundation (see p.122). More recently, again in association with Rupert, Anglo helped establish the Small Business Development Corporation and the Labour Intensive Industries Trust — both designed to ease unemployment. The Anglo Chairman's Fund has also financed a number of educational and training programmes for blacks. Anglo has been a leading advocate of, and participant in, the various government-business 'dialogues' organised by the Botha regime. With the 1982 split in the Nationalist Party (see p.145), it appears that links between Anglo and the Botha regime have become even closer, and that Anglo has effectively been

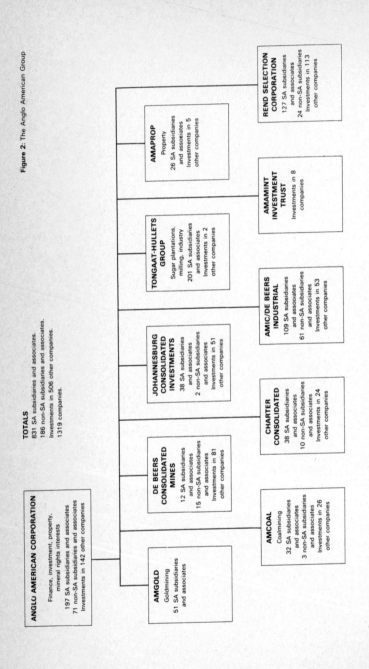

Figure 2: The Anglo American Group

co-opted as a crucial element in the monopoly capital/military alliance put together under the Botha regime. In a 1980 interview with *Business International*, Oppenheimer argued that while he would ideally prefer a PFP government, in practice he would work for changes acceptable to the 'reasonable people' (sic) in the Nationalist Party.

Anglo's vision of its desired social and economic changes in South Africa were spelled out in Oppenheimer's 1981 Chairman's Report. He argued that capitalist development in South Africa necessitated raising what he termed the 'capital intensity' of production. This would lead to an increased demand for more trained manpower which would increasingly have to come from the black population. Hence there was need for more education and training programmes for blacks. On the other hand he realised that greater 'capital intensity' would create more unemployment which could fuel 'black unrest'. To counter this, he advocated the establishment of small businesses and 'labour intensive' industries in the 'rural areas'. These would also create more opportunities for black entrepreneurs to become involved in the 'free enterprise' system.

Anglo's programme for making South Africa safe for capitalism does not differ markedly from the strategic thinking underlying the Total Strategy (see p.38). The training programmes are intended to optimise the conditions for capital accumulation, and the 'decentralisation' projects to ward off the struggles of the unemployed and create a supportive black middle class. No part of this programme would abolish any of the fundamental institutions of the apartheid system of capitalist exploitation and national oppression. The Corporation is on record as being in favour of modifications to, but not the abolition of, the migrant labour system. Oppenheimer is not in favour of equal political rights for all, but only of some form of 'power sharing' on a 'fair and acceptable basis'. Even the *Financial Mail* commented that Anglo's proposals to create low wage, labour intensive industries in the rural areas would necessarily imply 'an acceptance of continued influx control'.

The Corporation generally favours a paternalist approach to industrial relations, involving 'improvements' from above to forestall union organisation by its employees. Within the mining industry it has acted as a proponent of regular 'Social Audits' aimed at identifying workers' grievances in the hope of improving management-labour relations. However, Anglo subsidiaries have often been among the most reluctant of South African employers to negotiate with established democratic unions. Thus, one Anglo subsidiary, Scaw Metals, was identified as one of the most forceful advocates within SEIFSA of refusing to deal with any union which did not accept the industrial council system.

The differences between the Corporation and the Botha regime arise over the rate, pace, and precise extent to which changes should be made to secondary aspects of the apartheid system. The Corporation fears that the need of the Botha regime to respond to the demands and prejudices of white petty bourgeoisie forces leads it to make 'reforms' too slowly. It accepts the regime's bona fides in wanting 'reform' but argues that their slow implementation has 'increased the impatience' of blacks. 'Nothing is more dangerous than half-hearted reform', warns Oppenheimer in his 1981 report.

Important leaders:
    Retired Chairman and major shareholder: Harry Oppenheimer (who remains Chairman of De Beers)
    Chairman: Gavin Relly
    Vice-chairmen: Nicholas Oppenheimer (son of Harry and probable eventual Chairman)
    Gordon Waddell (Harry's former son-in-law)
Other key directors:
    Dennis Etheredge
    J. Ogilvie Thompson
    Dr Zac de Beer.

SANLAM (South African National Life Assurance Company)[4]

> The leading Afrikaner insurance and financial conglomerate, SANLAM is the second largest concentration of non-state economic power in South Africa. Its economic weight apart, the close historical and continuing links between SANLAM and key factions of the ruling Nationalist Party, make the group a crucial force in South African politics.

Structure of the Group

An accurate estimation of the extent of SANLAM's interests is difficult to make, as the group functions primarily as an investment house. Its declared total assets stood at R 3,100 million in September 1981. However, this figure appears to include only assets directly owned by the parent company and does not begin to reflect the range of the group's interests, nor extent of its influence. In particular, it does not include the asset of the groups which SANLAM controls through majority shareholdings. Thus, for example, the Gencor mining finance house is controlled by SANLAM, yet is listed in the *Financial Mail*'s tables as having a greater assets base than the parent company. Thus, the total assets of the groups and companies over which SANLAM exercised effective control in 1981 stood at R19,330.3 million. Furthermore, this figure does not reflect the influence SANLAM wields over other large companies in which it, or various of its subsidiaries, hold significant minority shareholdings. These include: 18% of the holding company of the Anglovaal conglomerate (whose own assets stood at R 1,249.8 million in 1981); 10% of the Volkskas banking groups with assets of R 4,770.0 million; 8% of the Rembrandt group with assets of over R2,000 million and 3.87% of the share capital of Barlow Rand, with assets of R 6,685.6 million.

SANLAM's vast interests are spread over all sectors of the economy and the group exercises a prominent influence in virtually every type of economic activity in South Africa. One of its major subsidiaries, *Federale Volksbeleggings* (FVB) was the second largest single non-state industrial conglomerate in South Africa after Barlow Rand in 1981 — the FVB chairman sits on the Barlow Rand Board. FVB held assets of R 1,400 million in 1980. Its interests include, *inter alia*: chemicals, heavy manufacturing and construction, furniture, motor works, tyres, electronics, clothing, property and retailing. SANLAM controls South Africa's second major mining house, Gencor, which itself has huge gold, coal, uranium and other strategic mineral interests, together with substantial holdings in forestry and agri-business. SANLAM's Bankorp subsidiary provides a full range of banking services through a number of different banks. SANLAM also holds 10% of the Volkskas banking conglomerate (which it controlled between 1974 and 1977), and 30% of the French Bank of South Africa. The group also has extensive interests in property, printing (through the *Nasionale Pers* group — see p.410) and an almost total monopoly of cinema outlets.

SANLAM also has heavy investments in the state sector: by November 1981 these stood at more than R 1,000 million. Reflecting this, SANLAM directors sit on the boards of a number of state undertakings, including SASOL, the Industrial Development Corporation and the South African Reserve Bank. In the past, senior SANLAM executives have been appointed to head key state undertakings. Thus Dr P.E. Rousseau moved from FVB to head SASOL in the 1950s (and on retirement was appointed Chairman of FVB), and the former Managing Director of SANLAM's mining interests holding company, T.F. Muller of *Federale Mynbou*, was named chairman of ISCOR (see p.101).

The parent company SANLAM is itself South Africa's second largest life assurance company, just behind the SA Mutual. In 1981 it had 1.2 million policy holders and a total premium income of R 938 million. This is the real financial base of the group. SANLAM's predominance reflects a crucial shift in the finance sector since the end of the Second World War — the emergence of insurance companies as a major source of investment capital and other forms of finance for all sectors of the economy. Through its life policies and various subsidiaries, especially Santambank, SANLAM is one of the leading non-state sources of agricultural credit.

SANLAM itself is what is known as a 'mutual' company. This means that in law it is owned not by shareholders, but by the holders of its life assurance policies. In effect this gives its directors total control of the company and means that no other monopolies can buy shares in SANLAM and so gain a foothold in the group's holding company. Thus, though directors of other monopolies such as Anglo American, Rembrandt and Volkskas sit on the boards of SANLAM subsidiaries, they are not represented on the board of SANLAM itself. This gives SANLAM greater independence than more conventionally structured monopolies. By contrast, SANLAM directors sit on the main boards of at least two other major South African monopolies (Barlow Rand and Anglovaal) and on the boards of subsidiary companies of many others.

This absence of control over SANLAM and its subsidiaries by minority shareholders led to a protracted and bitter public quarrel between SANLAM and Rembrandt in 1982. SANLAM policy demands absolute control over its subsidiaries and their directors. A disagreement between the then SANLAM Chairman, Andries Wassenaar and Gencor Chairman (and SANLAM Vice-chairman) W.J. de Villiers, over a Gencor investment in a company managed by Wassenaar's son, led to a move by SANLAM to oust de Villiers from the Gencor chair. This was intensely resisted by Rembrandt which has a large minority stake in Gencor (and which had in fact financed Gencor's takeover of the then Union Corporation in 1975 — which had made Gencor the second largest mining house). An intense, public dispute erupted over the rights and role of minority directors in a SANLAM subsidiary. This in effect pitted against each other the two most powerful Afrikaner monopolies, SANLAM and Rembrandt. Observers commented that the public and vitriolic nature of the quarrel (the Rembrandt annual report for 1982 uses the term 'abominable lie') was further evidence of the collapse of the solidity of Afrikaner nationalism. Equally importantly, the dispute reflected and further crystallised growing concern by other monopolies over their lack of control over 'institutional investors', and in particular the two giant insurance companies SANLAM and South African Mutual, whose status as mutual companies renders them non-accountable to other monopolies.

History and Political Position

SANLAM's close links with both state undertakings and the financing of agriculture, reflect its historic position as a crucial component of organised Afrikaner nationalism. The company was formed in 1918 by the same individuals who formed the Cape Nationalist Party three years earlier. From that date to this, SANLAM has been the major influence over the Cape Nationalist Party, giving it for many years both a different class basis and political perspective to the Nationalist Parties of the Transvaal and Orange Free State (see p.139).

SANLAM's early strategy of growth was to fasten on to the surplus profits and revenue of agricultural capital, centralise these under its control through life assurance policies, and so convert hoarded money into productive capital. It grew slowly in its early years. In 1939, in wary collaboration with the *Afrikaner Broederbond* (see p.266), SANLAM organised what came to be known as the 'Afrikaner economic movement'. This was the organised attempt to use nationalist ideology to mobilise the savings and all forms of loose money in the hands of Afrikaans-speakers of all classes, in a project to create a class of Afrikaner financial, industrial and commercial capitalists. This economic movement created the key SANLAM subsidiary, FVB, as its official invest-ment house. During the 1940s, while the Nationalist Party was still a deeply divided and relatively small opposition party, the economic movement first organised the alliance of class forces which the Nationalist Party was able to mobilise politically in 1948 and so come to power. In this period too, were formed the other crucial SANLAM subsidiaries, Saambou and Bonuskor (the latter sold later to Volkskas). But SANLAM was unquestionably the major beneficiary of the economic movement. The assets under its control rose from R 5 million in 1939 to R 30 million in 1948. The dominance of the economic movement by SANLAM led to great resistance by the more petty bourgeois elements in the north, and accusations that 'Cape Finance Power' was taking over Afrikaner nationalism.

But the real growth of SANLAM began with the Nationalist Party assumption of office in 1948. Through various measures such as favourable pricing policies, the award of contracts to Afrikaner companies, the transfer of government and local authority finances to Afrikaner finance companies etc, the NP government fostered the very rapid development of certain sectors of Afrikaner capital during the 1950s and 1960s. SANLAM's mining subsidiary, *Federale Mynbou*, was the direct recipient of state contracts for coal in the early 1950s. This gave it a growth impetus and a base to enter the mining of other minerals. So successful were these NP policies, that by 1960 SANLAM was no longer dependent on agriculture for its own accumulation. This was reflected in its own increasingly independent political positions.

This state support, however, is not enough to explain the very rapid growth of SANLAM into the second most powerful group in the South African economy by the mid-1970s. The most important explanation lies in the intense interpenetration of capital in South Africa which began in the 1950s, and took off in the 1960s. SANLAM was perhaps the single major beneficiary of this process. Following the flight of foreign capital from South Africa after the 1960 Sharpeville massacre, SANLAM took the opportunity to invest massively and cheaply in established undertakings in many sectors previously closed to Afrikaner capital. It was actively assisted in this process by the Chairman of the Anglo American Corporation (see p.65), Harry Oppenheimer, who saw the development of Afrikaner capital as a crucial means of transforming the policies of the Nationalist Party. In 1963, Oppenheimer virtually gave control of one of the major mining finance houses, The General Mining and Finance Corporation (now Gencor) to the SANLAM subsidiary, *Federale Mynbou*, beginning a long period of co-operation between SANLAM and the Anglo group.

By the 1960s, SANLAM and the Cape Nationalist Party were acknowledged to be the 'official opposition' within the Nationalist Party, and were advocating policies somewhat at odds with the Verwoerd government. SANLAM interests played a leading role as the bulwark of the *verligtes* ('moderates') in the struggles in the NP in the 1960s (see p.142). SANLAM was largely responsible for organising the replacement of *verkrampte* ('reactionary') Andries Treurnicht by the *verligte* Gerrit Viljoen as *Broeder-bond* Chairman in 1974. By the mid-1970s, SANLAM management was arguing that the economic and labour policies of the Vorster government were holding back economic growth. In an unprecedented move within the Nationalist Party, SANLAM's then Chairman, A.D. Wassenaar published a stinging attack on the economic policies of Vorster's government, lambasting

Figure 3: The Sanlam Group

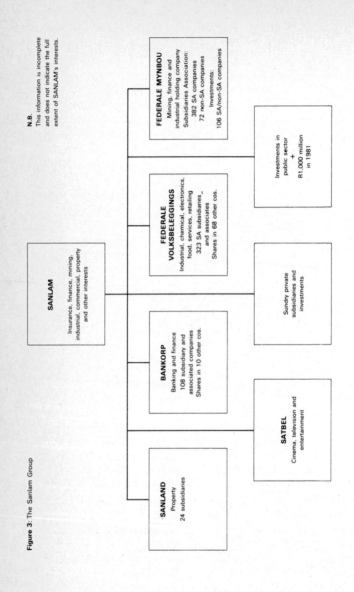

N.B.
This information is incomplete and does not indicate the full extent of SANLAM's interests.

SANLAM
Insurance, finance, mining, industrial, commercial, property and other interests

SANLAND
Property
24 subsidiaries

BANKORP
Banking and finance
108 subsidiary and associated companies
Shares in 10 other cos.

FEDERALE VOLKSBELEGGINGS
Industrial, chemical, electronics, food, services, retailing
323 SA subsidiaries and associates
Shares in 68 other cos.

FEDERALE MYNBOU
Mining, finance and industrial holding company
Subsidiaries Association:
382 SA companies
72 non-SA companies
Investments:
106 SA/non-SA companies

SATBEL
Cinema, television and entertainment

Sundry private subsidiaries and investments

Investments in public sector
+
R1,000 million in 1981

the many forms of state control over the free investment of capital in South Africa. In effect, it called for the lifting of all restrictions on the operation of market forces – and, by implication, state controls over the mobility and employment of African labour. The book created a sensation in white politics. And the company was widely regarded as having been involved in the manoeuvrings to remove Vorster and his heir apparent, Dr Connie Mulder, which culminated in the 'Muldergate scandal' (see p.144).

The election of P.W. Botha as Prime Minister in 1978 was clearly a triumph for SANLAM. The then Chairman announced that he was 'delighted' with the 'reforms' promised by the Botha government, though warned of anti-'reform' elements in the Cabinet. SANLAM is one of the moving forces behind the Total Strategy. Its new Chairman, Dr Fred du Plessis, is a member of the Defence Advisory Council – the state body in which the alliance between monopoly capital and the military is co-ordinated. In the current impasse of the Total Strategy and the continuing orchestrated attempts by monopoly capital to elicit a more powerful commitment to cosmetic reforms in apartheid, it can be safely concluded that the extremely powerful SANLAM group is playing a leading role.

Important leaders:
immediate past Chairman (retired in 1982): A.D. Wassenaar
Chairman: Dr F. du Plessis
W.B. Coetzer
P.E. Rousseau
C.J. Human.

The Barlow Rand Group[5]

Barlow Rand is the biggest industrial conglomerate in South Africa, with substantial mining interests as well. The company has self-consciously assumed the role of mobilising and organising the interests of all elements of monopoly capital. Its policy of 'social responsibility' is based on a clear need to win black support for the 'free enterprise system'. The group is a leading element in the alliance between the military and monopoly capital, crystallised in the Total Strategy.

The Barlow Rand group in 1981 consisted of some 300 operating companies organised into 14 broad divisions. The group employs over 200,000 people. In 1981 it controlled total assets of R 6,685.6 million. Important takeovers of three large food companies by Barlow Rand in early 1982 have significantly increased these assets. Barlow Rand's interests are concentrated in heavy industry, food products and mining; its various subsidiaries tend to dominate most of the sectors in which the group is involved. Where they do not, as in mining, the group nevertheless has substantial interests (see Table 2.6).

While most of its undertakings are based in South Africa, Barlow Rand also operates in the UK, USA, Belgium, Australia, Israel, Japan, Namibia, Zimbabwe, Botswana, Swaziland and Mozambique. Through an agreement with 'Hyster', Barlow Rand is the world's largest distributor of forklift trucks, and dominates the US and UK markets. While the group is keen to expand its foreign operations, strict exchange control regulations in South Africa are a major restriction. In 1980, foreign operations made up 7.4% of the group's total turnover and contributed 3% to pre-tax profits.

Barlow Rand has emerged into this position in the past decade as part of the broader process of the centralisation and interpenetration of capital into monopolies in South Africa. In 1970, the Barlow Group was a large industrial company concentrated in tractor dealership. In 1971 it took over one of the major mining houses, Rand Mines, changed its name to Barlow Rand, and began a programme of rapid expansion through the acquisition of existing companies.

The expansion of Barlow Rand in the 1970s was itself a major factor in the centralisation and interpenetration of capital in South Africa. The pattern of ownership of the group reflects this interpenetration of South African monopolies and points to possible struggles for control emerging between them. Until April 1982, SA Mutual (see p.80) held 5.2% of Barlow's shares, while Anglo American owned a further 12.7%. This large Anglo minority shareholding reportedly provoked fears in Barlow Rand of a possible Anglo takeover attempt. To guard against this, Barlow Rand concluded a complicated deal with the SA Mutual in April 1982. Barlow thus gained control of Mutual's two very large food products subsidiaries, Tiger Oats and Imperial Cold Storage. This made the Barlow food subsidiary, now renamed Tiger-Sugar, by far the largest of the five food product companies which dominate the South African market (three of the others are owned by the Anglo American, SANLAM and Anglovaal groups respectively. The fourth, Premier Milling, is owned by British Associated Foods). In return, SA Mutual's share of Barlow Rand was increased to 23%. Whilst some observers argue that the 'arrangement' will effectively give Mutual an industrial arm, to date SA Mutual has not sought to control companies in which it has significant holdings. Thus, increasing Mutual's share of Barlow Rand was seen by the latter as an effective hedge against Anglo's possible ambitions.

Barlow Rand is clearly strategic in the South African economy, not only because of its dominant position and size, but also because it is a major earner of foreign exchange and, in the words of the *Financial Mail*, 'supplies a wide range of strategic products', including military materials. Barlow Rand subsidiaries are among the most important private contractors in the burgeoning South African armaments industry. According to the *Financial Mail*, Barlow Rand's links with the Botha government are 'remarkably close'. Barlow Rand Chairman, Mike Rosholt, is a member of the Prime Minister's Defence Advisory Council. In 1979, Prime Minister Botha persuaded Barlow

Table 2.6
The Barlow Rand Group: Areas of Operation, Turnover and Profit Analysis (1980)

Divisions	Turnover R millions	% of group total	Post-tax profit R millions	% of Total
1. Mining and exploration: includes: gold mines, coal mines, chrome mines, asbestos mines, fluorspar, exploration drilling, forestry and timber	282.9	8.5	52.7	23.8
2. Cement and lime*	176.7	5.1	18.2	8.2
3. Ferro-alloy and stainless steel manufacture	154.3	4.5	19.7	8.9
4. Electrical and general engineering*	350.1	10.1	11.2	5.0
5. Earthmoving equipment*	291.4	8.4	21.2	9.6
6. Building materials and steel distribution*	504.5	14.6	26.7	12.0
7. Paint and allied products*	177.1	5.1	9.9	4.4
8. Engineering supplies, mechanical handling, equipment and motor vehicles	382.7	11.0	6.7	3.0
9. Household appliances and electronics*	299.9	8.7	14.2	6.4
10. Sugar and chemicals*	202.0	5.9	8.0	3.6
11. Floorcovering and textiles	228.6	6.6	4.1	1.8
12. Packaging*	371.2	10.7	17.9	8.1
13. Property	28.1	0.8	4.6	2.1
14. Administrative and financial services	–	–	6.8	3.1
Total:	*3,459.5*	*100.0*	*221.9*	*100.0*

* indicates Barlow Rand is largest operator in this sector

Rand to second to the state one of its senior directors in order to reinvigorate the state owned armaments company, ARMSCOR. Johan Maree spent three years at ARMSCOR as its executive Vice-president.

Among South African companies, Barlow Rand is also notable for its labour policies. It responded far quicker, and with a greater strategic vision to the heightened levels of working-class struggle at the end of the 1970s. Barlow managers believe that 'industrial relations and personnel practices will be the crucial determinants of the future climate for business in South Africa'.

In 1978 the group abandoned previous policy only to negotiate with company liaison committees. Black unions would be recognised, but only if registered under the 'new dispensation' (see p.329). Following the rejection by workers of a registered union in one of the group's subsidiaries, this policy was again changed to include recognition of unregistered unions which can prove representativeness. The group has also proclaimed its intention to eliminate discriminatory practices and introduce 'equality of service conditions, opportunities and rewards' for all employees. Chairman Rosholt has explained that

> unless the [black] workers get their share of the cake and accept the private enterprise system as something they should work for and participate in, we will have problems ahead. I don't believe any shareholder will object to this — it is for their ultimate benefit.

Reflecting the group's liberal position, and the relationship between liberalism and capitalism, the key manager in charge of labour relations, Personnel Director Reinald Hofmeyr, has been an executive member of the liberal pressure group, the South African Institute of Race Relations (see p.418), since 1964.

The Barlow Rand group is clearly in the lead in the attempts of the biggest monopolies to bring about the urgent modifications to apartheid needed to ensure renewed stability and profitability for capitalist undertakings. Its close relationship with the Botha government and leading role in the Total Strategy programme gives it great influence within the state. Its domination of the industrial sector enables it to influence the broad policy directions of the capitalist class as a whole. Barlow Rand's Chairman Rosholt has formed an informal grouping of the representatives of ten major companies employing 800,000 people. Representing mining, industrial and commercial firms, this group meets regularly to discuss labour practices and problems. All members have agreed to pressurise the government to change policies which 'discriminate against any group of workers'. After months of 'detailed research', a delegation from this grouping, headed by Rosholt, met with P.W. Botha in 1981 to put monopoly capital's minimum demands. Rosholt himself is a member of the Prime Minister's Defence Advisory Council. Press reports indicate that following strong pressure from this council, P.W. Botha was persuaded to force the ultra right wing to split from the Nationalist Party in February 1982 (see p.145).

Important leaders:
   Chairman: Mike Rosholt
   Vice-chairman: Gordon Dunningham
   Personnel Director: Reinald Hofmeyr.

The Volkskas Group[6]

The leading Afrikaner banking conglomerate and fourth largest banking group in South Africa, Volkskas is one of the 'big three' Afrikaner monopolies. For a short period, 1974-7, it was part of the SANLAM group, but is now again an independent group. Volkskas is a creation of the *Afrikaner Broederbond* (see p.266), and as such, a leading force in Afrikaner nationalist politics.

In 1981 the total assets of the group were listed as R 5,014 million. Though primarily involved in banking and financial services, since the late 1960s the group has diversified its interests into industry. In the financial year 1980/1, Volkskas became the first South African bank to derive more than half of its total profits from industrial interests. Through its two main industrial subsidiaries, Bonuskor and *Transvaal Suikerkorporasie*, Volkskas has extensive holdings in engineering, construction and mining equipment, motorcycle distribution, earthmoving, forestry, sawmilling, farming and property. Over and above these directly controlled operations, the bank has widespread industrial and mining investments. Volkskas owns 10% of SANLAM's mining subsidiary *Federale Mynbou* (which in turn owns Gencor, the second largest mining conglomerate) and an undisclosed portion of Rembrandt. In return, SANLAM owns 10% of Volkskas, and Rembrandt owns 20% of the bank. However, unlike these two other Afrikaner monopolies, Volkskas has kept its investments primarily within the realm of 'Afrikaner' business, although it did set up an 'international division' in 1982. Volkskas directors sit on the boards of a large number of Afrikaner companies, including *Federale Mynbou*. The dispute between SANLAM and Rembrandt in 1982 over the control of Gencor (see p.72) saw Volkskas allied with Rembrandt. Some observers believe that SANLAM is on the verge of moving Gencor's bank account from Volkskas to its own Bankorp subsidiary. It is also speculated that the 1981 transfer of the account of the *Afrikaanse Handelsinstituut* (see p.114) from Volkskas to Bankorp was initiated by SANLAM in an attempt to weaken Volkskas.

Volkskas has always been controlled by the *Afrikaner Broederbond*. It was formed as a co-operative bank by the *Broederbond* in 1934, with a paid up capital of R 3,000. It became a commercial bank in 1941. In 1944, after much conflict within the *Broederbond*, it was turned into a private company owned by *Broederbond* members. Although it is now a listed company whose shares are traded on the Johannesburg Stock Exchange, the company's Articles of Association restrict the voting rights of shareholders to ensure that it remains under *Broederbond* control. The official *Broederbond* history, published in 1979, admits that all members of the Volkskas board of directors are appointed by the Bond.

Together with SANLAM , Volkskas was the major beneficiary of the

'Afrikaner economic movement' jointly organised by SANLAM and the *Broederbond* in the 1940s. The bank's assets rose from R 26,000 to R 30 million from 1935 to 1948. However, as in the case of SANLAM, the spectacular growth of Volkskas dates from the assumption of power by the Nationalist Party in 1948. Primarily through the direct political transfer of government, local authority and various public body accounts to Volkskas, the bank's assets rocketed to R 168 million by 1960.

The position of Volkskas as a creation of the *Afrikaner Broederbond* gives it a somewhat anomolous role in ruling class politics. The *Broederbond* was for many years a mainly petty bourgeois based political organisation which tended to provide a base for the extreme right in nationalist politics. Whilst all important Afrikaner capitalists were members of the *Bond*, they have not succeeded in bringing it under their control. Thus, particularly under the present leadership of Professor Carel Boshoff, the *Broederbond* has re-emerged as a strong, independent, extreme right wing force and a major base of opposition to the Total Strategy of P.W. Botha's pro-monopoly regime (see p.270).

As key monopoly capitalists themselves, subject to some degree of *Broederbond* control, the managers of Volkskas have adopted a very low political profile. It is extremely difficult to characterise the bank's politics. It is certainly the most right wing and openly pro-apartheid of all South Africa's major private monopolies. Nevertheless, there are indications of struggles within the company — which also has important links with the pro-monopoly factions of the NP. The son of a former Volkskas Chairman is the present South African Defence Minister and architect of the Total Strategy, General Magnus Malan. At the 1980 General Meeting of the bank, he seconded the Chairman's address with a significant pro-Total Strategy speech.

Important leaders:
    Chairman: D.P.S. van Huyssteen
    Managing Director: Dr P.R. Morkel.

South African Mutual[7]

> Formerly known as the Old Mutual, South African Mutual is
> South Africa's largest life assurance company (being marginally
> bigger than SANLAM). It functions as an investment company
> with vast holdings in many sectors of the economy.

Like SANLAM, as a 'mutual' company, SA Mutual is 'owned' not by shareholders but by the holders of its life assurance policies. This gives the company and its management greater independence *vis-à-vis* the other monopolies, as the latter are unable to buy into the parent company of the group. It also means that far less information is available on the company and its assets than is the case for listed companies.

In 1981, the total assets controlled by SA Mutual stood at R 5,140.9 million. Its life assurance undertakings form the base of its operations. In 1981 the company had a total premium income of R 708.5 million. This provided the vast bulk of the investment capital at its disposal — estimated by the *Financial Mail* at R 2.5 million per day in 1980. The parent company itself is planning an asset base of R 10,000 million in 1985.

The group's investment policies differ markedly from those of other financial conglomerates: SA Mutual appears not to use investment capital to acquire direct control over operating companies; rather, most of its investments are concentrated in large, but still minority holdings in all sectors. The group thus functions primarily as a life assurance and investment operation rather than as an industrial holding company. Its takeover of control of the Tiger Oats food conglomerate appeared to be a significant exception to this policy. However, in early 1982 this control was traded with Barlow Rand in return for an increase in SA Mutual's holdings of Barlow's share capital to 23%, together with sizeable direct investments in various Barlow subsidiaries. Some observers argue that the deal has effectively given Mutual an 'industrial arm'.

Its other interests are widespread: life assurance apart, it controls South Africa's fourth largest short-term insurance company, Mutual and Federated, and supplies a wide range of other financial services. SA Mutual has a large holding in South Africa's third largest (and recently most profitable) banking group, Nedbank — which itself controlled assets of some R 4,608.9 million in 1980. The Chairman and Managing Director of SA Mutual sit on the Nedbank board.

Complementing its large investment in the highly profitable Barlow Rand group, SA Mutual owns 10% of the beer, retailing and hotel conglomerate, South African Breweries. The SA Mutual Chairman sits on the SAB board. Through its own investments and those of its Common Fund Investments subsidiary, the group has substantial holdings in virtually all of South Africa's other conglomerates and various of their subsidiaries.

SA Mutual has long been a leading element of 'local' capital in South Africa. Its original parent company, the Old Mutual, was formed in the Cape Colony in the 19th Century; its growth was slow but steady. However, with the coming to the fore of life assurance companies as a major source of investment finance in the 1950s and particularly the 1960s, SA Mutual began to acquire its very large holdings and played a leading role in the interpenetration of capitals.

The political role of SA Mutual is not as open as that of other conglomerates. Nevertheless, it is clearly an important force. Chairman J.G. van der Horst is known to be a close adviser to Prime Minister Botha. He is also a director of the state oil-from-coal company, SASOL and sits on the Prime Minister's Defence Advisory Council. The company is clearly supporting the Total Strategy of the Botha regime.

Important leaders:
    Chairman: J.G. van der Horst
    Managing Director: F. Davin.

The Rembrandt Group[8]

> A mainly tobacco and liquor based conglomerate with substantial
> industrial and mining interests. The Rembrandt group also has
> extensive investments in over 100 countries and until very recently
> was the third largest cigarette company in the world. As a leading
> 'Afrikaner' monopoly, Rembrandt is closely linked to specific
> factions of the ruling Nationalist Party. The group's founder and
> chairman, Anton Rupert, is a leading ideologist of 'reformist'
> Afrikaner nationalism.

Tracing the full extent of Rembrandt's interests is extremely difficult. The
company is notoriously secretive about its operations and has been granted
official exemption from the publication of information about its assets,
investments, shareholders etc. In August 1981, according to *Fortune*, the
group and associated companies controlled total assets of R3,700 million,
based on an annual turnover of R6,600 million. These figures do not, however,
include Rembrandt's extensive South African financial and industrial interests
held through large minority holdings in a number of crucial conglomerates
and their subsidiaries. Thus, Rembrandt owns 30% of the shares in SANLAM's
mining subsidiary *Federale Mynbou* (itself owner of the second largest mining
company, Gencor), 20% of the Volkskas bank, 20% of the Total South
Africa oil company, and many others. If these are included, an estimate
would put the total assets controlled by Rembrandt at over R6,000 million.
    Until recently almost all of the group's assets were concentrated in cigarettes
and liquor. However, over the past decade, fearful of international consumer
boycotts, and faced with a threat to its liquor interests by South Africa's
beer monopoly, South African Breweries, Rembrandt initiated extensive
diversification. It now has large interests in mining, banking, insurance,
engineering and petro-chemical undertakings inside South Africa. Moreover,
the 1981 sale of half of its controlling interest in Rothman's international
to the giant US cigarette company, Phillip Morris, means that the group now
has liquid funds of some R400 million outside South Africa and is poised for
a major overseas investment.
    Since the mid-1970s Rembrandt has been locked in a fierce struggle for
domination of the liquor industry with South African Breweries. Up to that
time, Rembrandt has virtually dominated the production of spirits, whilst
SAB had an almost total monopoly of beer production. Both companies
retained substantial interests in the wine industry and in liquor retail outlets.

Together they controlled not only the production of liquor, but also its sale. Eventually the competition between them grew so sharp that the state intervened in 1979 to regulate the industry and stop the 'war' between the two groups. Many observers suggested that the fact that Rembrandt seemed to be getting the worse end of the competition precipitated the state intervention. Nevertheless, both groups agreed to sell off their wine interests and retail outlets in return for a virtual state guarantee of their respective domination of spirits and beer production. However, recent events suggest that, with some state assistance, Rembrandt is gaining control of the wine company set up with SAB under the 1979 agreement. In 1982, Rembrandt and its Chairman, Anton Rupert, also became embroiled in a well-publicised dispute with SANLAM over control of SANLAM's mining subsidiary, *Federale Mynbou* (see p.72).

Rembrandt was formed (under another name) by leading members of the *Afrikaner Broederbond* in 1940 as part of the Afrikaner economic movement (see p.268). It began producing cigarettes under its current name in 1948. Through a combination of aggressive, nationalistically oriented marketing and a cheap labour policy which employed white female labour, it rapidly captured a large share of the South African market. During the 1950s, Rembrandt retained its very close links with Afrikaner nationalism through heavy financial contributions to the Nationalist Party, the running of regular training seminars for the NP and the sponsoring of a number of Afrikaner nationalist cultural projects.

In 1953, on a loan provided jointly by the two other major Afrikaner financial institutions, SANLAM and Volkskas, Rembrandt bought the Rothmans mail order cigarette company. This was rapidly transformed into the largest South African cigarette producer and began expanding overseas. A boycott of Rembrandt products by the African National Congress in the 1950s stimulated its expansion out of South Africa on a large scale in 1958. Coupled with the aggressively publicised 'moderate' business philosophy of Chairman Anton Rupert, this aroused the anger of the then leader of the NP and South African Prime Minister, Dr Hendrick Verwoerd. The quarrel between the two persisted until Verwoerd's assassination in September 1966. Nevertheless, by the end of the 1960s, under Rupert's innovative leadership, Rembrandt had grown into a vast cigarette multinational with interests in over 100 countries and was the third largest cigarette company in the world. The 1981 deal with Phillip Morris now gives Rembrandt its first entrée into the huge US market.

As a South African company investing in many Third World countries, Rembrandt is potentially vulnerable to consumer boycotts. Learning from the 1950s boycott launched by the ANC, it has coped with this threat in three ways. Firstly, it is intensely secretive about its interests. In countries such as Malaysia, Jamaica and Singapore, its operations have been concealed. Secondly, Rupert has evolved a 'philosophy' of 'industrial partnership' under which Rembrandt's foreign operations are all joint ventures with Rembrandt as a low profile minority 'partner' of local owners and managers. Thirdly, and most recently, it has extensively diversified its interests into other sectors.

Rembrandt, and particularly its founder and Chairman Anton Rupert, played an important role in the development of organised Afrikaner nationalism after 1940. In 1939, Rupert had been the firebrand editor of the Nazi-inclined student newspaper, *Wapenskou*. His early business associates were all leading members of the *Afrikaner Broederbond*, which helped finance the launching of cigarette manufacturing in 1948. The Deputy-chairman and Chief Secretary of the *Broederbond*, together with other leading *Broeders* sat on the first Rembrandt board. However this very close identification with the more conservative Transvaal wing of Afrikaner nationalism and the petty bourgeois *Broederbond* began to shift after 1948 as Rupert emerged as the leading and aggressive ideologist of Afrikaner capital.

As such, Rupert played a central ideological role in the transformation of Afrikaner nationalism from a largely petty bourgeois phenomenon into one based heavily on the newly emerging and powerful class force of Afrikaner capitalists. As early as 1950, Rupert had reconceived Afrikaner nationalism along the lines of its present day 'reformist' varieties, advocating co-operation with English monopolies, the cultivation of a black petty bourgeoisie through the state, 'co-operative' investments in emerging African states etc. In the early 1950s, outside SANLAM, these were decidedly minority views in Afrikaner nationalism, and contributed to Verwoerd's attempt to ostracise 'Sir Rupert' from Afrikaner nationalism. In the late 1950s and the 1960s, as the class conflict within the NP intensified, petty bourgeois nationalists attacked both Rembrandt and SANLAM as 'southern finance power'.

Rupert emerged from these struggles not just as an ideologist of Afrikaner capital, but as one of the leading ideologists of monopoly capital and most influential men in South Africa. As such he has played an extremely active role both internationally – in 'boosting South Africa's image' – and internally in organising and coalescing monopoly interests into many 'non-party' political projects. Thus, Rupert was the moving force in the establishment of the South Africa Foundation shortly after the 1960 Sharpeville massacre, as an organisation of South African businessmen dedicated to developing a 'balanced' image of South Africa abroad (see p.121). In recent years he has concentrated on attempts by monopoly capital to win support for capitalism from the black petty bourgeoisie. Together with Harry Oppenheimer of Anglo American, Rupert founded the Urban Foundation in 1977 as 'a business pressure group that has worked to modify laws against black property ownership' (see p.122). Recently, and again in concert with Oppenheimer, he organised and partly financed the Small Business Development Corporation, designed to finance business undertakings by blacks, particularly in the Bantustans. In keeping with his flowery descriptions of his own projects, Rupert defines the SBDC as 'the beautiful face of capitalism'.

Rupert is fully behind the Total Strategy of the Botha regime, and more reluctant than other important monopolists to criticise the regime openly. After the 1981 'Good Hope' conference of government and capitalists, in sharp contrast with other influential business leaders, Rupert pronounced himself satisfied with the 'reform' programme of the regime. He is certainly no liberal and firmly opposes the establishment of democratic rights in South Africa. *Fortune* magazine quotes him as saying: 'After many African countries became free they got dictatorships like Amin's. We have to find a solution that won't end up giving us one man one vote.'

Important leaders:
Anton Rupert
D.W.R. Hertzog.

Anglovaal[9]

A mining and industrial conglomerate, the Anglovaal group consists of a series of pyramid holding companies with final control vested in a partnership of the Hersov and Menell families. A total of 18% of the shares of the top holding company, Anglovaal Holdings, are held by the SANLAM subsidiary, *Federale Mynbou*. Anglovaal has minority holdings in, and directors on the boards of, various Anglo American Subsidiaries, and Anglovaal directors also sit on the board of Barclays Bank.

The total assets of all companies controlled by the group stood at R2,847.6 million in 1981. These are concentrated in mining and industrial undertakings. The group's mining interests are in gold, copper, zinc and manganese. It is also on the threshold of developing major coal-mining operations, and has applied to the state for permission to produce methanol from coal. This takes up an old lapsed interest of the company, as Anglovaal first initiated the investigation of production of oil from coal in South Africa, but when it could not raise the required capital, sold its interests and patents to the state in the 1940s. This later led to the development of SASOL (see p.102).

Outside mining, Anglovaal has extensive industrial interests controlled through its Anglo-Transvaal Industries holding company. Until very recently, it held a total monopoly of all bottles produced for South Africa's beer and soft drinks industries. Anglovaal's other industrial interests are concentrated in a few highly lucrative industries — food, packaging, textiles, engineering and construction.

Anglovaal first developed as a significant force among the mining finance houses with the opening up of the West Rand gold-field in the 1930s. Its industrial subsidiary, Anglo-Transvaal Industries, was established in the 1940s as a supplier to the controlling mining house. However, it began diversifying in the 1950s, and was selected for special focus in the 1981 *Financial Mail* 'Top Companies' survey because it had 'long been known for its aggressive and wide-reaching acquisitions policy'. The group is also notable amongst

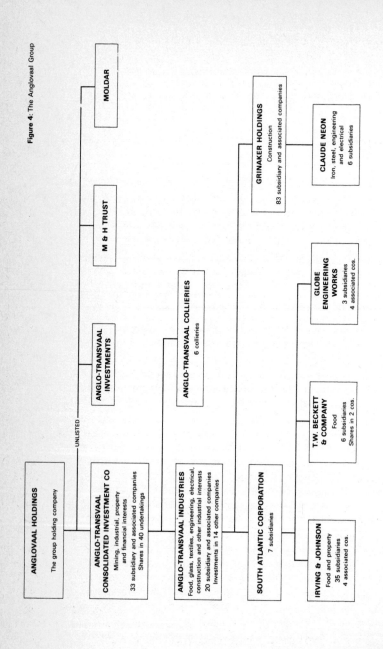

Figure 4: The Anglovaal Group

ANGLOVAAL HOLDINGS
The group holding company

— UNLISTED —

ANGLO-TRANSVAAL
CONSOLIDATED INVESTMENT CO
Mining, industrial, property
and financial interests
33 subsidiary and associated companies
Shares in 40 undertakings

ANGLO-TRANSVAAL
INVESTMENTS

M & H TRUST

MOLDAR

ANGLO-TRANSVAAL COLLIERIES
6 collieries

ANGLO-TRANSVAAL INDUSTRIES
Food, glass, textiles, engineering, electrical,
construction and other industrial interests
20 subsidiary and associated companies
Investments in 14 other companies

SOUTH ATLANTIC CORPORATION
7 subsidiaries

GRINAKER HOLDINGS
Construction
83 subsidiary and associated companies

IRVING & JOHNSON
Food and property
35 subsidiaries
4 associated cos.

T.W. BECKETT
& COMPANY
Food
6 subsidiaries
Shares in 2 cos.

GLOBE
ENGINEERING
WORKS
3 subsidiaries
4 associated cos.

CLAUDE NEON
Iron, steel, engineering
and electrical
6 subsidiaries

South African monopolies for the firm retention of control within the Hersov and Menell families — though its Chairman acknowledges that this could 'be a constraint on the capital base of the group [and] to its buying power at some time in the future'.

The company does not play as highly a visible role in South African politics as some other monopolies. Nevertheless, it has recently been advocating modifications to apartheid along the lines of those favoured by Anglo American. After the 1981 'Good Hope' conference between government and the capitalist class, the strongest statement of disappointment in the Prime Minister's programme was expressed by an Anglovaal director.

Important leaders:
    Basil Hersov
    Clive Menell.

South African Breweries (SAB)[10]

SAB is currently the largest monopoly operating in the consumer goods manufacturing and retailing sector. It has total control over the entire South African brewing industry and a 30% share in the Cape Wine and Distillers Corporation controlling most of the wine industry. It previously controlled almost a third of the retail liquor trade, but has now sold most of its liquor outlets in agreement with Rembrandt and under pressure from the government. In return, its absolute monopoly over the beer industry has been virtually guaranteed.

SAB also controls South Africa's largest retail chain, OK Bazaars, and took over another large chain-store group, Edgars, in 1982. It controls the highly lucrative Southern Sun hotel group as well as having interests in furniture manufacturing and retailing, shoe manufacturing, the soft drinks industry and property companies.

South African Breweries was formed through the amalgamation of a number of individual brewing companies in the 1940s — the Castle Wine and Brandy Company and Cape Breweries being two of the most important. It began to expand into other fields in the late 1960s when its management decided that a company 'dependent almost entirely on the beer industry could be economically and politically vulnerable'. Its major 'coups' were the acquisition of South Africa's largest retail chain, the OK Bazaars, in 1973, and the formation, in association with Sol Kerzner, of Southern Sun Hotels in the same year. The latter is currently the most profitable SAB subsidiary.

In 1981 the combined assets of the SAB group stood at R2,673 million.

Figure 5: The SAB group (1980)

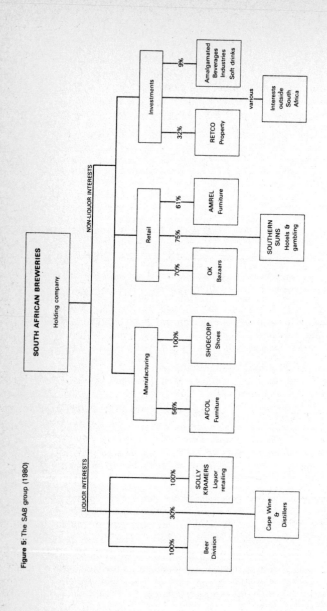

The group also has a prominent position in the consumer goods sectors of neighbouring countries. Its subsidiaries dominate the liquor industries of Botswana, Lesotho, Swaziland, Namibia and Zimbabwe, and although its Zambian subsidiary has been nationalised, SAB continues to manage the firm and receive royalties for the use of its brand names. OK Bazaars subsidiaries also operate in all these countries.

SAB's origins were local. However, as a result of the capital interpenetration in South Africa after World War II, SAB, like other large monopolies, is characterised by interlocking shareholdings with other conglomerates. Thus, 25% of SAB share capital is controlled by an Anglo American subsidiary with strong links to British capital, Johannesburg Consolidated Investments.

Despite its essentially domestic origins, SAB was not part of the Afrikaner economic movement associated with the governing Nationalist Party. It subsequently never benefitted from the particular state support given to Afrikaner capital after 1948; indeed, SAB complains today that government intervention tends to support its Afrikaner rivals. Cited examples of this are government assistance for the formation of a rival brewing company, by Louis Luyt in 1970 (later taken over by Rembrandt, and which subsequently disappeared in 1978); the use of liquor licensing rules to limit the expansion of SAB retail outlets so as to favour the rival Rembrandt chain (which controls most of the wine, spirit and remaining retail outlets); and the use of fiscal policy to promote the growth of distillate drinking (controlled by Rembrandt) at the expense of beer. The *Financial Mail* reported in December 1981 that the SAB management believed that their company 'has probably suffered more from government attempts to clip its wings than any other SA public company'.

In terms of its political stance, SAB basically supports the Total Strategy of the Botha regime but feels that it is not proceeding fast enough with secondary 'reforms'. SAB managers have participated in business/government dialogues, although they are not as vocal on directly political questions as managers of other prominent monopolies.

One area with political implications in which the SAB is active is the financing of sports functions designed to frustrate the international sports boycott of South Africa. It financed an unofficial and widely condemned English cricket tour early in 1982, but came badly unstuck when it attempted to do the same with an international football tour the same year. Massive rejection by football spectators, unlike those who watch cricket drawn largely from the oppressed population, and the subsequent refusal of key black clubs to play against the 'international' team led to the abandonment of the tour. SAB lost a sizeable sum of money and much prestige, leading its public relations spokesman to announce that the company would have to reconsider its sports sponsorship policy in the future.

Important leaders:
Chairman: Dr Frans Cronje (for many years the United Party parliamentary spokesman on finance)
Managing Director: Dick Goss

FOREIGN CAPITAL[11]

> The total foreign investment in South Africa in 1978 was esti-
> mated by *Business International* at R26,100 million. Other
> estimates put the figure at R30,000 million in 1981.
>
> Although direct control by foreign investors in South African
> production has undergone a relative decline, foreign investment
> continues to be of fundamental importance in South Africa's
> capitalist economy. It generates foreign exchange permitting the
> import of machinery and equipment upon which expansion
> depends. It gives local producers access to modern technology,
> and in recent years, foreign loans have financed large deficits in
> the state budget.
>
> The pattern of foreign investment also changed in the 1970s.
> The relative significance of direct investment in subsidiary opera-
> tions, and portfolio investment (in shares) has declined, while
> the relative weight of foreign loans has increased. Foreign com-
> panies have also been affected by the trend towards monopolisa-
> tion and interpenetration of capital in South Africa, giving rise
> to the centralisation of economic power in the hands of a few large
> foreign investors.
>
> Strong international pressure on foreign companies dealing
> with apartheid has resulted in the introduction of various 'Codes
> of Conduct'. These are supposed to regulate the treatment of
> black workers by foreign investors. While in no sense altering
> the exploitative conditions to which black workers are subjected,
> these Codes do provide an additional potential form of pressure
> on management. Some tendencies within the democratic trade
> union movement see this as an important weapon in the struggle
> for recognition.

The estimated R30,000 million of foreign liabilities in South Africa represents less than the combined assets of the two largest domestic monopolies. Nevertheless, there are good reasons to regard such a figure as a considerable underestimate. In order for the South African assets of a foreign investor to be included in the total of foreign direct investment, the external parent company has to exercise 'effective control'. The definition of such control is vague and under existing conditions permits a number of multi-national corporations to disclaim, where convenient, all involvement in their South African subsidiaries. Thus, the vast South African holdings of the British group, Consolidated Goldfields, are not included in such estimates because these are technically controlled by a separate South African registered company, Goldfields of South Africa. Similarly, all Japanese firms operate in South Africa through agency agreements with local companies. Thus, while

Toyota dominates the South African car market, and Japanese car and motorcycle firms offer substantial discounts to members of the South African Defence Force, the Japanese representative at the second SADCC meeting in 1980 was able to claim: 'In the field of economy, we prohibit any direct investment, including joint venture. Japan strictly observes relevant UN Resolutions on South Africa'. Such prohibitions however do not extend to the repatriation of profits.

Existing foreign investment in South Africa is of three types: direct investments, portfolio investments (purchase of stocks and shares) and loans. In recent years the proportion of portfolio and direct investment in the total has declined, whilst that of loans has increased. Such foreign investment is critical to reproduction of South African capitalism in a number of ways. Firstly it generates foreign exchange which permits the imports of capital goods on which the South African economy is heavily dependent (see p.54). Secondly, foreign investment gives South African capitalism access to technology not available domestically. One econometric study estimated that 60% of the economic growth between 1957 and 1972 could be attributed to technological changes, of which two thirds were the result of foreign technology. A 1973 survey found that 74% of the manufacturing firms interviewed said that 90% of their technology was of foreign origin. Access to such technology is particularly crucial to South Africa's burgeoning armaments industry (see p.104). With the rapid deployment of microchip technology in South Africa, access to such technology through foreign investment is a *sine qua non* of economic growth.

Foreign investment is vital thirdly, in the words of one study, because foreign borrowing has recently:

> played a predominant role in financing government expenditure, and above all the escalating defence budget; in financing the expansion programmes of public corporations; in financing the balance of payments deficit; and in financing imports of sophisticated plant and machinery. In short, it is foreign investment that has sustained the apparatus of the South Africa state; that has sustained the balance of payments and so permitted a measure of economic growth; that has financed imports of sophisticated technology; and that has financed strategically crucial infrastructural investment.

According to the 1981 *Business International* study, 'Apartheid and Business', there were in 1978 between 2,000 and 2,500 foreign controlled companies operating in South Africa. These were distributed by countries as follows:

Britain	1,200
West Germany	350
United States	340
Japan	70
France	50

Netherlands	50
Australia	35
Belgium	20
Italy	20
Switzerland	12
Sweden	10
Spain	6
Canada	5

There is, however, great unevenness of economic power among this relatively large number of foreign firms. Details of financial assets of foreign subsidiaries are often not published, thus making impossible an analysis based on assets. However, British firms have been pressured into supplying certain information about employment in their South African subsidiaries to the British parliament. This permits some conclusions about concentration of economic power to be drawn on the basis of size of the labour force. Table 2.7 shows that of 144 British parent companies giving information, nine firms (or 6.25% of the total) employed 44% of the total labour force employed by the British firms — while 35 firms (or 24.31% of the total) employed 89%. These major British multinationals, together with firms such as West Germany's Siemens and Volkswagen, the American Ford and General Motors, Japan's Toyota and Datsun, constitute the dominant force among foreign capital in South Africa. Moreover, most of these firms have close links with South African based monopoly capital as part of the overall interpenetration of capital.

In terms of employment policies and political stance during the 'golden age' of apartheid 1963-73, there was little perceptible difference between foreign investors and domestic capital. Numerous studies showed that ideological pronouncements by foreign capitalists about how they were 'undermining apartheid from within' were so much special pleading. They paid the going rate, refused to negotiate with black workers and had numerous links with the repressive apparatus of the apartheid state through defence contracts etc.

However, the intensified struggles of African workers after 1973, as well as action by the international working class movement, placed western multinationals with South African subsidiaries under pressure through, for example, the Sullivan and the EEC Codes of Conduct. These stipulated an improvement in working conditions and the recognition of the right to trade union organisation.

Although these Codes have had a minimal impact on wages and working conditions, it has been argued by some within the democratic trade union movement (see p.334), that the clauses relating to trade union recognition did provide a certain basis for unions to gain an initial foothold. The British *Guardian* newspaper nevertheless reported in March 1983 that of the 130 British companies with South African subsidiaries reporting to the British parliament on their employment practices, only 12 formally recognised black

Table 2.7
Distribution in 1979 by Number of Employees of 144 British Subsidiaries

Number of employees per firm	Number of firms in (a)	(b) as a percentage of total number of firms	Total Number of employees in (a)	(a) as a percentage of all employees
(a)	(b)	(c)	(d)	(e)
Less than 2,000	109	75.69	48,442	20.63
2,000–4,999	26	18.06	83,362	35.50
5,000 +	9	6.25	102.988	43.87
Totals	*144*	*100.00*	*234,792*	*100.00*

Top nine with more than 5,000 employees:*

Name of firm	Number of employees
Associated British Foods (Premier Milling)	16,200
Barclays Bank	19,730
Courtaulds	7,999
General Electric Co.	8,200
Imperial Chemical Industries	10,637†
Lonrho	7,863
Metal Box	8,765
Standard Chartered Bank	17,147
Unilever	6,447
Total	*102,988*

*Excludes Goldfields of South Africa (see p.70)
† Includes 9,865 employees in the Anglo American controlled AECI in which
  ICI has a very large interest.

trade unions. A substantial majority of these firms remained 'unwilling to
recognise unions under any conditions', while 13 firms refused to supply any
information.

For foreign capital, particularly in the 1960s, investment in apartheid
South Africa offered one of the highest rates of return anywhere in the world.
Its attractiveness in this regard was always offset by the potential threat of a
mass political challenge. By the early 1970s, and with increasing urgency in
the growing crisis of the mid-1970s, most foreign investors were urging the
need for cosmetic reforms of apartheid of the kind which later crystallised
in the Total Strategy. Foreign capital generally lent its weight to the regime's
public relations campaign to persuade the world that everything was changing
in South Africa. However the impasse in the Total Strategy in 1980 and
1981 reawoke fears of political confrontation and led to strong pressure from
foreign investors on the government. A major survey commissioned by the

influential *Business International* journal of the conditions facing foreign investors in South Africa in the 1980s, elaborated what is now in effect the programme of demands of foreign (and indeed all monopoly) capital in South Africa: 'If political stability can be maintained, a political dispensation acceptable to South Africa's black people introduced, inflation curbed and the training and mobility of the black workforce rapidly improved, South Africa's business environment in the 1980s could be excellent.'

THE MAJOR NON-STATE BANKING GROUPS[12]

> The South African non-state banking system is controlled by five major banking groups. In order of assets controlled these are: Barclays, Standard, Nedbank, Bankorp and Volkskas. The two largest groups, Barclays and Standard are controlled by parent British banks of the same name, Nedbank and Volkskas are South African-owned banks, whilst Bankorp is a subsidiary of SANLAM. Both Bankorp and Volkskas are leading elements of 'Afrikaner' capital.

Each of these five major groups offers a wide range of banking and other credit and finance services — based on strong commercial banks. Thus, each controls a network of subsidiary merchant, discount and industrial banks, leasing and hire-purchase companies, insurance brokers, and long- and short-term insurance companies. As such, both individually and collectively these groups meet much of the credit and finance needs of commerce and industry in South Africa. However, with the exception of Bankorp, whose subsidiary, Santambank, plays an important role in the provision of agricultural credit, these banking groups are not deeply involved in agricultural finance. The credit needs of agriculture are serviced primarily by the state-owned Landbank, which provides extensive credit to capitalist farmers at interest rates substantially lower than those charged by the major banks (although these rates were raised in 1981). In September 1982 Barclays announced its intention to begin competing with the building societies by entering the financing of individual private home ownership.

In addition to the five major bank groups, the banking system in South Africa is further characterised by a number of smaller, foreign-owned banks which provide supplementary services, the most important of which is the servicing of foreign trade. Thus, for example, the French Bank of South Africa — a subsidiary of the French *Banque de l'Indochine et de Suez* — has a dominant place in the financing of South Africa's wool exports.

In terms of total assets controlled, the five banking groups were ranked as follows in 1981:

Barclays	R11,696 million
Standard	R10,904 million
Nedbank	R 5,615 million
Bankorp	R 5,276 million
Volkskas	R 5,014 million

Other smaller banks between them controlled R2,777 million.

These figures of total assets are to some extent misleading, and conceal some of the differences between these groups. Barclays and Standard have the largest capital in absolute terms. Yet under current banking regulations, in 1982 the smaller Nedbank had the greatest proportional ability to lend funds as it had the greatest capital surplus. An aggressive advertising campaign by Nedbank concentrated on this fact, and in 1982 the group was judged by the influential *Financial Mail* to be the most efficient of all the banks in terms of 'handling their assets and meeting the demands of their customers'. In this ranking, Nedbank was followed by Barclays, Standard, Volkskas and Bankorp. Moreover, in terms of returns on total assets, Nedbank was judged to be 'roughly twice as efficient as its nearest rival' and the leader, by a more modest margin, in returns on shareholders' funds. For some years, Nedbank effectively followed policies contrary to the agreements of the 'Register of Cooperation', the informal cartel of the big banks, and when this collapsed in 1982, Nedbank became the first South African bank to pay interest on current accounts.

Apart from size of assets and general efficiency, the groups can be differentiated along other lines. Thus, Barclays, Standard and Volkskas all have large branch networks and depend for a large proportion of their assets on this source. These groups likewise have the highest proportion of total deposits in the form of current accounts, on which they paid no interest before 1983. Nedbank, and particularly Bankorp, have much smaller branch networks and are heavily dependent for funds on fixed deposits. In terms of the use of total funds, there is some discrepancy between these groups. The Bankorp group is deeply involved in hire-purchase and leasing; in 1981, 55% of its total advances were allocated to this sector. This means that Bankorp was not as heavily involved in industrial financing as the other groups, which lent the bulk of their funds to industrial and commercial undertakings. However there are clear differences among these four remaining groups as well. Barclays, Standard and Nedbank function primarily as lending institutions, the vast bulk of whose income is derived from interest on loans. Volkskas, on the other hand, has diversified its interests out of banking into industry. In the financial year 1980/1, Volkskas became the first South African based banking group to derive more than half of its total profits from industrial interests.

This points to the different linkages of these groups within South African monopoly capital. Barclays and Standard are British-owned banks which have not sought to transform themselves into wider conglomerates. Nedbank is now a South African-owned bank which has very close connections with the

South African Mutual insurance group, and through it, Barlow Rand (see p.80). But, like SA Mutual, Nedbank has generally confined its interests to the field of financial services and credit. Volkskas, formed and controlled by the *Afrikaner Broederbond* (see p.266) is the crucial component of northern 'Afrikaner' capital, and since the 1960s has diversified extensively into industry, and, in 1982, established an 'international division'. For a short period in the mid-1970s, Volkskas was controlled by the SANLAM group, but is now an independent conglomerate, and easily the most conservative — financially and politically — of all the major banking groups. Bankorp on the other hand is but part of the wider SANLAM conglomerate. It was formed in the late 1970s when the major SANLAM controlled bank, the Trust Bank, got into difficulties, and the group decided to concentrate all its banking interests under Bankorp. Within the SANLAM group, the banks grouped under Bankorp perform a number of specialised functions. But since the parent SANLAM insurance company operates to provide extensive industrial credit, and controls directly one of South Africa's largest industrial conglomerates (see p.71), Bankorp does not concentrate as heavily on industrial credit as the other major groups.

Before the 1960s, the banking sector was dominated by the two big British banks, with Nedbank a poor third. However the consolidation of Volkskas and the Trust Bank under Nationalist Party rule created a significant Afrikaner banking force in the 1960s. During this decade, all the banking groups were advocating cosmetic reforms to apartheid, with the Trust Bank (now part of Bankorp) perhaps the most outspoken. Because of its strong *Broederbond* connections, Volkskas did not go so far as the other banks, but generally did agree with the need to win black allies for South African capitalism. With the coming to power of P.W. Botha in 1978, the banks were an important force supporting the Total Strategy. Indeed, in the strategic vision of the state and its 'Constellation of Southern African States' proposals (see p.45), the banks are to play an important role in supporting one of the key institutions of the 'Constellation' — the proposed Southern African Development Bank.

STATE CORPORATIONS

South African Transport Services (SATS)[13]

> The largest state corporation and also the largest single employer of labour in South Africa. SATS controls the South African railways, harbours and South African Airways; it also operates a road transport service.
> Previously known as the South African Railways and Harbours

Administration (SAR & H) its name was changed in April 1982 as part of a reorganisation designed to adapt services to meet the changing demands of the market through a major cost-cutting and productivity offensive. SATS has adopted an extremely hostile attitude towards unregistered trades unions.

SATS is currently of crucial strategic importance in South Africa's regional policy. A number of neighbouring states are heavily dependent on South Africa's ports and railway system. Under the regime's Total Strategy, the withdrawal of specific transport services has been used as part of 'destabilisation' tactics *vis-à-vis* neighbouring states. More generally, SATS is engaged in an active competitive struggle to keep traffic from neighbouring states flowing through South African ports. This has the objective of maintaining leverage over these countries and frustrating SADCC alternatives.

SATS is the largest state corporation in South Africa and occupies first place in the *Financial Mail*'s 'Giants League'. As the country's largest single employer of labour, it had 271,342 employees in 1981. The Corporation has either a total monopoly or is the leading force in virtually all large-scale transport within the country. Its six major ports (in descending order of tonnage handled, Richards Bay, Durban, Saldanha Bay, Port Elizabeth, Cape Town and East London) handled a total of 77,045,543 tons in 1980/1. Its 35,697 km. of railway track transported 184,533,407 tons and nearly 750 million passengers in 1980/1. The Corporation's Road Transport Service is also the dominant force in road haulage within the country. Likewise, South African Airways, with a fleet of 38 jet aircraft, also has a monopoly of all but minor air transport in South Africa. These latter two have come under increasing attack from potential competitors in recent years. All sectors of the SATS operation were extensively 'modernised', mechanised and expanded in the 1970s. The Corporation's total assets rose from R2,634 million in 1970 to R10,186 million in 1980/1.

History and Role
The origins of SATS go back to the state controlled railways and harbours administration of the colonial and republican governments of the present four provinces of South Africa in the latter half of the 19th Century. With the union of the four colonies in 1910, these services were amalgamated into the SAR & H. When South African Airways was established in the 1930s, it too was placed under SAR & H control.

Ever since the opening of the gold-fields in 1886, transport policy has been a site of intense struggle within the South African capitalist class. After its formation the SAR & H was itself a major area of contest between competing capitalist interests. Its policies reflected the political balance of forces within the capitalist class, and have been designed to serve a number of specific social and/or political objectives of the state — as well as providing transport services to its clients. This is seen above all in two areas, labour and rating policies.

After 1907, successive railways administrations were drawn into state policies to provide employment for 'poor whites' on 'relief works' (see p.242). Such programmes were greatly accelerated under the Pact regime (1924-33). The railways became one of the key sites for the implementation of the Pact's 'civilised labour' policy. This obliged state departments to replace African employees with whites. Between 1924 and 1932 the number of unskilled white labourers employed on the railways increased from 6,363 to 12,042, whilst the number of Africans fell from 35,532 to 17,467.

During this period the SAR & H also adopted a discriminatory rating policy. This provided low rates to capitalist agriculture, now effectively subsidised by other customers. It also favoured industries sited on the Witwatersrand over those near the ports. The adoption of this policy was the result of the struggle between different capitals — mining capital and the major commercial interests were opposed. It was only made possible by the election of the Pact government in 1924 (see p.13).

These labour and rating policies were not applied with the same vigour during the periods of the fusion government (1933-9) and wartime coalition (1939-48). The accusation that the SAR & H had 'gone soft' on the 'civilised labour policy' was exploited by 'Christian National' trade unionists (see p.247) to build up support among white railway employees in the 1930s and 1940s. Another 'grievance' was the alleged discrimination against Afrikaans-speakers, many of whom were considered security risks during the war years. The first 'Christian National' trade union, *Spoorbond*, was established in 1934 around these issues, and succeeded in forcing the railways administration to recognise it in 1942. Moreover, during the war years the considerable pressure on capitalist agriculture was reflected in its loud complaints about rating policies.

After the coming to power of the Nationalist regime in 1948, the SAR & H administrative structure and policies underwent a major reorganisation. A Commission of Inquiry appointed by the new regime took evidence from 2,875 white railway employees. Its report alleged that during the war there had been widespread 'discrimination' against pro-Nationalist Afrikaners. This provided the ideological pretext for a major purge of senior officials associated with the old United Party regime and their replacement by persons loyal to the new Nationalist regime. Tariffs were restructured on a basis more favourable to capitalist agriculture and between 1948 and 1951 an initial attempt was made to return to full-blooded 'civilised labour' policies. Blacks were dismissed from all categories which had previously been filled by whites.

However, there could be no escape from the basic trends of class formation in the post-war period in which whites were steadily vacating manual positions and shifting 'up the ladder' to supervisory and clerical positions. As early as 1951, the railways reported that an 'acute shortage of applicants for the position of railworker [white]' was making it necessary 'to employ non-

Europeans on certain work previously undertaken by Europeans'. By 1959, the number of ungraded 'railworkers' had declined from 17,469 in 1950 to just 12,000. However, whilst the administration began in the 1950s to turn over to blacks tasks previously performed by white 'railworkers', throughout the 1960s, in accordance with basic government policies of the period, it steadfastly refused to do so in respect of graded positions.

These policies were placed under severe strain by a rapid expansion of the SAR & H during the 'boom' of the 1960s. The corporation's assets almost doubled from R1,410 million in 1960 to R2,634 million in 1970. Imports rose by 129% and exports by 75%. The closing of the Suez Canal in 1967 significantly increased the cargo handled by the existing ports, whose capacity became ever more extended. Major extension programmes were begun at the Cape Town and Port Elizabeth ports. Moreover, reflecting the large increase in the export of base minerals, which began in the late 1960s, by the 1970s two new ports were planned at Richard's Bay and Saldanha Bay, to handle much of this cargo. (In terms of total tonnage handled, these are now respectively the largest and third largest South African ports).

Reorganisation in the 1970s
In the context of this expansion, existing labour policies provoked a major crisis in the SAR & H in the early 1970s. Despite recruiting drives abroad, there was a shortage of whites to fill a number of graded posts. So acute were these shortages in the years 1970-2, that a number of services were curtailed with significant effects on the movement of cargoes. This led to wide-ranging complaints from capitalists and eventually resulted in a major restructuring of labour processes in the ports and railways. There were a number of aspects to this.

The first was the movement of blacks into graded posts. Originally this involved the reclassification of certain posts e.g. the introduction of the category 'train marshaller' to describe blacks doing the job of 'shunter'. In the three years 1972-5, 4,600 blacks had moved into former white categories, mostly on an officially designated 'temporary' basis. However, this process accelerated rapidly after 1976; by 1978, 22,000 blacks were employed in previously 'white' posts, only 6,889 of whom were still classified as temporary.

The second aspect of restructuring during this period involved mechanisation and 'modernisation' of labour processes. In part this was a further response to the labour crisis of the early 1970s, in part the result of competitive pressures and the introduction of new technologies (particularly the automation of train control after 1974 and containerisation in the ports in 1977) and in part a consequence of the initiation of major new projects such as the Sishen-Saldanha railway and port project and Richard's Bay port complex. During the 1970s, the South African railways and harbours emerged as a modern, mechanised service and established their current technological lead over other ports and railways in the region. As a rough index of the mechanisation during this period the tons handled per employee in the harbours service rose from 3,795 in 1971 to 4,286 in 1977 and then shot up to 7,604 tons by 1981.

This major reorganisation of all SATS operations reflected, and was part of, similar restructuring of all sectors of the economy during the 1970s. In this context, the political role of the corporation shifted somewhat.

With the advancing liberation struggle in the southern African region, marked particularly by the independence of Mozambique and Angola in 1975 and of Zimbabwe in 1980, South African Transport Services (as the corporation is now known) has come to be of critical strategic importance. The bulk of the imports and exports of neighbouring states goes through the ports and railways of South Africa -- 72% of the traffic to/from Botswana, 33% to/from Zambia and 75% to/from Zimbabwe in 1980. This gives the apartheid state a leverage over these states, well recognised by strategists of the regime. The 1977 Defence White Paper, which first spelled out the Total Strategy (see p.44), explicitly identified 'action in relation to transport services, distribution and telecommunications' as a key element in advancing the apartheid state's strategic interests in the region. In recent years 'action in relation to transport services' has been used, in co-ordination with other tactics, in attempts to 'destabilise' neighbouring states seen to be pursuing policies hostile to the apartheid regime. The clearest example was the withdrawal by South Afrcain Railways of locomotives from Zimbabwe and the jamming up of Zimbabwe goods using South African ports during 1981. Despite official denials, there is little doubt that this was linked with a series of other actions intended to pressurise the Zimbabwean government to modify certain limited measures planned against South African investors and to refrain from giving explicit support to the ANC. A further similar incident was the withholding of railway wagons from Mozambique at roughly the same time as the attack by South African military forces on ANC residences in Mozambique in January 1981.

More generally, SATS appears to be currently engaged in a major competitive offensive to keep traffic from neighbouring countries flowing through South African ports. This has the clear objective of maintaining the potential leverage of the apartheid state over these countries in the future and frustrating SADCC alternatives.

The corporation's name was changed to SATS in April 1982 as part of a major reorganisation designed to adapt its services to meet the changing demands of the market. Over the past two decades, the railways have come under increasing competitive pressure from private road hauliers (despite a strict licencing system which excludes much of the potential road competition). This, plus a deficit of R85.1 million in the three months April-June 1982, prompted SATS to launch a major cost-cutting and productivity offensive.

Partly as a consequence of this offensive, partly as a result of the fact that it is a state corporation which cannot be seen to undermine the regime's 'industrial relations' policies, and partly in consequence of its own past 'labour relations' practices, SATS has adopted an extremely hostile attitude towards unregistered trade unions. In 1982, the General Workers' Union, which had already won recognition from private stevedoring companies, began organising dockworkers employed by SATS. SATS management, however, refused to have any dealings with the GWU, giving the ideological justification that it had a closed shop agreement with what it acknowledged was a 'sweetheart' employees' association. When GWU members in the Port Elizabeth docks began a go-slow over this issue in September 1982, 900 dockworkers were dismissed. Eventually the union was forced to withdraw on this issue (see p.341).

General Manager:
  E.L. (Bart) Grové.

Iron And Steel Corporation (ISCOR)[14]

> A state-owned corporation currently controlling more than 75% of South African iron and steel production.

ISCOR was established by the 'Pact' government in 1928. The aim was for the state to take the initiative in the creation of basic industries so as to encourage the expansion of domestic industrial capital. The project was opposed at the time by mining capital, which objected to having to pay higher taxes in order to finance an undertaking which it thought would not directly benefit it.

Steel production began after the completion of the plant in 1934. Originally the Corporation had been committed to maintaining a 'civilised' (i.e. white) labour employment policy. However, soon after production began it found itself unable to compete in price terms with overseas steel cartels, and so resorted to a variety of protective measures and agreements with the International Steel Cartel. Subsequent complaints by mining and industrial interests about the resulting high prices later led to the abandonment of the 'civilised' labour policy and the resort to cheap black labour. The first large influx of black workers came in December 1937 when 875 previously 'white jobs' were turned over to blacks – an event known in the Corporation's folklore as the 'kaffirisation' of ISCOR.

The increased demand for steel products during the war years provided a major stimulus for expansion. Two new plants were opened and ISCOR became, for the first time, a cost efficient producer. Expansion continued after the war and by 1953 production reached the one million tons per year mark. By 1961 production reached two million tons, and during the post-Sharpeville 'boom', expanded even more rapidly to three million tons in 1968, four million in 1973 and five million in 1976. Today as well as producing well over five million tons of steel (about one and a half million for export and three and a half for local industries), ISCOR also controls the production and export of iron ore — a rapidly expanding key export earner, particularly after the coming into operation of the Sishen-Saldanha railway and port project in 1976.

In 1980, the Corporation made a profit of R140 million, following a loss of R38 million in 1979. Its total assets in 1980 amounted to R3,312 million, placing it 12th among South Africa's top 50 companies. By 1981 its total assets had increased to R3,457 million, but its position in the top 50 league had dropped slightly to 15th.

ISCOR employs a total of 68,000 people (31,200 whites and 36,400 blacks). Its production processes are generally highly mechanised and technically complex following major investments in the 1960s and 1970s. Consequently, it has a demand for technically qualified staff. Traditionally this was met from the ranks of white workers, however, along with other capitalist enterprises ISCOR has now found that the available pool of white labour is no longer sufficient to meet its needs. Indeed its management identifies a shortage of between 11% and 12% in the skilled categories as the most serious problem facing the Corporation.

Along with other capitalist employers, ISCOR's management has now announced its intention to seek certain modifications in the racial division of labour so as to allow them to employ blacks in skilled jobs. However, it faces opposition from its white labour force, part of which is affiliated to the militantly racist Mine Workers' Union (see p.258). Consequently it has principally relied on recruitment campaigns overseas to resolve its skill crisis.

With regard to its black labour force, ISCOR employs a high proportion of migrant workers housed in Corporation compounds. Indeed, one of its plants in Newcastle, Natal, was specifically located in a 'border area' in conformity with the government's policy of border industries (see p.212). As a prominent member of the Steel and Engineering Industries Federation of South Africa (SEIFSA), ISCOR adheres to the position of that organisation which refuses to deal with any unregistered union.

Chairman: Tommy Muller
General Manager: Floors Kotzee.

SASOL (Suid Afrikaanse Steenkool, Olie en Gaskorporasie)[15]

> State-owned oil-from-coal and chemical producing corporation
> and a key strategic installation in South African capitalism's
> struggle to thwart the effects of oil sanctions.

The idea of establishing an oil-from-coal plant in South Africa was first mooted in a White Paper published by the 'Pact' government in 1927. It was considered, though not acted on, by a number of private capitalist corporations in the 1930s and 1940s. The Anglovaal mining finance house went the furthest towards actually establishing a plant by acquiring the South African rights to US Kellogg and German Arge technology, but failed to raise the £15 million investment capital necessary to begin production. This led to state intervention in 1950: SASOL was formed as a state corporation in that year, taking over the rights to the Kellogg and Arge technology from Anglovaal. The first petroleum was produced five years later.

SASOL's growth during the next 15 years was relatively modest. By the 1970s it was producing a small, though significant, share of South Africa's total liquid fuel requirements. However, as the only commercially operative oil-from-coal plant in the world, SASOL made a number of technological advances which became of great importance later.

SASOL's real expansion dates from the sharp oil price rises after 1973. Partly as a result of the fact that SASOL's product rapidly became extremely competitive in relation to imported oil, and partly due to the threat to future oil supplies, the Cabinet decided in 1974 to authorise the building of a second plant, SASOL 2, at a capital cost of R2.4 thousand million. With the overthrow of the Shah's regime in 1979 and Iran's subsequent refusal to supply oil to South Africa, a further decision was taken to build SASOL 3 at a cost of R3.2 thousand million. SASOL 2 and 3 are claimed to represent the largest process project ever built in the world and are certainly the biggest financing operations ever undertaken in South Africa. Partly in order to raise the necessary capital, and partly to cement the alliance between monopoly capitalism and the Botha regime, shares in SASOL were sold in 1981 to private individuals and corporate investors. It is expected that SASOL will eventually emerge as a corporation with a substantial 'private' stake. Through SASOL South Africa now has a clear lead in the technology of producing oil from coal; indeed it is now in a position where it seems likely that it will sell its technological expertise in this respect to advanced capitalist countries. The SASOL projects have been a major factor enabling South Africa to withstand the effects of UN oil sanctions imposed in 1978, although 1982 reports suggest that output from the three projects will fall substantially short of the hoped for 50% of total liquid fuel demand. SASOL's clear strategic importance to the survival of South African capitalism has, not surprisingly, made it a target in the armed liberation struggle. In June 1980, *Umkhonto we Sizwe*, the armed wing of the ANC, attacked SASOL plants causing millions of Rands worth of damage.

Total assets in 1980 amounted to R1,061.1 million, and in 1981 to R1,232.5 million.

Managing Director: J.A. Stegmann
Chairman: Dr P.E. Rousseau.

Armaments Development and Production Corporation (ARMSCOR)[16]

State corporation responsible for the provisioning of arms to the South African military.

ARMSCOR was formed in 1964 to circumvent threatened arms boycotts against South Africa. Its task was to manufacture arms while the Armaments Board was meant to purchase arms abroad and maintain quality and cost control. Both functions were brought under ARMSCOR in 1976. ARMSCOR grew rapidly: its total assets rose from R200 million in 1974 to R1,200 million in 1980. In 1980 ARMSCOR was the 27th largest corporation in the *Financial Mail*'s 'Giants League'.

ARMSCOR and its subsidiaries manufacture weapons, ammunition, pyrotechnical products, aircraft, electro-optics, naval craft and missiles. This accounts for only about 40% of total arms production; the remaining 60% of local arms production comes from private contracting firms. In 1976 alone, 25,000 contracts were handed out to about 1,200 private arms contractors. Over 400 private companies now rely to a significant extent on defence contracts. ARMSCOR and its subsidiaries employ about 29,000 people and it is estimated that the armaments industry as a whole employs 90,000. The link between ARMSCOR and private manufacturing was well symbolised by the three year (1979–82) secondment of a key Barlow Rand director, Johan Maree, to ARMSCOR as Executive Vice-chairman.

In addition to organising domestic production, ARMSCOR is also responsible for purchasing weapons abroad. This aspect of ARMSCOR's work is shrouded in secrecy, but it is known that over the years it has arranged deals with, among others, France (to manufacture Mirage fighter-bombers under licence and to purchase submarines); Italy (to manufacture Impala fighter/trainer aircraft under licence); the United States (for technical assistance in developing 155mm artillery weapons) and West Germany — all in contravention of UN arms embargoes. However, ARMSCOR strives for 'self sufficiency'. Its spokesmen boast that the apartheid state now meets its own needs in respect of the majority of armaments. It was claimed that in one of the invasions of Angola in 1981 (so-called 'Operation Protea') over 90% of the weaponry used was of South African manufacture. Furthermore, the South African armaments industry claims now to no longer merely be producing externally-designed weapons systems locally, but also to be developing its own technology. One of the first examples of this was the development in the 1960s by a group of South African scientists in association with a French team of the Cactus-Croatle missile system. A more recent example was the announcement in September 1982 that a mobile version of the 155 mm artillery piece — the G6 — had been developed in South Africa.

The South African arms industry is now reputedly the tenth largest in the world. It has for a number of years been involved in arms exports to, among others, Paraguay, Chile, Taiwan, South Korea, Indonesia and Morocco. In September 1982 it announced plans to increase arms exports from the current level of about R10 million per year to about R100 million, partly in order to raise foreign exchange to finance new arms production projects.

The total value of arms produced and procured by ARMSCOR in 1980 was estimated at R979 million compared to R 32 million in 1968. The total production and procurement for 1981 rose to R 1,400 million.

Chairman: Comandant Piet Marais
Executive Vice-chairman: Fred Bell.

MAJOR CAPITALIST INTEREST GROUPS

South African Chamber of Mines (COM)[17]

> Organisation of mining capital to which all significant mining companies are affiliated. The Chamber of Mines serves as the employers' representative in negotiations with white unions, and as a lobby within state apparatuses for mining capital's interests. It also organises and controls the recruitment of African migrant labourers through its subsidiary, The Employment Bureau of Africa (TEBA) incorporating the former recruiting organisations, WENELA and the Native Recruiting Corporation.

The Chamber of Mines was formed in 1887 to co-ordinate and represent the interests of mineowners. Historically the Chamber played a decisive role in the creation of the migrant labour system (see pp.8–11). It lobbied successfully for the extension of pass laws and imposition of taxes to compel rural Africans to enter the labour market as low paid migrant labourers. It acted to discipline and control individual mining capitalists so as to prevent competition for labour supplies leading to wage increases. In 1897, members of the Chamber reduced their wage rates for African workers to an agreed 'maximum average'. As a result, wages of African miners fell from an average of R 78 per month in 1889 to R 58 in 1897. They remained at that level in real terms until the strike wave of the mid-1970s. The Chamber also assumed direct responsibility for the recruitment of African labourers. In 1896 it formed the Rand Native Labour Association, out of which the present recruiting organisation grew.

In the earlier years, when the mining houses were controlled by foreign capital, the COM was the organisation *par excellence* of foreign (imperialist) capital. Until the Second World War the Chamber was prominent for its resistance to tariff protection of the domestic manufacturing sector implemented after 1924.

Following the Second World War, differences between mining capital and industrial capital over the maintenance/modification of the migrant labour system resulted in the United Party regime being unable to produce a coherent response to the large influx of Africans to the cities during the 1940s. This was one factor which made it possible for the Nationalist Party to come to power in 1948 (see p.17).

During the 1950s and 1960s, the Chamber rapidly lost its 'foreign' complexion. With the emergence of monopoly capitalism in all sectors and the interpenetration of capitals, distinctions between 'foreign' and 'national' capital declined in importance. Within the Chamber, 'Afrikaner' capital first became involved with the entry of *Federale Mynbou* in 1953 and became much more importantly enmeshed with its takeover of General Mining in 1963.

In more recent years the Chamber has been heavily involved in researching and promoting the introduction of more mechanised production processes. It has also implemented an 'internalisation' policy to substitute workers recruited in neighbouring territories with workers recruited in South Africa. These developments were stimulated by: 1) the widespread strikes by black workers, including those employed in the mining industry, which erupted in South Africa in 1972/3 and have continued sporadically ever since (see p.83); 2) the rise in the gold price following the breakdown of the Bretton Woods fixed gold price system in 1971 (see p.54) and; 3) the changing political conditions in southern Africa (the Liberation of Mozambique, Angola and Zimbabwe) as well as Malawi's decision to prohibit labour recruitment following the death of Malawian migrants in an air crash in 1974. These developments made external sources of labour appear for the first time as unreliable.

The combination of the first two factors prompted an upward adjustment in the general level of wages for black mineworkers (which had hitherto remained unaltered in real terms since 1897). The first move in this direction came in mid-1972 when the Anglo-American Corporation withdrew from the 'maximum average' wage agreement and unilaterally increased its African wage rates. During the next two years competitive pressures compelled the other mining houses to make similar adjustments.

These wage adjustments in turn stimulated the mechanisation and internalisation policies pursued from the mid-1970s. The higher wage levels prompted mining capital to try to raise productivity by introducing more mechanised production techniques. In mid-1974 the industry announced a ten year programme for the introduction of new techniques for rock-breaking and the removal of blasted ore. Where these techniques have been introduced, in the newer higher technology mines, machinery operated by a relatively small number of semi-skilled operatives has replaced large gangs of manual labourers thereby reducing the total demand for labour.

The wage increases and growing unemployment in South Africa (estimated at 20% by 1980) also made it feasible for mining capital to extend its recruitment operations within South Africa itself. This, plus the growing awareness that external sources were becoming unreliable, led to a dramatic change in the composition of the mine labour-force. The foreign labour component, which had reached 79.5% in 1973, fell to 44% in 1980. Particularly affected were countries such as Mozambique, where the number of workers fell from 118,000 in 1975 to about 40,000 by 1981.

The Chamber has also attempted in recent years to negotiate a relaxation of job colour bar regulations in the industry. However, the mining industry has historically had the most rigid and extensive system of job colour bars. Moreover, the white mining unions are relatively strong and the Mine Workers' Union in particular (see p.258) has taken a firm stand against any undermining of 'job reservation'. These negotiations have thus been rather more protracted than in Manufacturing industries. The Sixth Report of the Wiehahn Commission (see p.325), released in 1981, recommended that statutory job colour bars in the industry should be abolished through agreement between mining capital and white unions. By the end of 1982 no such agreement had been reached, although some mining capitalists were reportedly 'optimistic' that one would emerge.

The Chamber's active involvement in the suppression of the African Mineworkers' Union following the 1946 African miners' strike (see p.322) and the general climate of repression and control within the compounds have stifled the emergence of African miners' unions. However, it is known that with the resurgence of militant struggles by black workers in recent years, intense discussions took place within the COM on the tactics to deploy to try to delay the emergence of union organisation among black miners as well as over what to do if and when such unions emerged. While all members of the Chamber agreed, as a secret 1976 Report of a joint COM–Department of Mines Commission made clear, on the need to retain the migrant labour and compound systems, some of the more 'liberal' mining houses, e.g. Anglo-American, also argued for a policy of codes of conduct, improved conditions, fringe benefits, and regular 'social audits' in the hope of 'improving management labour/relations'. Other members of the COM, e.g. Goldfields, are regarded as 'laggards' in making social improvements. By 1982 the Chamber appeared to have agreed on a pre-emptive strategy of permitting an affiliate of one of the more moderate democratic trade union groups – the National Union of Mineworkers formed by CUSA in 1982 (see p.345) – to begin organising black miners.

The Chamber of Mines has in recent years become less important as an organising force among mining capital. Contradictions between members of the COM were already evident in the mid-1960s when Anglo American attempted unsuccessfully to bring about certain changes in job colour bar regulations (see p.260), and again in 1972 when Anglo unilaterally broke the 'maximum average' agreement. Currently the major members of the Chamber are: Anglo American; Gencor (SANLAM); Johannesburg Consolidated Investments (in which Anglo American has a controlling interest); Goldfields (of which Anglo American controls 28% of share capital); *Federale Mynbou* (SANLAM); Rand Mines (Barlow Rand); Anglovaal; Lonrho and RTZ. Of these it is clear that at least Anglo American, SANLAM and Barlow Rand no longer restrict themselves to acting in and through the Chamber of Mines, but also act independently and through other channels (such as business-government dialogues) to press for the adoption of particular strategies and tactics to defend the interests of monopoly capital.

South African Federated Chambers of Industry (FCI)[18]

One of several organisations of industrial capital, drawing its membership mainly from domestic 'non-Afrikaner' capital. The FCI strongly supports the Total Strategy whilst pushing for a faster pace of 'reform'.

The FCI was founded in 1907 to represent the specific interests of the incipient industrial bourgeoisie, some of which were then in conflict with those of mining capital. Up until the mid-1920s the FCI's major activity was lobbying for an effective system of tariff protection for local manufacturers. This was then opposed by mining capital and blocked by regimes allied to it (see p.14).

Industrial capital's victory on the tariff question came after the election of the Nationalist-Labour Pact government in 1924. The 1925 Customs Tariff Act introduced an effective system of protective tariffs. Throughout the period of both the 'Pact' and 'Fusion' governments (1924–33, 1933–9) relations between the FCI and government were extremely cordial. Among other things, in 1934 the FCI put forward proposals which formed the basis of the regime's efforts to promote the employment of 'civilised' (i.e. white) labour at the expense of blacks. During the war the FCI played an even more important supportive and co-ordinating role. With the emergence of monopoly capitalism in industry in the years after 1945, contradictions began to develop within the industrial bourgeoisie. The FCI basically came to represent larger and more firmly established domestic industrial capital.

After 1948 the FCI found itself in some conflict with the Nationalist regime over specific apartheid measures. It opposed the introduction of tighter influx control designed to relocate to white farmers part of the reserve army of black labour then in the towns. It argued that it was more convenient for industry to have a certain labour 'surplus' at hand. It also opposed the introduction of statutory job reservation in 1956, fearing that industry would be tied down by bureaucratic controls. It argued that the 'natural economic process' would guarantee continued 'white supremacy' anyway.

On the question of union organisation by African workers, prior to the 1973 strikes the FCI's position was that African workers be granted 'some (negotiating) facilities *short of full trade union rights* e.g. by way of mixed unions or branch unions under the supervision of established unions'. This represented a certain compromise between those of the FCI's regional centres, notably the Transvaal, which were opposed to any form of negotiation with organised black workers whatsoever and those centres, notably the Cape, which favoured controlled recognition of African unions. However, during the decade of 'industrial peace' 1963–73, when all forms of worker organisation were heavily repressed by the state, the FCI was noticeably feeble in pushing for even the limited forms of restructuring envisaged in its formal policy. Most of its members were generally content with the status quo in which trade union struggle by black workers was not a major threat.

The mass strikes of 1973 and the trade union organisation which followed forced the FCI and all other organisations of the capitalist class to make some new response. The FCI was prominent among employers' organisations calling for a 'new labour dispensation', particularly in the period after the mass uprisings in Soweto and elsewhere in 1976. When the Wiehahn Commission published its first report in 1979 (see p.325) the FCI endorsed it unreservedly, stating that the Commission had 'welded together a coherent approach permitting a new integrity to South Africa's system of labour relations'.

In the post-Wiehahn period many unions refused to accept the limitations and restrictions implied in participation in statutory bodies. The FCI, like all major employers' organisations, strongly favours the bureaucratic, centralised Industrial Council system. However, it takes a more 'liberal' approach than some other organisations, notably SEIFSA (see p.110), on the tactics to adopt in order to achieve the objective of incorporating democratic unions into the Industrial Council system. Basically, it seeks to 'encourage' unions into the system through limited plant level bargaining. This tactic aims to win the 'confidence' of unions, whilst holding out the prospect of more substantial negotiations should they join the Industrial Council. As part of this tactic, the FCI also favours reducing the control element in the registration procedure in the hope of persuading unions to accept registration.

In the current period of the Total Strategy and the monopoly-military alliance, the FCI's role has become relatively less important than that of individual corporations and groups of companies. It attended the various business-government dialogues (the 'Carlton Conference' of 1979 and the 'Good Hope Conference' of 1981) but is not really the major body through which monopoly industrial capital puts its demands. In response to the recent apparent decline in the importance of Chambers as organising forces among the capitalist class, partly engendered by the emergence of large conglomerates spanning all sectors, the FCI began exploratory talks with ASSOCOM (see p.111) in 1982 over a possible merger; this project collapsed, however.

Moreover, a number of important foreign multinationals are not members, nor are many 'Afrikaner' capitalist firms. Further, some other bodies such as

SEIFSA appear to be more important in their particular sectors (in this case the iron and steel industry). Consequently, the FCI cannot be regarded as *the* voice of industrial capital. It nevertheless has an importance as one of the forms of organisation of domestic industrial capital.

Steel and Engineering Industries Federation of South Africa (SEIFSA)[19]

> Centralised employers' organisation grouping all major state and private firms in the metal industries. SEIFSA is known for its hard line in dealings with unions outside the Industrial Council system.

The first specific metal industries employers' organisation on a national level was formed in 1942. Some 440 such employers came together in the South African Federation of Engineering and Metallurgic Associations (SAFEMA). SAFEMA was a direct response to the labour unrest which engulfed the metal industries during the early war years. A wage freeze, and the appointment of a Controller of War Supplies with powers to 'direct labour' to different centres in the interests of the 'war effort' led to a number of strikes by both black and white workers. At the same time the *Broederbond* was attempting to take over the Iron and Steel Union (see p.266).

In 1941 an informal meeting of metal industries employers decided to co-ordinate efforts to assert their interests; SAFEMA was formed the following year. It set about to centralise the then regionally dispersed industrial councils into an industry-wide bargaining system. At the same time employers concluded closed shop agreements with various white unions; a move which, in the view of SEIFSA's official history, 'certainly made them [the unions] less militant because the arrangement carries reciprocal obligations'. A centralised Industrial Council system was established shortly after the war. SEISFA adopted its present name in 1947 when SAFEMA's constitution was amended to permit it to absorb a number of other employers' associations then operating in the metal industry.

SEIFSA's principal role has been to act as the employers' representative on the Industrial Council. In the period 1950–73 the Industrial Council functioned as a cosy cartel. Together with the bureaucrats of white unions, SEIFSA determined at national level the wages and conditions for all workers in the metal industries. A rigidly defined grade and wage scale was adopted in which the higher paid grades were, under racially exclusive closed shop agreements, open only to (white) union members. From time to time such categories were redefined and turned over to black workers at lower rates of pay. This was possibly the most organised system of 'floating the colour bar' to operate during the pre-Total Strategy period.

By the mid-1970s, however, in the face of economic crisis and the growing mass challenge, capitalists in the metal industries also began to seek certain modifications to the system of job reservation and racially exclusive closed shop agreements. In what was seen as a pioneering step in the development of the so-called 'new labour dispensation', SEIFSA negotiated the abolition of racially exclusive closed shops in the metal industries in 1978, before the publication of the Wiehahn Report (see p.325).

However, SEIFSA has taken a hard line against negotiating outside the Industrial Council system. Like other employers' organisations, it is firmly committed to maintaining this system, which in the metal industry has worked for many years very effectively, from the bosses' point of view. SEIFSA opposes any move by employers which might undermine the Industrial Council in the industry. It regards any form of 'in house' bargaining with unregistered unions, even over issues not dealt with by the Industrial Council, as a threat. It accordingly takes a different approach to that now favoured by the FCI (see p.108). In a set of 'Guidelines' issued in 1979 it instructed its affiliates that:

> Recognition of or negotiation with black trade unions should be . . . through final legal registration of trade unions in terms of the Industrial Conciliation Act and contingent upon the trade unions concerned becoming parties to the National Industrial Council. . . .

One of the major forces in the Federation behind this position is the Anglo American subsidiary, Scaw Metals, regarded as a major influence in SEIFSA.

Association of Chambers of Commerce (ASSOCOM)[20]

The national federation of all local Chambers of Commerce, grouping almost all major 'non-Afrikaner' white private undertakings, with the exception of the mining companies.
ASSOCOM is thus perhaps the most representative of all the individual economic groupings of the capitalist class. Since the 1950s, it has been dominated by larger national undertakings and has called for the lifting of restrictions on the operation of 'market forces'. It currently vigorously supports the Total Strategy, yet argues that its programme of 'reforms' to apartheid do not go far enough.

The roots of ASSOCOM go back to the emergence of local chambers of commerce in important commercial centres during the 19th Century. ASSOCOM itself was formed as a national body in 1892. Until World War I, it was dominated by the large imperialist-orientated import-export wholesale houses which controlled the commercial sector in South Africa, and upon whom smaller retailers were totally dependent for supplies. Under their domination, ASSOCOM adopted a fiercely pro-free trade position and was an important force arguing against the erection of protective tariffs around South African industry. However, with the emergence of some local industry during World War I, and the steady collapse of the influence of these great merchant houses following the war, ASSOCOM was taken over by local merchants. It began to echo the demands of local manufacturers for protection of local industry. During the 1920s it lost much of its character as a body solely representing commerce as such. Most industrial firms affiliated in order to give themselves yet another institutional voice apart from the FCI (see p.108) through which to advocate protectionism.

By 1932, important industrialists had been elected to the presidency of all leading local chambers of commerce and to ASSOCOM itself. During this period ASSOCOM emerged as perhaps the single most representative and influential organisation of national capital, and adopted a militantly 'South Africanist' position. In the period of party political crisis during the Great Depression and the Gold Standard crisis of 1932 (see p.158), ASSOCOM fought hard for a National Government, uniting all sections of the capitalist class within a 'businessman's party'. The coalition of the Nationalist and South African Parties in 1933, and their 'fusion' into the United Party in 1934 (see p.157), was proclaimed by ASSOCOM as its own individual achievement.

The unity of all major sections of capital was undermined with the passage of the Agricultural Marketing Act of 1937. This provided for single channel marketing of agricultural produce, in effect guaranteeing prices for agricultural producers. ASSOCOM fiercely opposed what it depicted as 'state interference' in the market, and the protection of 'less efficient' producers. While the FCI supported the Marketing Act, retailers and traders within ASSOCOM were able to get the organisation as a whole to oppose it.

ASSOCOM's opposition to the Marketing Act persisted during World War II. By 1944, the Association was campaigning vigorously for the abandonment of a system of controlled marketing of agricultural produce, and earned the fierce wrath of organised agriculture. This was one of the issues which shattered the political unity of the capitalist class in the later war years. By 1945, ASSOCOM was ranged together with the Chamber of Mines and FCI favouring the implementation of a 'cheap food' policy through the lifting of controls over marketing, whilst the South African Agricultural Union was joined by the *Afrikaanse Handelsinstituut* in arguing for the use of control machinery to raise agricultural prices.

The labour question was the second great issue which divided the capitalist class in this period and so, in effect, led to the defeat of the ruling United Party in 1948. On this issue, ASSOCOM was broadly aligned with the FCI in advocating a policy of labour stabilisation, the training of African labour for skilled positions and a general easing of all restrictions on the mobility of labour. The other major organisations of capital opposed these notions, in favour of tightened controls over the influx of black labour to the cities, and the maintenance of the migratory labour system. In the event, these policies were implemented by the Nationalist Party government after 1948.

In the early years of Nationalist Party rule, ASSOCOM saw apartheid as an attempt to deprive industry of its African labour, and openly opposed such 'interferences in the free market economy', and 'the traditional attitude which prevents certain classes of the population from making their full contribution to the economy'. However, as it became clear that far from undermining the interests of industry and commerce, apartheid would facilitate higher rates of accumulation, ASSOCOM moderated this pious tone. Its evidence to the Viljoen Commission on Tariffs supported an extension of the protection of local industry.

The mass struggles against apartheid in the late 1950s, and particularly the crisis following the Sharpeville massacre (see p.26), again forged a measure of unity amongst the various organisations of the capitalist class. In July 1960, together with the FCI, AHI, SEIFSA and Chamber of Mines, ASSOCOM submitted a memorandum on 'native unrest' to the government. This called for the retention of the system of influx control, but argued for a fundamental division of the black population into urban and rural sections, and the granting of a series of vested rights to Africans living in the urban areas. Throughout the 1960s, ASSOCOM clung to this position and opposed what it saw as further state restrictions over labour mobility and training.

With the developing crisis of the 1970s, and the growing consolidation of monopoly capital in a few conglomerates, these demands by organised capital for tactical 'reforms' to apartheid intensified. ASSOCOM in particular now advocated lifting restrictions on labour mobility; the use of trained African labour in skilled positions; a programme of rights of permanent residence and freehold land title for Africans in the urban areas; the rapid reduction of state control over marketing systems and the reduction of its share in industry; and a system of controlled recognition of emerging African trade unions to contain their growing militancy. In 1975 all the major capitalist organisations formed the South African Employers' Consultative Committee to 'co-ordinate and crystallise employer thinking on labour affairs'.

The worsening economic and political crises after the 1976 Soweto uprising intensified these demands, and eventually led to the replacement of John Vorster by P.W. Botha as Prime Minister. Together with other capitalist organisations, ASSOCOM played an active role in the formulation of the strategy of the newly emerging alliance of monopoly capital and the military. The 'new dispensations' of the Wiehahn and Riekert Commissions (see p.38-9) were warmly welcomed by ASSOCOM as in line with its own policy of 'harnessing private initiative to a greater extent, and . . . harnessing its [South Africa's] total human resources more effectively'.

As such, ASSOCOM vigorously supported the Total Strategy of the Botha regime, while pressing it to greater reforms. In 1981, together with most capitalists, ASSOCOM began to express dismay at the slow pace of 'reform'.

Its 1981 national congress warned the state that unless the ruling class won black support for 'free enterprise', the 'appeal of Marxism' would spread. In the words of one speaker: 'Our future will be either mixed, Marxist and dominated or mixed, capitalist and free'.

Chief Executive: Raymond Parsons.

Afrikaanse Handelsinstituut (Afrikaans Commercial Institute – AHI)[21]

An umbrella body representing the interests of 'Afrikaner business', the AHI seeks to bring together all Afrikaner undertakings, on the grounds that 'the Afrikaner' still does not have his 'rightful share' in South African capitalism. The growth in membership and influence of the AHI during the period 1948-78, together with its now waning influence, are important indices of the changing position of Afrikaner capital in the political and economic relations within the capitalist class. Since 1962, the AHI has been riven by intermittent conflict between small entrepreneurs and big business undertakings, with the latter emerging as the dominant voice by the end of the 1960s. However, the AHI is no longer the most important forum for the representation and expression of the interests of 'Afrikaner' monopolies.

The AHI was an extremely important force within the Afrikaner nationalist class alliance after 1940. Since the late 1960s, it has strongly advocated the 'modifications' to apartheid which finally emerged in the Total Strategy. In the current divisions within Afrikaner nationalism, the vast majority of AHI members probably support a strategy of 'reform' against the forces of the far right. However, only the largest undertakings are clearly identified with the P.W. Botha faction of the NP. The remainder are more likely to identify with more 'centrist' groups.

The AHI was formed by the *Afrikaner Broederbond* (see p.266) in August 1942. This was the period of the 'Afrikaner economic movement' – the attempt, organised by the *Broederbond* and SANLAM to transform a substantial element of the large Afrikaner petty bourgeoisie from 'spectators in the business life of our country' into financial, commercial and industrial capitalists. This was to be achieved primarily through the collective organisation of the money and resources of all Afrikaans-speakers mobilised through nationalist ideology. The AHI was the single most important co-ordinating body to emerge out of the economic movement. It was formed in the first instance to bring together, and to provide advice and guidance to, small

Afrikaner traders. In the early years when, 'Afrikaner business' was a new phenomenon, through its journal *Volkshandel*, the AHI helped to mould and direct the interests of emerging Afrikaner business. Its main activities were attacks on 'foreign capital and foreign monopolies', an attempt to displace 'alien' Indian traders and an insistence that 'cheap labour' policies were not eroded in the rapid development of industry in South Africa during the Second World War. As such, the AHI played an important role in the development of the policies and ideology of apartheid.

With the election of the Nationalist Party government in 1948, the AHI was recognised by the state as the official organisation of Afrikaner business, and given representation on a wide variety of state economic boards and committees. The NP government fostered the rapid growth of Afrikaner undertakings through various measures (see pp.23-4). During this period the AHI gave enthusiastic support to all aspects of apartheid policy. In particular it saw the system of labour bureaux, pass laws and influx control as crucial mechanisms to ensure accumulation by Afrikaner capital. Its other main preoccupation was the extension of the network of protective tariffs around South African industry, finally concretised in the recommendations of the 1958 Viljoen Commission.

By 1960, a few large Afrikaner financial groups had developed to the extent that they were no longer dependent for accumulation on the savings of Afrikaner workers and petty bourgeoisie, and the hoarded profits of Afrikaner capitalist farmers. Particularly in the Cape, the largest Afrikaner undertakings began to pursue policies somewhat independent of those of the NP. This gave rise to a protracted struggle within all organisations of Afrikaner nationalism, culminating in the split of the 'Hertzogites' from the NP in 1969 (see pp.142-3). The AHI too was deeply affected by these struggles. Here, however, they took the form of a battle for control of the organisation between smaller and generally Transvaal-based undertakings, and the large groups, particularly SANLAM and Rembrandt. The 1964 AHI congress saw an attempt by smaller business, organised through the *Broederbond*, to drive SANLAM and Rembrandt representatives out of all positions of influence in the AHI. This conflict grew so intense that the organisation was unable to hold its 1965 congress. The main point at issue was the growing tendency of the larger undertakings towards open co-operation with non-Afrikaner monopolies at the cost of 'advancing the struggle of the Afrikaner for his rightful place in the economy'.

By the late 1960s, the AHI was again under the firm domination of the bigger undertakings. After the assassination of Prime Minister Verwoerd in September 1966, and in the context of fierce divisions within Afrikaner nationalism (see p.142), these larger undertakings used the AHI to advocate a number of 'reforms' in labour policy. As a result they were attacked by the *Broederbond* for 'slackening the economic struggle of the Afrikaner'. Essentially, the AHI advocated the lifting of some restrictions on the mobility and training of African labour and the gradual erosion of job reservation. As part of this, it argued that 'urban Bantu' were now permanently settled in the cities, and, in opposition to apartheid dogma that all urban Africans were 'temporary sojourners', that they should be given wider economic and political rights. This led to a rift between the Vorster regime and the AHI during the period 1971–3. At the same time, the AHI strongly attacked state control of certain key sections of industry, arguing that 'creeping socialism' was taking root in South Africa.

With the growing political and economic crises of the mid-1970s, together with all other organisations of the capitalist class, the AHI became much more strident in the expression of these demands. In 1975 it joined with all other groupings in the formation of a new employers' organisation concerned solely with the problem of labour. The dominant grouping within the AHI argued for a 'drastic change' in the organisation's ideas about industrial relations. Prior to 1976, the AHI had opposed all forms of recognition of African trade unions, preferring the system of liaison committees provided for in the 1953 Bantu Labour (Settlement of Disputes) Act (see p.174). However following the crisis of Soweto, and the perceived need by all sections of monopoly capital both to win 'the African middle class' for capitalism and to find an institutional framework to contain industrial conflict, the AHI recognised the need for some form of African trade unionism under strict state controls. It therefore warmly welcomed the Report of the Wiehahn Commission with its 'new labour dispensation'. In the post-Wiehahn period, however, it has consistently maintained that only registered trade unions should be tolerated, and that the Industrial Council system should in no way be by-passed by plant level negotiation of wages and working conditions.

The AHI is an enthusiastic supporter of Botha's Total Strategy. Although it has taken no official position on the splits within the Nationalist Party, its most influential members would clearly support the pro-Botha faction which has implemented most of the demands of the AHI. However, in the elaboration and implementation of the Total Strategy, and in the context of the increasing centralisation of economic power in the hands of the leading conglomerates, the influence of the AHI *per se* has waned somewhat. The Botha regime relies more heavily on the support of the conglomerates as such, rather than on organisations which bring together large and small undertakings.

South African Agricultural Union — SAAU[22]

Organisation of capitalist agriculture with great influence on the governing Nationalist Party. After the late 1940s it demanded and received state support to tighten up controls over black labour and redirect part of the reserve army of labour from the cities to farms. It also demanded and received a wide range of state subsidies and concessions. During the decade 1960–70, the SAAU pushed for state support for the mechanisation and 'modernisation' of capitalist agriculture. It also received state support for the removal and forced resettlement in the Bantustans of over a million 'surplus' squatters and former labour tenants. Power within the SAAU has now passed into the hands of a more mechanised, more profitable minority of capitalist farmers. The present SAAU leadership has close links with Afrikaner monopolies. It has remained loyal to the Nationalist Party despite the support for far-right parties from many farmers. The SAAU currently advocates a reduction of certain industrial protective tariffs in return for a reduction of certain controls over agricultural marketing.

The South African Agricultural Union was formed to represent the specific interests of capitalist agriculture. Agriculture has always been the most backward sector of capitalist production. This has historically resulted in a number of contradictions between it and other capitals, centering on state policies in relation to: 1) pricing of agricultural commodities; 2) protection against cheap food imports from abroad; 3) credit, technical assistance and subsidies and; 4) controls over black labour.

Until 1924 capitalist agriculture found its demands partly frustrated by regimes committed to the 'free trade' economic policies favoured by mining capital (see p.14). However, under the Nationalist Labour 'Pact' and 'Fusion' governments (1924-33 and 1933-9 respectively) a number of protectionist measures were introduced to benefit capitalist agriculture. Under the Pact, cheap food imports were subjected to high tariffs and effectively excluded. Cheap credits were made available to capitalist farmers and certain control measures over black labour were tightened. Under the 1937 Agricultural Marketing Act, a comprehensive system of Agricultural Marketing Boards was established to market agricultural commodities at high prices.

The larger capitalist farmers of the Transvaal, who clearly derived most benefit from these measures, broadly supported the United Party. Smaller and more vulnerable capitalist farmers in the Transvaal and OFS, together with Cape agricultural capitalists, deserted to the Purified Nationalist Party formed in opposition to the Fusion in 1934. Prior to 1939, however, the dominant elements in the SAAU broadly supported the Fusion government.

This changed dramatically during and after the Second World War. All major sections of capitalist agriculture now found themselves in acute conflict with other capitals and the United Party regime. The rapid development of manufacturing industry during the war years resulted in a large migration of black workers from 'white' farms. It is estimated in fact that about 40% of the increase in the urban African population in these years came from 'white' farms. Particularly in the Transvaal and OFS, agricultural capital faced an acute labour crisis. Moreover, as part of its 'cheap food' policies favoured by manufacturing and mining, the United Party regime now applied the Marketing Act in such a way as to hold prices down.

During the war years, those sections of capitalist agriculture which had

117

hitherto remained with the UP finally deserted to the Nationalists. Throughout these years, the SAAU pressed for a policy of dividing the African work-force into 'two streams, agricultural and industrial', regulated by a system of labour bureaux. It also fought for a tightening up of the Agricultural Marketing Act. As these demands found a decreasingly sympathetic hearing from UP officials, the SAAU moved closer to the Nationalist Party. By 1948, its new political alignment was openly expressed; the SAAU president hailed the Nationalist victory in the elections of that year, declaring that 'the farmer's boat has now entered calmer waters'.

During the first 12 years of Nationalist rule, the SAAU demanded and achieved a tightening up of pass laws, new 'influx control' measures (to the towns), 'efflux control' measures (from the farms) and a labour bureau system. All these measures served to limit further black labour flows from 'white' farms and redirect part of the reserve army of black labour from the towns to agriculture. The marketing system was also restructured into a comprehensive system of control boards with powers to intervene and protect prices. A wide range of subsidies was also introduced.

During the decade 1960–70 capitalist agriculture entered a new phase in a continuing process of mechanisation. The SAAU demanded and secured various forms of state intervention to advance this process. These included further subsidies, loans and technical assistance. They also included the forced removal and compulsory 'resettlement' in the Bantustans of over a million 'squatters' and former 'labour tenants' who had become 'redundant' with the introduction of more mechanised production techniques.

This process of mechanisation and consequent concentration of capital also brought about a significant centralisation of capital in agriculture. This involved, firstly, the elimination of a significant number of capitalist farmers from production and, secondly, the concentration of economic power in the sector in fewer hands. Thus, between 1960 and 1980, the number of 'white farmers' fell from 106,000 to 70,000; one study using tax revenue data con-cluded that even by 1966, 'white agriculture [was] dominated by *a very small group* of rural capitalists'. It has recently been estimated that 40% of white owned farming land is held by just 5% of white farmers. After 1960 it appears that power within the SAAU passed decisively into the hands of that 'very small group' of more profitable, more mechanised capitalist farmers. This was reflected in the fact that the SAAU argued before the 1970 and 1972 Commissions of Inquiry into Agriculture for a centralisation of power in the hands of 'economic' farmers and the discouragement of 'uneconomic' farming. This represented an important policy change. The SAAU had previously supported measures designed to keep the maximum number of white farmers in business. This it presented ideologically as 'socially and politically desirable' in order to prevent the 'blackening' of the countryside.

During the period of Total Strategy, the SAAU has remained staunchly loyal to the mainstream Nationalist Party, despite the fact that many smaller capitalist farmers now identify with far-right parties. The present SAAU leadership now has important links with Afrikaner monopolies. For example, in seconding SANLAM's annual report in 1982, its president spoke of his 'high esteem' for SANLAM in its role as a long term assurer and provider of finance for capitalist agriculture.

The SAAU is currently campaigning for a reduction in protective tariffs for industries supplying agriculture. This campaign is now notably conducted in terms of the aggressive 'free enterprise' ideology also promoted by the monopolies. In return, the SAAU offers its support for the lifting of various controls and protective measures over the marketing of agricultural produce — despite the fact that such controls remain crucial for smaller farmers. The SAAU, however, continues to favour a system of rigid controls over black labour as the *sine qua non* for capital accumulation in agriculture.

President: Jaap Wilkens.

National African Federated Chambers of Commerce (NAFCOC)[23]

The leading organisation of African capitalists in South Africa. In 1978 NAFCOC consisted of 97 local chambers of commerce with a total of 7,000 individual and company members. Reflecting the contradictory position of the African bourgeoisie in apartheid South Africa, NAFCOC plays an ambivalent role. It is courted by both state and monopoly capital as a crucial organisation in the strategy to 'develop a black middle class' and preserve 'free enterprise values' in South Africa. On the other hand, NAFCOC advances the demands of the existing and aspirant black bourgeoisie and fights against those apartheid provisions which restrict its development. It is, however, firmly opposed to 'extreme elements' and seeks to develop 'responsible African leadership' in South Africa, imbued with 'a love for capitalism'. It is committed to a view of the 'liberation' of blacks in South Africa through the development of black capitalism, in which 'the black man will have to move rapidly from a society of complainers and dependents to a society of doers and planners'.

NAFCOC grew out of the African Chamber of Commerce formed in the Johannesburg area in 1955. Following new restrictions imposed on African traders in 1963, initiatives were launched to link all African businessmen in a single organisation. In April 1964, groups from different parts of South Africa formed the National African Chambers of Commerce (NACOC). Throughout the 1960s, NACOC sought to represent the interests of African businessmen and make representations to the government, but these were consistently ignored because of the organisation's refusal to fragment into separate ethnic components based on the Bantustans. However, the state eventually agreed to accept an umbrella body linking together 'ethnic' chambers of commerce. In May 1969, NACOC reorganised itself as a federation of regional organisations representing the various Bantustans as well as black traders throughout the rest of South Africa; it also changed its name to NAFCOC. In 1978 it consisted of 15 regional organisations in all four provinces and each of the ten Bantustans. Since 1968, the President of first NACOC and then NAFCOC has been Sam Motsuenyane.

NAFCOC appears to be pursuing three broad objectives. The first is the removal of all legal restrictions on African private enterprise, whilst simultaneously utilising the potential protection of apartheid barriers to white capital in the 'black' group areas and Bantustans. Secondly, consciously emulating the development of Afrikaner capital in the 1940s and 1950s, NAFCOC seeks to mobilise, through an appeal to nationalist sentiment, all savings in the hands of South Africa's blacks for the development of explicitly African capital. And, thirdly, whilst operating within the framework of apartheid, NAFCOC's claims to urban leadership and emphasis on the crucial stabilising and moderating role of an expanded black middle class, seek to advance the interests of its members through concessions from the government. Its demands and appeals to the apartheid state are often cast within apartheid ideology. Thus, in a 1972 appeal to lift restrictions on African business outside the Bantustans, NAFCOC argued that

> in the broadest and fairest interpretation of the policy of Separate Development, we would expect the state to allow Africans to serve Africans, and African money to build African progress.

NAFCOC has promoted the emergence of a number of new African enterprises in South Africa. With the active assistance and heavy investment from South Africa's five leading commercial banks, plus a number of overseas financiers, NAFCOC set up the African Bank of South Africa, with Motsuenyane as Chairman. The bank was registered in July 1975 with a paid-up share capital of R 1.3 million, 23% of which was provided by the big banks, and the remainder by private African subscribers; NAFCOC itself contributed 19% of the capital. In 1979, the Bank held a total of R 6.7 million in deposits and had advanced loans of some R4.2 million. Most observers agree, however, that it has not succeeded in mobilising a significant part of the savings of South Africa's blacks, and is kept afloat only through 'substantial' deposits from 'sympathetic white-controlled companies'. Other NAFCOC attempts to co-ordinate the establishment of black business have seen the setting up of an insurance company in collaboration with an American company, and a proposed supermarket group entitled Black Chain.

In the wake of the 1976 Soweto uprising and the scramble by the ruling class to set up a 'stable black middle class with a meaningful stake in the free enterprise system' (in the words of ASSOCOM), NAFCOC has been accorded a leading role by both the state and monopoly capital. Motsuenyane was made a director of the Urban Foundation (see p.122). He was extensively quoted by the now defunct State Information Department as a figure who 'through his many business and lecturing visits overseas, has been able to put South Africa's case in more perspective and to promote international trade with various countries'.

NAFCOC has used this recognition in an attempt to win concessions from the state. Sponsoring a proposal to launch an African Leadership Development Trust, NAFCOC stressed the grievances of the 'urban black community' and the inability of Bantustan regimes to 'exercise effective leadership'. The resulting power vacuum led to 'the growth of extreme elements' and the organisation stressed the need for action to facilitate 'the selection and development of responsible black leadership'. NAFCOC suggested that it liaise with the state, Bantustan regimes and leading employers and employers' organisations to bring about the necessary 'leadership identification' and capital development for the emergence of such 'responsible' leadership which would clearly be a 'firm supporter of free enterprise'.

By thus bidding for a leading role in the black community, NAFCOC seems to be pursuing the twin related objectives of developing support for capitalism within the oppressed population — thus weakening mass support for the national liberation struggle — whilst through pragmatic co-operation with the state, hoping to promote slow change towards a de-racialised capitalist society. In the current impasse of the state's Total Strategy, NAFCOC is making little headway in either of these objectives, and is being forced into an ever closer identification with the ruling class.

In mid-1982 Motsuenyane was appointed to the Prime Minister's Economic Advisory Council. He has claimed that he advocated the idea of a 'constellation of states' before P.W. Botha, and also claims to be establishing 'contacts' with the Southern African Development Coordination Conference (SADCC). These statements were lauded by the South African Broadcasting Corporation.

Referring to these attempts to create black capitalism in South Africa, the South African Allied Workers' Union has commented:

> Quite a sizeable number of blacks are becoming employers and people must not see them as our brothers . . . people must not be fooled just because they are black — they are exploiters.

OTHER ORGANISATIONS OF THE CAPITALIST CLASS

South Africa Foundation[24]

Business lobby group with wide general support among South African capitalist interests. Its role is to 'sell' South Africa abroad as a stable, prosperous haven for foreign investment. The Foundation was formed in 1960 soon after the

Sharpeville massacre with the immediate intention of counteracting the post-Sharpeville 'loss of confidence' which led to large outflows of foreign capital.

The Foundation maintains permanent representatives in London, Paris, Bonn and Washington. It has links with the United Kingdom-South Africa Trade Association (UKSATA), the *Deutsch-Sud Afrikanische Gesellschaft* (DSAG) in Bonn, the *Comite France Afrique du Sud* in Paris and similar organisations in the Netherlands, Switzerland, Canada, Brazil, New Zealand and Scandinavian countries. The organisation lobbies among western governments, officials, editors, business organisations etc., particularly in opposition to proposals for sanctions against South Africa. It also organises and pays for visits to South Africa by potentially sympathetic prominent personalities from western countries. Ostensibly designed to allow these persons to 'see South Africa for themselves', these visits are carefully orchestrated public relations exercises. No expense is spared and visitors are introduced to white and black members of the political and business establishment and provided with trips to game reserves and other holiday facilities. Among the several hundred personalities who have visited South Africa as guests of the Foundation are Frans Joseph Strauss, the West German right-wing politician, and Geoffrey Howe, the then British Chancellor of the Exchequer, as well as numerous Senators and Congressmen from the United States. The Foundation appears to have almost unlimited funds at its disposal. It had 'excellent links' with the former Department of Information though it claimed during the 'information scandal' that it did not receive any funds from the Department.

President: Gavin Relly, Chairman of the Anglo American Corporation.

The Urban Foundation[25]

> Organisation formed and dominated by monopoly capitalists
> to mobilise the resources of the capitalist class in the project to
> create a black middle class.

The Urban Foundation emerged out of the extreme concern of the capitalist class with the paralysis of the Vorster government following the mass uprisings in Soweto and other townships in 1976 (see p.37). During this period, all capitalist groupings put very strong pressure on the government to modify apartheid policies so as to permit the development of a pro-capitalist black middle class, and wean this middle class away from a revolutionary alliance with workers. The *Financial Mail* called for 'Business Power' to assert itself over the government.

The idea of the Urban Foundation was first put forward at a meeting in a London hotel between the two 'giants' of English and Afrikaner monopoly capital, Harry Oppenheimer of Anglo American and Anton Rupert of Rembrandt. Over and above their management positions in these conglomerates, Oppenheimer and Rupert have long been the two most noted ideologists of and strategists for monopoly capital as a whole. Their concept of the Urban Foundation was launched at a 'Businessman's Conference' and began operations in March 1977.

The Foundation's clearly stated objective is to contribute towards the development of a black middle class with

> western-type materialistic needs and ambitions [because] only by having this most responsible section of the urban black population on our side can the whites of South Africa be assured of containing on a long term basis the irresponsible economic and political ambitions of those blacks who are influenced against their own real interests from within and without our borders (Statement 1977).

Its objective — to win black allies for the embattled ruling class — is thus identical to that of Prime Minister Botha's Total Strategy. Not surprisingly, the organisation has been commended by top military commanders, who in the words of Maj.-Gen. Charles Lloyd, agree with it about the need to 'secure through administrative and socio-economic action' the support of certain elements 'by alleviating friction points, grievances and dissatisfaction; improving their standard of living; giving them something to defend in the revolutionary war.'

The Urban Foundation seeks to make its own particular contribution to the common strategic objective of the ruling class by financing and initiating projects aimed at 'improving the quality of life' in black townships. It has given priority to housing and has initiated a number of housing projects throughout South Africa. These are aimed at two class constituencies in the African population: firstly, with respect to the black petty bourgeoisie, the Foundation seeks to have relaxed the social segregation measures and restrictions on black property rights under apartheid, so as to extend 'the free market in housing'. This will enable blacks to 'choose to live near others of a similar socio-economic background'. As the black petty bourgeoisie 'sell their existing houses or buy or build new homes', the Foundation envisages, secondly, that less well-to-do Africans will then be able to occupy such state-provided housing previously occupied by the *nouveaux riches*'. For this vision to be implemented, a change in land tenure laws in the urban areas was necessary. The Foundation played a central role in successfully pressurising the government to introduce the '99 year leasehold' scheme which now permits a form of African home-ownership in black townships in the 'white' areas. Many of the large monopolies now provide loans to certain categories of white collar and skilled manual employees, thus deliberately attempting to create ties of dependence with employers.

The other major area of the Foundation's activity has been in education: here it has involved itself in training schemes, literacy work and other types of pre-school and adult education. Its general aim is to upgrade black education in a context of a severe shortage of trained manpower.

Like its involvement in housing, the Foundation's activities in education should be seen as a collective attempt by the capitalist class to prod state policies in certain directions and collectively to undertake projects which are not sufficiently profit-worthy for individual undertakings. A spokesman has argued that the Foundation 'should be perceived as precisely what it is — an extension of commerce and industry, expressing the opinions of the nation's leading businessmen and industrialists'. Its status as an organisation of monopoly capital is clearly seen in its financial structure. The Foundation claims that the involvement of small business in its affairs is 'impractical at the current moment'. By May 1981 it had received R 32,011,683 from 233 donors. Over 90% of this money was donated by 58 donors, 14 of whom appear in the *Financial Mail*'s 'Giant's League', and a further 13 in its 'Top 100'. More than half of the total donations were provided by seven large donors. The Anglo American Group alone donated R 11 million or 34% of the Foundation's funds; all the other major South African monopolies and banks, with the notable exception of Volkskas, each donated over R 750,000, and some considerably more than this. The Foundation has also raised some R 40 million in loans from foreign banks.

The Urban Foundation's activities have met with a mixed reception amongst South Africa's black petty bourgeoisie; some have openly welcomed it. Sam Motsuenyane, Chairman of the African Bank and President of NAFCOC (see p.119), together with a number of other prominent black businessmen, sit on its board of directors. In Natal, the pro-capitalist Inkatha Movement led by the head of the KwaZulu Bantustan (see p.387), co-operates closely with the Foundation. Others have responded with some hostility. Before its banning in 1977, the Black Consciousness students' organisation, SASO (see p.302), attacked the UF for 'sabotaging the interests of blacks in South Africa by creating a black middle class; other black organisations have repeated these charges. One Cape community organisation has attacked the Foundation as 'Mr Big of Big Business, controlling as much of the lives of people in the townships as possible, wherever stooges can be found to collaborate'. As a result of a fairly widespread hostility from popular organisations, the UF has been forced somewhat on the defensive; it has now instructed its officials to avoid reference to 'the black middle class', and tends to negotiate out of the public eye.

Important leaders:
  Executive Director: Judge J.H. Steyn
  Chairman: Harry Oppenheimer (Anglo American)
  Deputy Chairman: Anton Rupert (Rembrandt)
  Directors include: Zac de Beer (Anglo)
    Clive Menell (Anglovaal)
    Frans Cronje (SA Breweries)
    Sam Motsuenyane (NAFCOC and African Bank)

Vem Tshabalala (NAFCOC and African Bank)
Pat Poovalinham (prominent businessman of Indian origin).

Free Market Foundation[26]

One of several organisations founded by members of the capitalist class in
the period immediately following the 1976 Soweto uprising to 'spread the
message of free enterprise to young blacks'. The Foundation was supported
by the Associated Chambers of Commerce, the Federated Chambers of
Industry, the Chamber of Mines, the *Afrikaner Handelsinstituut*, the National
African Federated Chambers of Commerce, the Trade Union Council of
South Africa and the Confederation of Labour (see respective entries).
Despite such backing, however, the Foundation now seems to have been
surpassed as a vehicle for the inculcation of bourgeois ideology among blacks
by such organisations as the Urban Foundation (see p.122).

Its main activity at present seems to be the presentation of awards to
ideologues of capitalism on 'Free Enterprise Day', 1 July each year. In 1982
it announced that 30 'prominent personalities' had become individual patrons
of the organisation. These included leading monopoly capitalists such as
Oppenheimer and Rupert and also two officials of the collaborationist labour
organisation TUCSA, Arthur Grobelaar and Lucy Mvubelo (see p.250).

Officials:
Leon Louw
Dr S.P. du Toit Viljoen

BIBLIOGRAPHICAL NOTE

General

The most valuable single source on the South African economy is the
Johannesburg weekly *Financial Mail*. A regular reading of this source over
a number of years provided much of the information used in this chapter.
The quarterly index published by the *Financial Mail* is especially useful.
The Annual Special Survey on 'Top Companies', published each May, was a
basic source.

In addition to the specific sources cited below, the following newspapers
have also been consulted regularly: *Rand Daily Mail* (Johannesburg); *Sunday
Times,* Business Times (Johannesburg); *The Star Weekly* (Johannesburg);
ANC Weekly News Briefing (London).

Each of the organisations covered in this chapter puts out a range of
publications, annual reports and position papers too numerous to list here.
The reader is advised to consult these.

In this chapter, references are divided into: a) sources used to write the
entry, and; b) further general reading and sources of information.

Specific Entries
1. a) see 'General' above.
   Clarke, S., *Changing Patterns of International Investment in South Africa and the Disinvestment Campaign*, London, Anti-Apartheid Movement, 1978.
   Clarke, S., *Financial Aspects of Economic Sanctions on South Africa*, Geneva, IUEF, 1980.
   Kaplan, D., 'The Current "Upswing" in the South African Economy and the International Capitalist Crisis: A Reinterpretation of South African "Development" ', *Work in Progress*, 16, 1981.
   Fransman, M., *The South African Manufacturing Sector and Economic Sanctions*, Geneva, IUEF, 1980.
   b) Houghton, D. Hobart, *The South African Economy*, Cape Town, Oxford University Press, 1976.
   South African Journal of Economics.
   South African Reserve Bank, Quarterly Reports.
   South African Reserve Bank, Annual Economic Review.
2. a) See 'General' above.
   Financial Mail, annual Special Survey on 'Top Companies' published each May.
   McGregor, R., *Who Owns Whom*, Somerset West, 1980, 1982.
   Report of the Commission of Enquiry into the Regulation of Monopolistic Conditions Act of 1955, Pretoria, 1977.
   b) Innes, D., 'Monopoly Capitalism in South Africa', in *South African Review*, Ravan, 1983.
3. a) see 'General' above.
   Business International, *Apartheid and Business: An Analysis of the Rapidly Evolving Challenge Facing Companies with Investments in South Africa*, Multiclient Study, 1980.
   Innes, D., 'Accumulation and Expansion in the South African Gold Mining Industry 1945–1960', Sussex University Seminar Paper, 1976.
   Innes, D., 'The Mining Industry in the Context of South Africa's Economic Development 1910–1940', London, Institute of Commonwealth Studies, *Collected Seminar Papers*, Vol 21, 1977.
   McGregor, R., op.cit.
   b) *Fortune*, 10 August 1981 (New York).
   Innes, D., *Anglo American and the Rise of Modern South Africa*, London, Heineman, 1983.
   Optima (Johannesburg)
4. a) see 'General' above.
   Financial Mail, Special Survey on *Federale Volksbeleggings*, 31 July 1981.
   McGregor, R., op.cit.
   O'Meara, D., *Volkskapitalisme: Class, Capital and Ideology in the Development of Afrikaner Nationalism, 1934–1948*, Cambridge, Cambridge University Press, 1983.
   b) du Plessis, E.P., *'n Volk Staan Op: Die Ekonomiese Volkskongres en Daarna*, Cape Town, Human & Rousseau, 1964.
   Volkshandel (Johannesburg)
5. a) see 'General' above.
   Financial Mail, Special Survey on Barlow Rand, 13 February 1981.

McGregor, R., op.cit.
6. a) see 'General' above.
  McGregor, R., op.cit.
  O'Meara, D., op.cit.
  b) *Financial Mail*, Special Survey on Volkskas, 14 September 1979.
  du Plessis, E.P., op.cit.
  Volkshandel
7. a) see 'General' above.
  McGregor, R., op.cit.
8. a) see 'General' above.
  Fortune, op.cit.
  McGregor, R., op.cit.
  O'Meara, D., op.cit.
  b) du Plessis, E.P., op.cit.
  Volkshandel.
9. a) see 'General' above.
  Financial Mail, Special Survey 'Top Companies', 30 April 1982.
  McGregor, R., op.cit.
10. a) see 'General' above.
  Financial Mail, Special Survey 'SAB Focus on You', 27 July 1979.
  McGregor, R., op.cit.
11. a) see 'General' above.
  Business International, op.cit.
  Clarke, S., 1980, op.cit.
  First, R., Steele, J. and Gurney, C., *The South African Connection*,
  Harmondsworth, Penguin, 1973.
  South African Labour Education Project, *Profiteering from Cheap
  Labour: Wages Paid by British Companies in South Africa*, London,
  1980.
  Volkshandel, March 1949.
  b) Numerous publications of anti-apartheid groups in western Europe
  and North America.
  Corporate Data Exchange, *Bank Loans to South Africa*, New York,
  UN Centre Against Apartheid, 1979.
  Foreign Relations Committee of the United States Senate, 'US Corpor-
  ate Interest in South Africa', 1978.
  House of Commons Expenditure Sub-Committee, *Investigation into
  Wages and Working Conditions of African Workers Employed by
  British Firms in South Africa*, HMSO, 1973/4.
  I.R.R.C. Directory of US Corporations in South Africa, New York,
  1982.
  International University Exchange Fund, *Economic Sanctions Against
  South Africa* (series), Geneva, 1980.
  Study Project on External Investment in South Africa and Namibia
  (series), London, Africa Publications Trust, 1975.
  UN Commission on Transnational Corporations, *The Activities of
  Transnational Corporations in the Industrial, Mining and Military
  Sectors of Southern Africa*, New York, 1979.
12. a) see 'General' above.
  Financial Mail, Special Survey on 'Top Companies', 8 May 1981.
13. a) see 'General' above.

Davies, R., *Capital, State and White Labour in South Africa 1900-1960*, Brighton, Harvester Press, 1979.

SADCC 2, Southern African Transport and Communications Commission: *Transport and Communications Projects*, Maputo, 1980.

South African Institute of Race Relations, *Survey of Race Relations in South Africa*, annual, Johannesburg.

South African Transport Services, *Annual Reports*, Pretoria.

b) House of Assembly Debates, Vote of the Minister of Transport in Budget debates.

Financial Mail, Special Survey on SATS, 26 September 1980.

14. a) see 'General' above.

Financial Mail, Special Survey on Iscor, 7 November 1980.

Morris, M. and Kaplan, D., 'Labour Policy in a State Corporation: A Case Study of the South African Iron and Steel Industry' in *South African Labour Bulletin*, 2, 6, 1976 & 2, 7, 1976.

15. a) see 'General' above.

Financial Mail, Special Survey on SASOL, 16 November 1979.

Financial Mail, Special Survey on Energy, 5 March 1982.

16. a) see 'General' above.

Financial Mail, 11 September 1981.

International Defence and Aid Fund, *The Apartheid War Machine*, London, 1980.

b) *Paratus*, Supplement on Armscor, November 1982.

17. a) see 'General' above.

Bardill, J., Southall, R. and Perrings, J., 'The State and Labour Migration in the South African Political Economy with Particular Respect to Gold Mining', Geneva, ILO, 1977.

Clarke, D., 'The South African Chamber of Mines: Policy and Strategy with Reference to Foreign African Labour Supply', Pietermaritzburg, Development Studies Research Group Paper, Natal University, 1977.

Johnstone, F.A., *Class, Race and Gold: A Study of Class Relations and Racial Discrimination in South Africa*, London, Routledge & Kegan Paul, 1976.

Webster, E., 'Background to the Supply and Control of Labour in the South African Gold Mines' in E. Webster (ed.) *Essays in Southern African Labour History*, Johannesburg, Ravan Press, 1978.

b) South African Chamber of Mines, *Annual Report(s)*.

18. a) see 'General' above.

Kaplan, D., *Class Conflict, Capital Accumulation and the State: An Historical Analysis of the State in Twentieth Century South Africa.* D.Phil. dissertation, Sussex University, 1977.

Kaplan, D., and Morris, M., 'Manufacturing Capital and the Question of African Trade Union Recognition', *South African Labour Bulletin*, 7, 1 and 2, 1981.

Morris, M., 'Capital's Response to African Trade Unions Post Wiehahn', ibid.

19. a) see 'General' above.

Kaplan, D. and Morris, M., 1981, op.cit.

Morris, M., 1981, op.cit.

The Steel and Engineering Industries Federation of South Africa,

Organisation and Structure of the Metal and Engineering Industries in the Republic of South Africa, Johannesburg, n.d.
20. a) see 'General' above.
    Bozolli, B., *The Political Nature of a Ruling Class: Capital and Ideology in South Africa 1890–1933*, London, Routledge & Kegan Paul, 1981.
    Financial Mail, Special Survey on Assocom, 15 October 1982.
21. a) see 'General' above.
    O'Meara, D., op.cit.
    Afrikaanse Handelsinstituut, *30 Jaar Afrikaanse Handelsinstituut*, Pretoria, 1972.
   b) *Volkshandel.*
22. a) see 'General' above.
    Financial Mail, Special Survey on Agriculture, 17 May 1982.
    Kaplan, D., 1977, op.cit.
    Morris, M., *The State and the Development of Capitalist Social Relations in the South African Countryside: a Process of Class Struggle.* D.Phil. dissertation, Sussex University, 1979.
    Wilson, F., Kooy, A. and Hendrie, D., (eds.), *Farm Labour in South Africa*, Cape Town, David Philip, 1977.
   b) *Farmers' Weekly*
23. a) see 'General' above.
    Financial Mail, 25 March 1983.
    Southall, R., 'African Capitalism in Contemporary South Africa', *Journal of Southern African Studies*, 7, 1, 1980.
24. a) see 'General' above.
    Africa Bureau, *The Great White Hoax: South Africa's International Propaganda Machine*, London, 1977.
    First, R., Steele, J. and Gurney, C., op.cit.
25. a) see 'General' above.
    Financial Mail, Special Survey, 'The Urban Foundation – Two Years On', 16 February 1979.
    Karon, T., 'The Urban Foundation' in Cooper, L. and Kaplan, D., (eds.) *Selected Research Papers on Aspects of Organisation in the Western Cape*, University of Cape Town, 1982.
26. a) See 'General' above.

3. Political Organisations of the Ruling Class and Its Allies

INTRODUCTION: STATE POLITICAL STRUCTURES[1]

Historical Development, 1870-1910

The form of state which came into existence in South Africa with the union of the four British colonies in 1910 is perhaps best described as a racially exclusive bourgeois democracy. The vast bulk of the black population was excluded from all representation in, and access to, state structures. On the other hand, however, all classes of the white population, and certain limited categories of blacks (see below p.133) were incorporated into representative institutions characteristic of bourgeois democracy — parliament, political parties etc.

This form of state emerged as the result of the specific processes of class formation and class struggle in which capitalist relations of production were established on a large scale in South Africa. As indicated in Chapter 1 (pp.7-11), the opening up of the diamond, and more particularly gold, mining industries at the end of the 19th Century inaugurated a process in which capitalist forms of production rapidly developed in all sectors and regions of South Africa. This rapid transition to capitalism gave rise to new forms of social relations with new contradictions and struggles. In the process political relations and the form of state were transformed.

Most fundamentally, the development of capitalism transformed large numbers of the oppressed colonised masses into wage labourers. However as indicated pp.7-14, capital accumulation in all sectors was critically dependent on the availability of *cheap* labour. Accordingly, the development of capitalism in South Africa subjected blacks to a range of specific highly coercive measures such as racially discriminatory land laws, the pass system regulating their mobility, special taxes to drive them into wage labour, the compound system etc. All these measures were explicitly designed to ensure that black peasants provided the necessary cheap labour power in sufficient quantities.

On the other hand, the development of the mining industry after 1870, and the subsequent transition to capitalism in agriculture 1870-1920, also transformed the previous exploiting classes, leaving capitalists as the only exploiting class. However, the particular path of capitalist development in South Africa gave rise to acute contradictions and conflicts within this capitalist class itself (see pp.14-28).

South Africa's racially exclusive parliamentary system was forged in the concrete struggles arising out of the contradictions generated by the transformation of social relations after 1870. The specific forms of capitalist exploitation which emerged reinforced the imperatives for the capitalist ruling class to maintain one crucial feature of all the state forms generated by colonialism since 1652 — the exclusion of the vast majority of blacks from any representative institutions. The state was required to secure the availability of a cheap labour force for capital. Through the state the racial division of the land was effected and legitimated. The state also administered an array of controls and coercive measures over this labour force — the most important being Pass Laws and the Masters and Servants Laws (see pp.171-3). Any access by the bulk of the black exploited masses to the representative institutions of even bourgeois parliamentary democracy would have fundamentally impeded the development of such a cheap labour system. This was clearly recognised by the exploiting classes. Thus the various attacks on the relative economic independence of the African peasantry after 1880 were accompanied by demands that the very small number of enfranchised black property owners in the Cape Province be deprived of the vote and all political rights. Moreover, the fact that under the migrant labour system African workers retained some base in the peasant economy of the labour reserve areas, made it possible to present the 'tribal' structures based in the reserves as an alternative to representation of blacks in the central state.

On the other hand, these transformations placed severe strains on the earlier state forms, particularly those that had developed in the Boer republics after 1852. Based on societies dominated by pre-capitalist agrarian rentier landlords, these state forms proved too unwieldy and inefficient to implement a number of the specific measures demanded by mining capital to secure its cheap African labour force in the 1890s. Moreover, agrarian landlords who dominated the Transvaal Boer republic sought to exclude mining capital from effective representation in its representative institutions, whilst simultaneously siphoning off revenue from the mining industry to subsidise various of their own projects. These factors eventually led mining capitalists to organise together with British imperialism to overthrow these Boer regimes in the Anglo-Boer war of 1899-1902.

This war resulted in the imposition of direct colonial rule throughout all of what is now South Africa. This, however, created its own conflicts, as much of the settler population — and particularly the emerging agrarian bourgeoisie in the Transvaal and Orange Free State — were excluded from any specific representation of their interests in the colonial states until 1906/7. These four colonies merged into the Union of South Africa in 1910, creating a racially exclusive bourgeois democracy (partially qualified by the enfranchisement of black property owners in the Cape). The major bourgeois interests were organised into competing political parties (see chart p.159). This form of state, which excluded the exploited masses from its representative institutions, served to secure the necessary conditions of accumulation of capital. It also provided an effective forum for the resolution of contradictions within the capitalist class, and a vehicle for uniting it in pursuit of the common objective of maintaining bourgeois domination over the exploited masses.

In addition to the bourgeoisie, however, South Africa's racially exclusive bourgeois democracy also included within its representative institutions other white classes — the white petty bourgeoisie and white workers. This can be explained by two main factors: firstly, that these classes were too small and too weak to ever effectively challenge bourgeois hegemony on their own. Secondly, under the existing conditions of class struggle the bourgeoisie needed some degree of support from other white classes in order to maintain its rule over the colonised masses.

Particular minority categories of the black population were also initially granted a degree of access to representative institutions. In the Cape, Africans, coloureds and Asians who met certain property and income qualifications (not applicable after 1928 to whites — the year in which white women also received the right to vote) were eligible to vote *though not themselves to stand* in parliamentary and provincial council elections. This Cape qualified franchise had been introduced in 1854 and was retained in that province after union in 1910. The qualification admitted only the propertied strata of the black population whom it was expected might identify with the bourgeoisie. The specific path of capitalist development, particularly in the countryside, assured that such strata would always be small and unable to challenge bourgeois hegemony. The subordination of the reserves as sources of labour power rather than of agricultural commodities severely curtailed any process of peasant differentiation and consequent emergence of a rich African kulak class in the reserves. The effects of the 1913 Land Act finally wiped out the embryonic African kulak stratum which had begun to emerge in the 'white' rural areas after 1870.

Outside the Cape, the exclusion of African middle strata, no matter how small, was virtually complete. In Natal an additional educational qualification meant that not more than 50 blacks were ever registered as voters, whilst *all* persons other than white males were totally excluded from the franchise in the Orange Free State and Transvaal from the outset.

After 1910, the position of the approximately 12,000 African voters in the Cape came under steady attack. Finally under the Representation of Natives Act of 1936, Africans were removed from the common voters roll in the Cape. Instead, Cape African males were given the 'right' to elect three special (white) MPs, and a purely advisory Natives' Representative Council, consisting of appointed members as well as elected members from all provinces, was set up.

Institutions of South Africa's Racially Exclusive Bourgeois Democracy During the Period of Segregation 1910–1948

South Africa's racially exclusive bourgeois democracy was based on the British Westminster system. This provided for a 'separation' and degree of autonomy for the legislative, executive and judicial branches of government. South Africa was part of the British Commonwealth – enjoying Dominion status as a 'fully autonomous and sovereign state' after the 1931 Statute of Westminster. The British monarch was the head of state, represented locally by a governor-general appointed by the South African government.

Broadly speaking, the legislative branch was dominant throughout the period of segregation, although there were some signs of a partial undermining towards the end of the 1930s. Its major institutions at the national level were a parliament consisting of the House of Assembly, directly elected by the overwhelmingly white electorate, and the Senate, elected on a provincial basis by an electoral college consisting of the Members of the House of Assembly and Members of the Provincial Council from each province. Parliament was responsible for the passage of laws. Through the party system it provided an appropriate forum for the representation of diverse interests within the ruling class and its allies, as well as for the resolution of contradictions.

At the provincial level, Provincial Councils directly elected by the white electorate had responsibility for formulating ordinances on white education, health, roads and local government affairs, whilst local authorities elected by white adult residents formulated local by-laws and regulations.

The executive branch consisted, at the national level, of the Cabinet appointed by the leader of the majority party in the House of Assembly, who himself became Prime Minister. The Cabinet was responsible for the administration of State Departments and introduced new legislation. During the segregation period, as distinct from that of apartheid after 1948, the Cabinet was generally subjected to a degree of real control and scrutiny by parliament. At the provincial level, the Provincial Administrator appointed by the central government, himself appointed an Executive Committee which reflected the balance of the parties in the Provincial Council.

The judicial branch consisting of judges and magistrates was appointed by the Governor-General on advice from the legal profession and was constitutionally independent of the legislature.

Developments 1948–1976

The coming to power of the Nationalist Party regime in 1948 in the wake of the crisis of segregation and the subsequent transition from segregation to apartheid (see pp.16–19) brought about a number of changes in state forms. Apart from the establishment of a Republic outside the British Commonwealth in 1961 – which brought about few substantive changes in the state form apart from substituting a figurehead President for the Governor-General — there were two major developments.

Firstly all categories of blacks were removed from access to the representative institutions of the central state. Persons of Asian origin had been removed from the common voters roll in Natal by the previous United Party government in 1945, which provided instead for separate representation by four (white) senators. Asians lost this 'right' as well in 1948. A long complex constitutional struggle from 1951 to 1956 removed so-called coloureds in the Cape from the common voters roll. Initially they were given the right to elect four (white) representatives to parliament and two to the Cape Provincial Council. However, in 1968 the Separate Representation of Voters Amendment Act removed this 'right' as well. Finally under the 1959 Promotion of Bantu Self Government Act, the three MPs elected by African male voters in the Cape since 1936 were abolished. By the 1970s all categories of the black population were totally excluded from the representative institutions of the central state. Africans were supposed to exercise their 'political rights' through tribally orientated structures based on the Bantustans (see p.197ff). (The Natives' Representative Council had been abolished in 1951.) Coloureds were supposed to be represented by the Coloured Representative Council and Asians by the South African Indian Council.

The other noteworthy trend in the period 1948–76 was the growing dominance of the executive over the legislative and judicial branches of government, and a corresponding trend towards greater authoritarianism. The offensive of the Nationalist Party regime against the living standards and popular organisations of the masses, together with the specific forms of state intervention to promote the interests of the class forces organised in the NP, are discussed in p.23ff above. Both necessitated more authoritarian forms of government. The offensive against the masses required a 'strong state', not overly burdened with legalistic 'safeguards' on human rights. The promotion of specific interests likewise required a certain reduction in legislative scrutiny and greater discretionary powers for the executive.

The result was a major shift in power towards the executive and the rise in importance of the repressive apparatuses of the state — at this stage particularly the police and security services such as BOSS. During the 1940s and 1950s, the courts had been used to some extent by the liberation movement and other progressives to thwart temporarily various moves by the regime. By the early 1960s the judiciary was systematically subordinated through a combination of political appointments to the bench and legislation reducing the discretionary powers of judges. Similarly, the legislature was reduced in importance through the granting of more and more discretionary powers to ministers and such manoeuvres as the blatant 'packing of the Senate' in 1956 in order to ensure the passage of the acts removing coloureds from the common voters' roll. As a consequence, the executive branch, and more particularly the Cabinet, became the dominant apparatuses of government whilst, from the early 1960s, security services and the police received ever more discretionary powers. The pre-1976 apartheid state can thus be described essentially as an authoritarian police state.

Developments after 1976: The Rise of the Military

As indicated on pp.32–36, the late 1970s and the 1980s have been a period of acute crisis for the apartheid system and its state form. In response to the growing mass challenge, a new alliance of monopoly capital and the military has now become the dominant force in the ruling class and the state. Important changes in state political structures have resulted – most importantly, the growing militarisation of the state.

The pursuit of the Total Strategy following the election of P.W. Botha as Prime Minister in September 1978 (see p.144) has propelled the military into a significant role within the executive branch, formulating not just military policy in the narrow sense but the overall strategy of the state. The specific mechanism of this growing military influence within the executive has been the State Security Council (SSC). Originally set up in 1972 as an advisory body, under Botha's premiership, the SSC has become the major decision-making body in the state, with a network of links embracing all government departments (see entry on the military, pp.179–92). But the perceived need for the ruling class to seek 'black middle class' allies, together with its evident failure to win widespread support for the Total Strategy among the NP's traditional white petty bourgeois and wage earning mass base (see p.152), has prompted the regime to seek more far-reaching institutional institutional changes.

In 1980, the Senate was abolished and replaced by a State President's Council, consisting of white, so-called coloured, and Asian appointees. Its brief was to formulate proposals for a 'new constitutional dispensation'. In accordance with the basic premises of the Total Strategy, this would give the *appearance* of inaugurating a system of 'power sharing' with certain categories of the oppressed population, whilst in reality ensuring that real power remained firmly in the hands of the present ruling alliance. This new dispensation was also required to free the ruling alliance from pressures from disgruntled white labour and petty bourgeoisie which impeded the introduction of socio-economic changes essential to the Total Strategy.

The President's Council proposals were presented in May 1982 and approved in a somewhat amended form by the Cabinet and Nationalist Party caucus (purged of its far right by the engineered split leading to the formation of the Conservative Party – see p.149). Through skillful manoeuvring the Botha faction ensured their endorsement first by a federal congress of the Nationalist Party (the first in over 40 years) and then by each of the four provincial congresses. Legislation will be presented to parliament in 1983 and, according to the envisaged timetable, the new 'dispensation' will be implemented in 1984.

Under the new system, certain changes will be made in the legislature so as to incorporate 'representatives' of the coloured and Asian population groups in what the official ideology describes as 'consociational democratic structures'. More specifically, there are to be three separate legislative chambers – one for whites, one for coloureds and one for Asians – which would relate to one another through a series of joint committees. Africans will not be included: they are to exercise their 'political rights' in the Bantustans, whilst municipal structures with slightly increased 'powers' will be set up in large 'black' urban areas, such as Soweto.

At the same time, however, the executive will be given even greater powers than at present and be freed from virtually any obligation or accountability to the 'representative' institutions of the 'consociational democracy'. Under the new system, South Africa will have an Executive President elected indirectly by an electoral college consisting of 50 members chosen by the largest party in the 'white' legislative chamber, and 25 and 13 respectively by the 'coloured' and 'Asian' chambers.

The President will appoint a cabinet consisting of members of the three chambers and will also have the power to decide which matters to be discussed by the legislature are matters of exclusive concern to one chamber, and which are of 'common concern'. In matters of 'common concern', a system of joint committees of the three chambers will be set up to 'try to achieve consensus' and take 'the major debate out of the debating chamber'. In cases where the three chambers disagree, the final decision will be taken by the President's Council. This will consist of 60 members: 25 personally appointed by the President; 20 by the white legislature; 10 by the coloured chamber and five by the Asian chamber.

The dictatorial powers to be assigned to the Executive President are intended to ensure firstly that the legislative chambers for coloureds and Asians do not become effective vehicles for the promotion of popular demands or the thwarting of 'executive' measures; and secondly, that the various petty bourgeois class forces still represented in the Nationalist Party (or in other parties in the white legislature) cannot use their parliamentary position to block the 'reforms' envisaged under the Total Strategy. As a final reserve, the Executive President will have the power to dissolve the legislature.

These proposals clearly imply a change in the role of political parties in state structures, but not the end of the party system as a means of organisation of the ruling class and its allies. The Executive President and candidates for the presidency will still need some form of political organisation behind them, and the legislatures will still be organised on party lines. However, the implementation of the 'consociational democracy' will clearly limit the effectiveness of parties in the minority legislative chambers for the coloured and Asian populations. It probably also implies a more authoritarian form of organisation of the largest party in the white chamber, which would in effect be a tool of the presidency.

THE NATIONALIST PARTY[2]

The governing party in South Africa since May 1948, currently led by Prime Minister P.W. Botha. Historically, the Nationalist Party (NP) organised an alliance of various class forces under the banner of Afrikaner nationalism. It regards itself as the political representative of the 'Afrikaner *volk*'. Its programme is apartheid — or, as its current euphemism has it — 'white self-determination' based on 'healthy powersharing'.

Since the mid-1970s, the NP has been deeply divided between so-called 'reformists' and 'conservatives'. The former favour minor modifications to apartheid in the hope of winning black support for 'capitalism'. The latter also claim to recognise the need for 'reforms' but reject anything which, in their view, weakens white domination. The reformists emerged as the dominant group under P.W. Botha after 1978. In early 1982, the conservatives were outmanoeuvred and forced out of the NP. Sixteen former Nationalist Party MPs formed the Conservative Party to oppose Botha's so-called 'reformist' policies.

For much of its history the NP was, and remains today, an organisation operating simultaneously at a number of distinct levels of politics. Thus, on the one hand it is a mass, white, racist political party which organises and mobilises outside the state apparatus, an alliance of class forces under the banner of Afrikaner nationalism. As such, it depicts itself as the political representative of all classes of white Africaans-speakers in South Africa. On the other hand, however, the NP is also the ruling party in the capitalist state. Its function at this level is both to represent within the state apparatus the interests of its class base, and to secure the favourable conditions for accumulation by all sections of the capitalist class.

At each of these distinct levels of politics, the NP functions differently and is subject to a different, yet intersecting array of pressures and class conflicts. However, since 1948 its role as the ruling party in the capitalist state has largely shaped the way in which it has represented the interests of the different class forces organised by the party outside of the state apparatus. To some extent, the intense conflict within the Nationalist Party and government during the period 1976–82, grew out of conflict between these two levels of the party's operation. In other words, various policies of the NP government aimed at securing favourable conditions of accumulation for the capitalist class as a whole, came into conflict with certain interests of sections of the Afrikaner petty bourgeoisie and white wage earners 'traditionally' organised in the NP since 1948. Furthermore, the transformation of the NP's class base after 1948 induced strenuous conflict between the constituent forces of the Afrikaner nationalist class alliance.

Organisational Structure

The NP is not a single 'unitary' party, but rather a loose federation of four autonomous provincial Nationalist Parties. Each of these four parties has a distinct social base, party organisation, membership, constitution, press and political and ideological style. Each is a site of differing struggles and represents widely varying interests. A knowledge of the structure of the NP is vital to an understanding of its operation, as the real locus of power within the party itself lies in the provincial party organisations rather than the national institutions of the party. Within the provincial NPs the provincial leaders often have greater influence than the national leader of the party. Within the party itself (as distinct from the Cabinet) the provincial leaders wield as much influence as the national leader himself. These provincial parties have always jealously guarded their particular interests, prerogatives and identities from each other and the 'national' institutions of the party.

The 'regionalist' or 'provincialist' conflicts which have always characterised Afrikaner nationalist politics thus rest on four separate party structures. However, the regionalism is more fundamentally explained by the fact that these parties each have a distinct class basis. As separately-organised, separately-led and separately-financed political institutions with different class bases, each provincial Nationalist Party is the institutionalisation of a distinct form of class alliance, differing in important respects from those of its federal partners. Moreover, in the period of Nationalist party rule from 1948 to the present, the class forces organised in the Afrikaner nationalist alliance in each province have been affected in different ways by the policies and strategies of the NP-ruled state to secure overall capitalist prosperity. Thus the conflicts between the class forces organised in the Nationalist Party have often taken the form of regionalist confrontation. The recent struggle between the so-called reformers and conservatives was often depicted as a struggle for dominance by the Transvaal NP (then led by Andries Treurnicht) over the Cape NP (led by Prime Minister Botha).

Early Class Basis in Each Province

When the NP came into office in 1948, the composition of the Afrikaner nationalist class alliance differed in the various provinces. In the Transvaal, the NP organised, for the first time, an alliance of capitalist farmers (who were losing labour to industry); specific strata of white labour; the large Afrikaans-speaking petty bourgeoisie (who, like white wage earners, were threatened with displacement by Africans 'from below') and emerging out of this petty bourgeoisie, a small group of aspirant commercial and financial capitalists organised in the 'Afrikaner economic movement'. This latter group was heavily dependent on the reinvested surpluses of agriculture and the savings of Afrikaans-speakers of all classes.

Moreover, alongside the NP, Transvaal Afrikaner nationalist politics were dominated by the secret *Afrikaner Broederbond* (Afrikaner Brotherhood). This was effectively the institution through which the specific interests of the Afrikaner petty bourgeoisie came to be independently organised and articulated. The *Broederbond* assumed a self-conscious role as the vanguard of Afrikaner nationalism. Through it, the Afrikaner petty bourgeoisie exercised ideological dominance over all class forces organised in the Transvaal NP and other organs of Afrikaner nationalism in the province. Thus, within the Transvaal NP, an Afrikaner nationalist ideology was developed which stressed a particular form of anti-British sentiment and emphasised the interests of the (white) 'small man' against the large, and predominantly English-speaking monopolies which dominated the economy.

The situation in the Cape differed markedly: here, the NP had long rested on an economic and political alliance between the wealthier capitalist farmers on the one hand, and a small group of financial capitalists in SANLAM, and later Rembrandt, on the other (see entries pp. 75 and 84).

The moving spirits of SANLAM had in fact dominated the Cape NP since they first formed it in 1915. Thus the Cape NP was always far more openly capitalist in orientation and sympathies than the other provincial NPs (particularly the Transvaal). Its interpretation of what constituted the Afrikaner *volk* and 'its' interests, likewise varied considerably from the petty bourgeois 'anti-capitalism' which dominated the Transvaal NP. Significantly, the *Broederbond* did not develop into a strong force in Cape Afrikaner nationalist politics. Indeed the *Broederbond* was often characterised in the Transvaal as the major oppositional force to 'Cape finance power'.

In the Orange Free State, a province of little industry, dominated by agriculture, and later gold-mining, the petty bourgeoisie and rural capitalists were the real base of the NP. This gave it a more rural orientation than both the Cape and Transvaal parties. Here too, the *Broederbond* was a significant force amongst the petty bourgeoisie of the province. However, compared with the Cape and Transvaal, the Orange Free State is a small province and its party was eclipsed by the NPs of the two major provinces. Similarly in Natal, the Afrikaans-speaking population was relatively small, and the Natal NP did not develop into a significant force.

The NP in Power: Policies and Internal Conflicts

The acute political crisis which brought the NP into power under Dr D.F. Malan in 1948, is discussed pp.16-19. The Nationalist Party mobilised an Afrikaner nationalist class alliance organised around a programme of 'apartheid' — a programme pledged to a restructuring of the conditions of capital accumulation in such a way as to defend and advance the material interests of Afrikaner capitalist farmers, wage earners, petty bourgeoisie and small and aspirant capitalists on the basis of intensified repression and exploitation of African workers.

Three broad phases of NP rule can be identified: 1948–60; 1960–73;

1973 to the present. Each of these is marked both by distinct policy directions, and internal conflicts between the class forces within the NP.

1948–1960

The apartheid policies of the Nationalist Party after 1948 created the conditions for rapid capital accumulation by all capitalists, and improved living standards for all whites. These measures are discussed pp.21–5. Also, capital accumulation was further fostered by policies which encouraged the centralisation and interpenetration of capitals. The rule of the self-proclaimed 'anti-monopolist' and 'anti-capitalist' NP, saw both the rapid development of monopoly capitalist relations of production and an extremely high rate of capitalist growth.

Apart from these generalised policies to secure rapid accumulation for all capitalists, the NP government also directly fostered the interests of the class forces it represented. A policy of strict 'influx control' through rigid pass laws, together with a system of labour bureaux, removed the large reserve army of unemployed African workers from the cities and dumped them in the rural reserves. This enabled the state to control and channel the flow of labour to all sectors of capitalist production, and in particular solved the acute labour crisis which confronted capitalist farmers. The system of job reservation and destruction of African working-class organisations protected the niche of privilege of white labour. Various segregationist measures enhanced the position of the Afrikaner petty bourgeoisie and removed the threat of displacement by a black petty bourgeoisie. The Group Areas Act drove small Indian traders out of the cities, enabling Afrikaner commerce to take their place. Government and local authority accounts were switched to Afrikaner finance companies, which facilitated their extraordinarily rapid growth. Government contracts were awarded to Afrikaner firms. Afrikaner businessmen were appointed to vital positions on numerous state economic boards and to senior management positions in state industries. In short, various forms of state support to Afrikaner capitals ensured their integration on favourable terms into the emerging relations of monopoly capitalism. In many ways, this class force was the major beneficiary of NP rule. In 1948 there existed hardly any Afrikaner business undertakings worth talking about. Today, SANLAM is the second biggest conglomerate in the country, and two other Afrikaner monopolies, Volkskas and Rembrandt, are amongst the eight non-state conglomerates which dominate the South African economy (see entries pp.70, 79, 82).

Thus, while all sections of the original NP class base benefited directly from NP rule, they did so unevenly. From the early 1950s, conflicts began to develop within the Nationalist Party between the various class forces from which it drew support. These conflicts centered on the question of which class force was the 'real' representative of the Afrikaner *'volk'*. Increasingly they developed into a struggle between on the one hand, the petty bourgeoisie of the Transvaal and Orange Free State, also organised into the *Broederbond* and on the other, the financial capitalists in SANLAM and Rembrandt in the

Cape. These conflicts also arose out of the changing character of the Nationalist class alliance. By 1960, so successful was the NP government's promotion of Afrikaner financial institutions that they had ceased to depend on the surplus profits of Afrikaner capitalist farmers as their major source of finance. Thus particularly in and through the Cape NP, Afrikaner capital began to advocate independent policies. By 1960, the Cape NP was seen as 'the official opposition' within the Nationalist Party. The class-based conflicts in the NP this appeared as 'regionalist' struggles between the Cape and Transvaal NPs.

1960-1973

The year of the Sharpeville massacre, 1960, marked a new phase of NP rule. Faced with mounting mass resistance to apartheid, the regime, now led by Dr H.F. Verwoerd, launched a two-pronged strategy. Firstly, under the supervision of Justice Minister John Vorster it greatly intensified repression. In April 1960 the African National Congress and Pan Africanist Congress were proscribed; detention without trial was introduced; torture of prisoners became standard practice; and heavy prison sentences, and a number of death sentences were handed out to organisers of political opposition to the regime. At the same time, the 'political solution' of the Bantustan programme was introduced. This took national oppression and dispossession to the logical conlusion by decreeing that the African majority of South Africa's population were not South Africans, but rather citizens of one of ten 'ethnic homelands' (see entry p.197).

By 1964, the mass political struggles of the 1950s and early 1960s had effectively been defeated. Various rural revolts had been brutally suppressed, the independent unions organised in the South African Congress of Trade Unions 'bled white' through repression, and the underground network of the liberation movement effectively destroyed. Through its repressive measures, the regime had managed to 'stabilise' the political situation and attract back even more massive inflows of foreign capital than had fled the country during the Sharpeville crisis. This repression was decisive in holding African wages down to minimal levels and created the conditions for the apartheid economic 'boom' which lasted from the early 1960s to the early 1970s (see pp.27-30).

During these years, the conflicts within Afrikaner nationalism burst violently into the open in bitter and public struggles between so-called *verligte* (enlightened) and *verkrampte* (reactionary) nationalists. Most significant in these struggles was the emerging open co-operation between SANLAM and Rembrandt on one hand, with the non-Afrikaner financial, mining and industrial monopolies on the other.

In 1963, a SANLAM subsidiary was virtually given control of the major mining house, General Mining, by Anglo American. This move provoked a deep division within the Nationalist Party, leading one nationalist newspaper to argue that 'it would be tragic to the future existence of Afrikanerdom, and eventually the whole white civilisation, if the (Afrikaner) capitalistic and political powers should split'. To still these criticisms, the SANLAM subsidiary donated R 10,000 to the NP.

In the early 1960s, within the NP itself the forces of petty bourgeois Afrikaner nationalism coalesced around the Prime Minister and Transvaal leader Dr H.F. Verwoerd. The Cape NP was treated within the NP as an opposition force. Verwoerd was able to mobilise against Cape Afrikaner finance all the other class forces in the Nationalist alliance. This was achieved largely through the *Afrikaner Broederbond* and by centralising power in both party and government into Verwoerd's two functions as national leader of the NP and Prime Minister respectively. This was unprecedented in the history of the NP — which was now transformed into a simple vehicle of support for the government. During the years 1960-6, the intense conflicts within the nationalist class alliance were displaced from the party itself to all other organs of Afrikaner nationalism, which saw a fierce struggle for dominance between *verligtes* and *verkramptes*.

The assassination of Verwoerd in September 1966 brought these conflicts into the open and back into the NP itself. The new leader, John Vorster, tried to play a Bonapartist role within the party by standing above the squabbling factions and relying for his major personal basis of support on the security apparatus generally, and in particular, the Bureau of State Security (BOSS — see entry p.193). Yet Vorster could not remain neutral as the NP underwent its most serious splits since the 1940s. He and other leading 'centrists' eventually allied themselves with the *verligtes* in the struggle against *verkramptes*. By 1969 the conflict led to a formal split: four *verkrampte* MPs led by former Cabinet Minister and senior *Broederbonder*, Dr Albert Hertzog, were expelled from the NP. They formed an ultra-right wing *Herstigte* (reconstituted) NP based on 'the true Afrikaner nationalism of Strijdom and Verwoerd' (see entry p.153).

The immediate issue provoking the split was a modification of sports policy to allow visiting international teams to include black players. However, the *verligte-verkrampte* conflict was essentially a class-based struggle between those who wished to preserve the nationalist alliance of 1948 as a class alliance dominated by the interests of small farmers and the petty bourgeoisie (*verkramptes*) against those who realised that in 20 years in power, the social basis of Afrikaner nationalism had shifted profoundly, and who sought to transform its ideology and politics to suit the changing class composition of the *volk*. The *verligte* phenomenon was a response to the emergence, particularly in the 1960s, of a class of aggressive, self-confident Afrikaner capitalists, whose interests now went beyond those of the narrow class alliance out of which they had emerged. Significantly, these struggles no longer primarily took the form of regionalist conflicts. By the late 1960s, the *verligte* influence was no longer confined to the Cape, but was emerging as a strong element in the Transvaal as well. Just as had occurred in the Cape a decade earlier, Transvaal businessmen were no longer totally economically dependent on an alliance of all classes of Afrikaans-speakers, and were beginning to push, even within the *Broederbond*, for new economic and political policies.

1973 to the Present

The third phase of NP rule, from 1973 onwards, can be characterised as a period of rising mass, and particularly working class, struggles in the context of economic crisis. The interaction between the two gave rise to the removal of Vorster as Prime Minister in September 1978, the adoption of the Total Strategy (see p.37), and the reopening of severe conflicts within the party, conflicts which had remained largely dormant from 1969 to 1974.

The gathering political and economic crisis of the mid-1970s is discussed on pp.32-6. By late 1976, in the wake of the Soweto uprising, it had become abundantly clear that capitalist 'stability' could not be re-established solely on the basis of repression and Bantustan policies. Various powerful forces, in particular monopoly capital and senior military officers, began to push for modifications to apartheid, both to defuse black support for the liberation struggle and to facilitate the reorganisation of industrial production.

The latter period of Vorster's government (1976-8) saw the beginnings of attempts to restructure aspects of political and social relations. However, given the balance of forces within the party, the Vorster government was increasingly paralysed on crucial policy issues. This culminated in the 'Muldergate crisis', which in effect condensed three distinct political crises: 1) a crisis for individual capitals and the capitalist class as a whole in the economic and political conditions of accumulation in South Africa; 2) a crisis for the Nationalist Party as the ruling party in the capitalist state and 3) a crisis for the Nationalist Party and the alliance of class forces outside the state apparatus, on which it had been built since 1948.

Vorster resigned in September 1978. The Cape NP leader and Defence Minister, P.W. Botha, defeated Transvaal NP Leader Connie Mulder in the election for NP national leader and Prime Minister. Botha's victory was the result of an alliance between all elements of monopoly capital – both inside and outside the NP – together with senior military officers, against the petty bourgeois right grouped around Mulder. It also marked a shift in the balance of class forces within the NP, with Afrikaner capital establishing itself as the dominant force within the Afrikaner nationalist class alliance.

On his accession to the prime ministership, Botha declared that the state was confronted by a 'total onslaught' by the 'Marxist threat'. It would adopt the Total Strategy (previously worked out in Botha's Defence Ministry) in response. Based on an organised political alliance between the military, all sections of monopoly capital, and Botha's faction of the NP, the Total Strategy represents an attempt to defuse mass opposition and the national liberation struggle through a programme seeking to break up the alliance of class forces on which this struggle rests (see pp.38-40).

The achievement of dominance within the NP by Afrikaner monopoly capital in the 'Muldergate' crisis, and the consequent implementation of the pro-monopoly Total Strategy, sharply antagonised forces amongst the Afrikaner petty bourgeoisie, small farmers and strata of wage earners. The result was a sharp escalation of class-based conflict within the NP. The far right petty bourgeois opposition crystallised around the post-1978 leader of the Transvaal NP and Minister of State Administration and Statistics, Dr Andries Treurnicht. At the same time, this situation provoked the growth of a far right opposition to the Total Strategy organised outside the NP, largely by defectors from the Nationalists. Thus, in the 1981 elections, the far right parties increased their share of the vote five and a half fold. Throughout 1981, these groups, and particularly the largest of the, the *Herstigte Nasionale Party* (see p.153), continued to win increased support. Significantly, the *Afrikaner Broederbond* reversed its longstanding policy of exclusive support for the NP, and appeared to be under the control of a majority faction opposed to the Total Strategy.

Finally, in early 1982, the far right within the NP were provoked to vote against P.W. Botha in a motion of confidence over his 'healthy power-sharing' policies. Sixteen MPs led by Transvaal leader Andries Treurnicht were expelled from the NP and established the Conservative Party (see entry, p.149). In order to win support for new 'reform' proposals based on an executive presidency, appointed cabinet and separate parliament for whites, coloureds and Indians, Botha convened the first meeting of the NP Federal Congress for 40 years.

Important NP leaders:

Cape NP:
P.W. Botha: Cape leader, national leader and Prime Minister
C. Heunis: Minister of Constitutional Development and Planning

Transvaal NP:
F.W. de Klerk: Transvaal leader, Minister of Internal Affairs
H. Schoeman: Minister of Transport
S.P. Botha: Minister of Manpower Utilisation
R. Botha: Minister of Foreign Affairs
M. Malan: Minister of Defence

OFS NP:
P. du Plessis: OFS leader, Minister of Agriculture

Natal NP:
O.P.F. Horwood: Natal leader, Minister of Finance

THE PROGRESSIVE-FEDERAL PARTY (PFP)[3]

Currently the major 'opposition' party within South Africa's whites-only parliament. The progressive-Federal Party (PFP) represents liberal monopoly capitalism. It advocates a 'national convention' of all except 'those groups advocating violence' to write a new constitution. Its programme calls for universal adult

> franchise 'in a system' of 'checks and balances' in which a minority
> of 10-15% could veto legislation. The PFP is led by Dr Frederick
> van Zyl Slabbert.

The origins of the PFP go back to 1959 when 12 United Party MPs broke away
over the UP's increasing abandonment of earlier commitments – in this case
over land for Africans. Led by Dr Jan Steytler they formed themselves into
the Progressive Party ('Progs') on a 'non-racial' programme which would
enfranchise those South Africans who possessed both property and a minimum
of ten years schooling. The party argued that the mass national liberation
struggles led by the ANC could best be defused through state policy to
encourage the development of a black middle class committed to 'free
enterprise'. It advocated respect for certain bourgeois democratic rights
undermined by the Nationalist regime.

In the period 1961–74, the Progressive Party remained a small party
drawing support from a minority of liberal, wealthy whites. In three general
elections it never won more than 4% of the votes cast. Throughout this period
it had only one MP – Helen Suzman, who represented the wealthiest
constituency in the country. The party was kept going by large donations
from Harry Oppenheimer, Chairman of the Anglo American Corporation
(see p.65), and was in fact widely seen as his personal political creation.

The intensification of mass struggles against the regime in the early 1970s
finally shattered the confidence of non-Afrikaner monopoly capital in the
hitherto major parliamentary opposition, the United Party (UP) (see p.157),
and was the key factor in the transformation of the Progressive Party into a
viable parliamentary party.

In the 1974 general elections the Progressive Party increased its parliamentary representation from one to seven. The growing crisis provoked a
split between the more conservative and 'reformist' wings of the United Party,
and the ousting from the UP of the reformist 'young Turks' led by Harry
Schwartz. They initially organised themselves into the 'Reform Party' which
then merged with the 'Progs' to form the Progressive Reform Party (PRP)
under the leadership of Colin Eglin in 1975.

The defeat of the South African army in Angola 1975–6, together with the
Soweto uprisings and general strikes, led to great pressure from leading
capitalists on the United Party to unify the parliamentary opposition to the
Nationalist Party. A committee under retired judge and former *Broederbond*
member, Kowie Marais, produced a 14 point plan for unity between the
United Party and Progressive Party in 1977. This plan split the UP three ways.
Its most right wing MPs formed the South African Party (SAP – which has
since joined the Nationalist Party), while the majority merged with the
miniscule Democratic Party to form the New Republic Party (NRP) (see
p.153). Six former UP MPs joined the PRP which changed its name yet again
to the Progressive-Federal Party. In the 1977 General Elections the PFP now
emerged as the major parliamentary opposition party, winning 16.6% of the

votes and 17 seats (to 10 for the NRP, 3 for the SAP and 134 for the Nationalist Party). In the 1981 elections the PFP increased its share of the total vote to 18.1% winning 26 parliamentary seats.

The growth of the party in the 1970s induced a number of political conflicts between the so-called 'principled' liberal old guard of the old Progressive Party, generally rallying around Helen Suzman, and the 'pragmatic' new elements of the 1970s. The issues revolved around the question of whether the PFP should maintain its role as strident liberal critic of the regime's policies to 'retain credibility amongst blacks' or should concentrate on expanding support amongst the white electorate, which involved a watering down of hallowed 'Progressive Party principles'. Cutting across this issue, many elements in PFP, particularly those grouped around its Afrikaans journal, *Deurbraak*, began to attack the political strategy and performance in parliament of party leader Colin Eglin. In 1979, Eglin was replaced by Frederick van Zyl Slabbert as party leader. Slabbert is an Afrikaner, former professor of sociology, and one of the new Progressive Party MPs of 1974. A strong proponent of the view that the PFP should seek wider support amongst the white electorate, he has written that the PFP's most important role is to persuade 'both black and white that negotiation was preferable to confrontation and that an acceptable constitutional solution could be negotiated at a national convention'. According to the Johannesburg *Financial Mail*, as leader of the parliamentary opposition Slabbert 'has had considerable impact . . . his performance in parliament is outstanding'.

In the process of these changes and conflicts within the PFP, its policy of a qualified franchise has been replaced by a call for a 'national convention' to write a new constitution for South Africa. This is accompanied by PFP 'proposals' for such a convention which would turn South Africa into a federation of 'self-governing states', based on a federal parliament elected through 'universal adult franchise', but in which 'consensus would be necessary for new laws as a minority of 10–15% could veto legislation'. The economic programme of the PFP calls for heavy state spending on education and social services in order to protect the basic 'free enterprise economy'.

The differences between the PFP and the ruling Nationalist Party are essentially strategic — that is, how best to secure and maintain the political conditions for capitalist stability and prosperity. Since 1959, the 'Prog' view has been that this will best be secured through winning the support of a large black middle class, committed to capitalism as a 'strong bulwark against revolution'. Its 12 point 'alternative' to Botha's 12 point Total Strategy emphasises negotiation and 'planning together with members of other population groups, not for them'.

Unlike the NP, whose recent Total Strategy is now based on a similar strategic conception, the PFP recognised the need to co-opt fully the black petty bourgeoisie into an alliance with the ruling class, through much greater concessions than the NP will consider. This is clearly seen in what PFP leader Slabbert considers to be the four crucial differences between his party and the NP: 1) whites alone should not decide on the constitution, there

should rather be 'joint decision making' through 'negotiation and compromise';
2) the government should not enforce 'racial or ethnic group membership',
the PFP stands for 'natural pluralism based on voluntary association';
3) unlike the NP, which denies that blacks are South African citizens, the PFP
'accepted the African as a fellow citizen with whom a constitutional solution
had to be found'; 4) the PFP 'questioned whether it was necessary to use
means such as detention without trial and bannings to maintain law and order.
Extraordinary security measures could not be ruled out, particularly in times
of change, but laws could however not be devoid of justice'.

These differences were borne out in the reaction of the PFP to the new
Constitutional Proposals of the President's Council in May 1982 (see pp.136-7)

While welcoming the inclusion of coloureds and Asians in political institutions,
the PFP rejected the undemocratic 'concept of an Executive President' and
attacked the exclusion of Africans from the institutional arrangements
recommended by the Council. In reply, PFP leader Slabbert held a series of
public meetings with the 'Chief Minister' of the KwaZulu Bantustan, Gatsha
Buthelezi, in which they recommended the findings of the so-called
Buthelezi Commission as laying a basis for progress towards 'peaceful change'
(see p.394).

In short, while the NP is committed to maintain the rule of capital and
racial privileges for all whites through ever increasing repression and the
Balkanisation of South Africa, the PFP stands in the tradition of monopoly
capital in Europe of controlling mass struggles through incorporation. This is
clear in its 'social democratic' (sic) economic programme which has been
described as reconciling 'the two poles of capitalism and socialism'.

However, this liberal and 'reformist' rhetoric should not conceal the fact
that the PFP favours the retention of all the essential structures and institutions of capitalist exploitation in South Africa. It remains totally opposed to
one person one vote, and supports the Botha regime's aggression against
neighbouring states. Its finance spokesman, Harry Schwartz, in fact advocates
even more drastic action against 'states harbouring terrorists'. Since the
formation of the Progressive Party in 1959, it has been a party of monopoly
capital. Despite its recent acquisition of some support amongst the white
urban petty bourgeoisie, the party remains essentially a representative of
monopoly interests. Its programme represents in effect, the maximum demands
of monopoly capital in South Africa and the furthest monopoly capital is
prepared to go in conceding the demands of the masses.

Its links with the most powerful monopoly in South Africa, the Anglo
American Corporation, are particularly close. Former Anglo Chairman, Harry
Oppenheimer, remains the most important source of financial support for the
PFP. His ex-son-in-law and chairman of numerous Anglo subsidiaries, Gordon
Waddell, was a 'Prog' MP (whose campaign was managed by Tony Bloom,
the Managing Director of South Africa's second largest food conglomerate,
Premier Milling). Another key Anglo Director, Dr Zac de Beer, was one of the
original 12 Progressive MPs in 1959, and was re-elected as a 'Prog' MP in 1977
(but has recently resigned to concentrate on business). However, both

Waddell and de Beer remain in vital positions on the PFP Federal Executive. Other PFP MPs (e.g. Alex Boraine) are former Anglo managers, and many of the leaders of its youth wing end up on the Anglo American payroll.

Although the PFP is a party of monopoly capital, it stands almost no chance of achieving office. Since 1948, the NP government has effectively secured the conditions for monopoly profits. It has done so on the basis of a mass white class alliance which the PFP could never organise. In other words, in the eyes of the white petty bourgeoisie (particularly Afrikaners) and white wage earners, the PFP is too much the tool of monopoly interests ever to be able to develop a mass electoral base for itself. As a party of monopoly capital, its role is to fight for the maximum demands of this class force, and so to act as a strong source of pressure on the regime. This was very well expressed in 1981 by the major PFP patron, Harry Oppenheimer:

> Since we're not going to get the Nationalists out of power so quickly — much as I'd like to, and see the Progressive-Federal Party come in — one has got to find a means of doing social justice in a way that the reasonable people [sic] in the Nationalist Party might go for.

Important leaders:
Leader: Frederick van Zyl Slabbert
Federal Executive Chairman: Gordon Waddell
National Chairman: Colin Eglin
National Vice-chairman: Ray Swart
Spokesman on Justice: Helen Suzman
Chairman of Economic Commission: Harry Schwartz.

THE CONSERVATIVE PARTY OF SOUTH AFRICA — KONSERWATIEWE PARTY (KP)[4]

A far right wing parliamentary opposition party formed out of a split in the ruling Nationalist Party in March 1982. Led by former Transvaal leader of the NP, Dr Andries Treurnicht, the KP opposed NP plans for 'healthy power sharing' contained in the Report of the President's Council (see p.136). It has committed itself to the NP constitutional proposals of 1977, arguing that the Botha government has departed from these and is slowly introducing 'integration' in South Africa. At the end of 1982, the KP had 18 MPs, making it the third largest parliamentary party. It appears to have substantial support in the rural constituencies of the Transvaal, and amongst the Afrikaner petty bourgeoisie. It has brought under its wing the various far right movements which proliferated after 1978, but has so far not succeeded in co-operation attempts with the even more right wing *Herstigte Nasionale Party* (HNP).

Although the KP was formed in 1982, its genesis goes back to the mid-1960s, and the emergence of the so-called *verligte-verkrampte* (moderate–reactionary) split in the Nationalist Party (NP). This split essentially pitted the newly emerging Afrikaner monopoly capitalists and their ideologues against the more reactionary class forces of the petty bourgeoisie, white labour and small farmers (see pp.138–45). Eventually, in 1969, the four leading *verkramptes* were expelled from the NP and formed the HNP. The present leader of the KP, Dr Andries Treurnicht, was at that time the main publicist of the *verkramptes*, in his capacity as editor of the Pretoria daily, *Die Hoofstad*. He was a leading member of the *verkrampte* inner circle, together with the later leaders of the HNP. When the latter were expelled from the NP and formed the HNP, Dr Treurnicht was elected to the HNP executive at its founding congress. However, in a move which was to produce lasting bitterness with the HNP leaders, he argued against the formation of a new party and insisted that he would continue to fight for *verkrampte* principles within the NP. He was soon thereafter elected to parliament and gradually promoted. By 1978 he was a junior minister.

The formation of the HNP in 1969 did not remove the basic cause of the *verkrampte-verligte* split in the NP – i.e. the changing class basis of the NP and the now conflicting interests of its various component class forces. However, after 1969, under the leadership of John Vorster, a centrist group allied with the *verligtes* established firm control over the party and was able to eliminate overt struggles for power between the *verkrampte* and *verligte* factions. This tenuous unity began to shatter in the gathering political crisis of the mid-1970s (see pp.32–6). All elements of monopoly capital. including those Afrikaner elements hitherto politically organised in the NP, intensified their agitation for rapid 'reforms' to save capitalism and re-establish stable capitalist prosperity. These moves were intensely resisted by the political representatives of white labour, the Afrikaner petty bourgeoisie and small farmers, particularly in the Transvaal. The result was a sudden reopening of intense *verligte-verkrampte* struggles within the NP. The latter were led by the then Minister of Information and leader of the Transvaal NP, Dr Connie Mulder, with Andries Treurnicht as his close ally.

Politically pressurised from all quarters, and riven by intense internal political differences in the period 1976-8, the NP government was in effect politically paralysed. It was able neither to introduce the 'reforms' fought for by English and Afrikaner monopoly capital, nor cling to 'old style apartheid'. New constitutional proposals for three ethnic parliaments were introduced in 1977, but little action was forthcoming. The political log jam was finally broken in the 'Muldergate' scandal, when the combined manoeuvres of monopoly capital and the top echelons of the military over irregularities in Mulder's Department of Information discredited Mulder as the leader of the right. When Vorster resigned from the premiership in September 1978, Mulder was unable to enforce party discipline in his own Transvaal NP. The *verligtes* in the Transvaal supported the candidacy of Defence Minister and leader of the Cape NP, P.W. Botha, and Mulder was defeated. He was soon hounded from the NP and formed the far right National Conservative Party (see pp. 155-6).

The 'Muldergate' crisis severely discredited the forces of the far right in the NP. However, these remained sufficiently strong to elect Treurnicht as the leader of the Transvaal NP in late 1978. With the introduction of Botha's 'reform' programme under the Total Strategy (see pp.37-41), the right had strong institutional base from which to resist these 'reforms'. Led by Treurnicht, the NP *verkramptes* fought a determined and often successful rearguard action over the next three and a half years, earning Treurnicht the title of 'Dr No' in the English language and *verligte* press. During this period, the NP lost much support amongst its traditional mass class base in the Transvaal, the Afrikaner petty bourgeoisie, small farmers and white labour. The HNP captured 14.08% of the vote in the 1981 general elections. In the Transvaal, analysis of the results put their share of the vote at 25% and a *verligte* newspaper, *Rapport*, argued that 38% of Afrikaners had voted against the NP. Treurnicht himself came fairly close to losing his Waterberg seat to the leader of the HNP, Jaap Marais. In the months which followed, a number of far right wing splinter groups continued to attract support from disgruntled Afrikaner nationalists (see p.155). Prime Minister Botha skilfully sought to use Treurnicht to attack the far right, and he began to lose credibility amongst the mass of NP supporters in the Transvaal.

By the end of 1981, the government's strategy of internal 'reforms' was stalled. Its external 'Constellation of States' plan was also in ruins. At the November 'Good Hope' conference between the government and 600 leading capitalists, the representatives of monopoly capital put very strong pressure on Botha to remove Treurnicht. Moreover, the monopoly capitalists seated on the Defence Advisory Committee finally persuaded the Minister of Defence and architect of the Total Strategy, General Magnus Malan, to pressurise Botha to force a break with the far right in the NP, and Treurnicht in particular.

In early 1982, an official NP organ 'NAT 80' said in an editorial that 'there could only be one government' in South Africa. This conflicted with Treurnicht's insistence that the forthcoming 'new constitutional dispensation' would set up three separate parliaments – for whites, Indians and coloureds, each with its own cabinet and prime minister. The Botha faction argued that above these three groupings would stand a supreme 'Cabinet Council' drawn from all three groups and which would wield full state power. The Treurnicht groups objected and Botha called for a vote of confidence in the NP parliamentary caucus insisting on a mandate to interpret party policy at his discretion. Twenty-two MPs voted against this resolution. The Treurnicht faction further lost control of the Transvaal NP when the centrist groups led by F.W. de Klerk and Hendrik Schoeman allied with the *verligte*, pro-Botha faction. After 16 of the original 22 dissenters refused to accept the discipline of the majority in the NP caucus, they were then all expelled from the party.

In March 1982 these elements came together with the National Conservative Party of Mulder and *Aksie Eie Toekoms* (see p.155) to form the Conservative Party of South Africa. Its founding meeting was held in the

Skilpadsaal (Tortoise Hall) in Pretoria, giving rise to many jokes about the tortoise politics of the new party. Shortly afterwards, a further two NP MPs left to join the KP. Its programme promotes a policy of racial separation. Unlike the HNP, the KP accepts the need for some of the 'reforms' which have been introduced since 1977, such as the amendments to the Industrial Conciliation Act, mixed sports, etc. But it argues that the new constitutional arrangements planned by the Botha regime are a violation of the 1977 NP constitutional proposals and imply a logic of the gradual abandonment of racial separation. The HNP initially refused co-operation with the KP on the grounds that it (the HNP) is the authentic and proved party of the right wing 'Afrikaner' opposition, and that it is not prepared to accept the 1977 proposals, nor many of the petty changes introduced since the death of Dr Verwoerd in 1966. Despite intense press speculation of an electoral agreement between the HNP and KP, the two parties have opposed each other in a number of by-elections with the KP consistently drawing more votes than the HNP. However, in a number of such by-elections the combined KP/HNP vote has exceeded that of the victorious NP and negotiations for co-operation between the two parties continue.

The formation of the KP has increased the drainage of support from the NP, particularly in the Transvaal. All except two of the present 18 KP Members of Parliament represent Transvaal constituencies, mostly in the rural areas. The KP and the NP are engaged in a fierce battle for control of all of the traditionally important institutions of Afrikaner nationalism, especially the Dutch Reformed Churches and the *Afrikaner Broederbond* (see entries pp.271 and 266). Treurnight is a former *Broederbond* Chairman. Its present Chairman, Dr Carel Boshoff, is all but publicly identified with the KP. It is also widely acknowledged that the KP enjoys substantial support. A number of former NP cabinet ministers, including the architect of the NP Bantustan Policy, D.C. de Wet Nel, together with the wife and much of the family of former NP Prime Minister Hendrik Verwoerd, have joined the KP. A poll conducted by the authoritative pro-Botha NP weekly, *Rapport*, in late 1982 indicated that 38% of Afrikaners in the Transvaal support the KP, compared with 44% for the NP. Its support in other provinces is substantially weaker. However, control of the Transvaal is the key to control of the present South African electoral system. The KP has very strong support amongst smaller agricultural capitalists, all levels of the Afrikaans petty bourgeoisie and white labour. It is possible that in any future election is could significantly increase its parliamentary representation, and displace the Progressive-Federal Party as the official opposition. One factor impeding its prospects of growth is its inability to achieve an electoral pact with the HNP — which has split the far right vote to the benefit of the NP in a number of by-elections. Another potential factor is the rumoured tussle for the leadership of the KP between its present leader Dr Treurnicht, and his predecessor as leader of the Transvaal NP, the considerably more experienced Dr Connie Mulder.

Important leaders:
    Leader: Dr A.P. Treurnicht
    Dr F. Hartzenberg
    Dr C. Mulder.

NEW REPUBLIC PARTY (NRP)

Parliamentary opposition party formed out of a merger of the rump of the
old United Party (see pp.157–8) and the miniscule Democratic Party in 1977.
The NRP won the allegiance of 23 of the former UP MPs (the largest grouping).
W. Vause Raw and Radclyffe Cadman became its leaders after the UP leader,
de Villiers Graaff and Democratic Party leader (and former Nationalist
Interior Minister) Theo Gerdener, surprisingly withdrew from the leadership
despite being the main forces in the group's original constitution. The party
supports the traditional UP policy of a federal South Africa under 'white
leadership'. In the 1977 elections it retained only ten seats in parliament
(representing a loss of 13). It held onto eight of these in the 1981 elections.

The NRP however, retains control of the Natal Provincial Council (the
only Provincial Council not controlled by the NP). In 1982 the NRP rejected
the proposals of the Buthelezi Commission for 'consociational power sharing'
between the KwaZulu Bantustan and the 'white' Natal provincial administration (see p.384). The NRP argued that the proposals did not offer cast iron
guarantees to whites – despite the fact that they allowed for a minority
veto. This NRP position led to intense conflict with the PFP in Natal, which
favours the proposals and has sought to promote them in a series of joint
meetings with Inkatha.

The NRP has cautiously endorsed the Botha regime's proposals for a 'new
constitutional dispensation', but sees these as the first step in a continuing
process which will eventually include Africans in a white-led federal system.

Current Leader: W. Vause Raw

HERSTIGTE NASIONALE PARTY (RECONSTITUTED NATIONALIST PARTY) (HNP)[5]

Far right wing *verkrampte* party formed in 1969 by a breakaway
group of four Nationalists MPs led by former Minister of Posts and
Telegraphs, Albert Hertzog (son of first Nationalist Party Prime
Minister, General J.B.M. Hertzog). It favours a return to fully
fledged Verwoerdian apartheid based on the 1966 principles of
the Nationalist Party.

The immediate issues leading to the 1969 formation of the HNP were the Vorster government's announced intention to 'relax sports apartheid' (when and where this would help get white sportsmen readmitted to international tournaments), and its 'outward looking' foreign policy offensive in Africa. More fundamentally the HNP's establishment reflected the growing fears of certain strata of the Afrikaner petty bourgeoisie and smaller capitalist farmers that their interests were being betrayed by a party dominated increasingly by Afrikaner monopoly capital (see pp.142-5).

The HNP's original programme was a typical petty bourgeois manifesto. It called for the vigorous implementation of 'pure apartheid' and the assertion of Afrikaner dominance. It demanded restriction of urban residential rights for blacks, stricter separation of housing and social facilities and reduced expenditure on black education, housing and social amenities. It also advocated that Afrikaans be recognised as the sole official language and that citizenship should only be conferred on white immigrants fluent in that language. It further proposed that the economic growth rate be restricted to a level governed by the availability of domestic white labour and local capital — so as to protect the country from being 'contaminated' by external 'money influences'.

For many years the HNP remained in the political wilderness challenging the Nationalist Party in by-elections but failing to win a single seat. In the 1981 elections, however, it benefited from the growing petty bourgeois revolt against the Total Strategy of Prime Minister Botha (see p.151). It won 192,000 votes (14.08% of the total), although it narrowly failed to win a seat in parliament.

Since the 1981 elections the HNP visibly grew in strength with a number of defections to it from the ranks of the Nationalist Party. It tended, however, to stand aloof from other far right organisations and from attempts to forge unity among them. With the formation of the Conservative Party in March 1982, however, its relative position began to weaken (see p.149).

The HNP has important differences with the Conservative Party. The HNP calls for a return to Nationalist Party policies as outlined in its 1966 Manifesto, while the KP advocates a return to its interpretation of the 1977 NP manifesto. These are not merely sectarian differences about when the NP departed from the 'true principles' of Afrikaner Nationalism. At issue are some more substantial policy differences. The KP opposes 'power sharing' with blacks, but accepts the need for certain 'reforms' in the economic and social spheres. The HNP favours a return to full blooded Verwoerdian apartheid in all spheres including, for example, statutory job reservation, and fully segregated facilities. To date the two parties have been unable to reach an electoral pact, thereby splitting the far right vote to the NP's advantage in a number of by-elections. However, negotiations between them continue.

Important leaders:
  Leader: Jaap Marais
  Editor of *Die Afrikaner* (the HNP newspaper): Beaumont Schoeman

Loui Stofberg
Willie Marais.

OTHER FAR RIGHT POLITICAL ORGANISATIONS

The current polarisation of class forces 'traditionally' organised by Afrikaner Nationalism since 1948, reflected in the growing support for the *Herstigte Nasionale Party* and the formation of the Conservative Party in March 1982, also produced a proliferation of smaller far right political organisations, particularly in the period 1978–82. The most important of these include:

The National Conservative Party (NCP)

Formed in 1979 by Dr C.P. Mulder, the former leader of the Transvaal Nationalist Party, Minister of Plural Relations and Information and candidate (against P.W. Botha) for the premiership. Mulder was forced to resign after being implicated in the 'information scandal'. In many respects the NCP functioned as a personal vehicle of Mulder in his campaign to clear his name and take revenge on Botha. But together with the *Herstigte Nasionale Party* (see p.153) it was also a mouthpiece for reactionary petty bourgeois strata. The NCP's programme promised to resist constitutional proposals which might 'undermine the sovereignty' of the white parliament and criticised the 'trend towards concession-making' in domestic and foreign policies. The party opposed the legislation arising from the Wiehahn Commission Report (see p.325), and rejected any moves to grant more land to Bantustans under 'consolidation' proposals. In the 1981 elections the NCP put up nine candidates who polled 19,000 votes (1.52% of the total) but failed to win a single seat. Mulder was later, however, elected as a councillor on the Randburg municipality, where one of his first actions was to call for the segregation of a local public toilet. On the formation of the Conservative Party in 1982, Mulder was elected as a member of its executive and subsequently announced the dissolution of the NCP. It is believed that he has ambitions to replace Treurnicht as Conservative Party leader.

Aksie Eie Toekoms (Action Own Future) (AET)

Group formed by dissident *Broederbond* members early in 1981. A small number of candidates contested the April 1981 elections as independents but under the Action Own Future slogan. They received only a small number of votes. After the election support built up and in November 1981 it constituted itself as a formal political party. Like the NCP, however, AET dissolved itself into the Conservative Party.

Afrikaner Weerstand Beweging (Afrikaner Resistance Movement) (AWB)

A semi-terrorist, Nazi-inclined organisation formed in 1979 and led by Eugene Terrèblanche. In 1980 it formed a political party — the *Blanke Volksstaat Party* (White People's State Party) — which advocated the establishment of a racist Nazi-type state. Its emblem is a three legged swastika. The AWB also has a 'military wing', the *Stormvalke* (Storm Falcons). It, too, supported the formation of the Conservative Party and dissolved its own political party but not its 'military wing' in March 1982. Early in 1983, eight AWB members including Terrèblanche, were arrested on charges of illegal possession of arms. Released on bail, Terrèblanche launched a hysterical denunciation of the Botha regime's constitutional proposals. He accused Botha of building the future of South Africa on a series of unstable foundations: 'The first foundation stone will be laid on curry and samoosas, the second on the Cape Coloureds, the third on Bantu beer and the fourth on Harry Oppenheimer's big hole in Kimberley.

Kappie Komando

A women's pressure group known for the sporting of *voortrekker* (pioneer) costumes — particularly the *kappie* (bonnet) — as a symbol of its commitment to the 'traditional values' of Afrikaner nationalism. The *Kappie Kommando* became embroiled in a controversy in 1982 when its leader suggested that women who had served with South African forces against the fascist Axis powers in the Second World War were basically field prostitutes. It, too, supported the establishment of the Conservative Party.

South Africa First

A far right pressure group, mainly English speaking and Natal based. A number of its leading personalities are British immigrants previously associated with the British fascist group, the National Front. South Africa First has been prominent in organising a campaign against proposals to allow blacks a certain access to the previously all-white Durban beach front.

Wit Komando (White Commando)

A terrorist organisation involved in bombings and other attacks on *verligte* Nationalists, liberals and progressives. Some of its members are now serving prison terms for such attacks.

In September 1981 all the above groups agreed to form an alliance under the banner 'Action Save White South Africa'. A 'unity conference' was held in Pretoria and was also attended by Dr Albert Hertzog, the founder and former leader of the HNP. A former Surgeon-General of the Defence Force, Lt.-Gen. C.R. Cokroft, who described himself as a 'concerned Christian not affiliated to any of the parties', was appointed spokesman of the front. However, the then largest of the far right parties, the HNP, stayed aloof, arguing that whilst not opposed in principle to alliances, it would only enter one on its own terms. As indicated above most of the smaller far right groups have now associated with the Conservative Party.

THE UNITED PARTY[6]

> Main opposition party in whites-only parliament until 1977 when it split three ways. Some MPs merged with the Progressives (see p.145), some formed the South African Party which later merged with the Nationalist Party, while the majority constituted themselves as the New Republic Party (see p.153).

The United Party was formed in 1934 by the 'Fusion' of the two major parliamentary parties then in existence, the Nationalist Party led by J.B.M. Hertzog and the South African Party led by J.C. Smuts. The 'Fusion' represented the coming together of the major capitalist interests, in the face of the crisis over the abandonment of the Gold Standard in 1933. 'Fusion' was opposed from the outset by certain groupings of capitalist agriculture and sections of the Afrikaner petty bourgeoisie which broke away to form the Purified Nationalist Party led by D.F. Malan. The United Party represented all major capitalist interests until the outbreak of World War II. South Africa's participation in World War II and wartime economic policies, however, divided the capitalist class. Capitalist agriculture opposed the war and favoured a separate peace with Nazi Germany, while industrial and mining capital favoured participation in the war. During the war years capitalist agriculture deserted the UP for the Nationalist Party (renamed *Herenigde Nasionale of Volksparty* – Reunited Nationalist or Peoples' Party) leaving the UP to represent an unstable alliance of mining and industrial capital. Hertzog, the UP leader since 1934 and Prime Minister, resigned over the war question. He was replaced by Smuts who was Prime Minister until 1948.

The United Party's demise as governing party occurred in the context of the heightened mass struggles of the war and post war period. The party proved incapable of producing a decisive response to the challenge of the oppressed and exploited masses, wavering between increasing repression and attempting a co-optive strategy towards certain classes within the black population. It was effectively outbid in the 1948 elections by the Nationalists who were able to unite around its apartheid programme those sections of the exploiting and privileged classes most vulnerable to the challenge of the masses (see p.16).

For the first few years in opposition, the United Party put up a fairly vigorous opposition to certain measures introduced by the new Nationalist government, fearing that these would either hamper the development of monopoly capitalism or provoke an uncontrollable 'black uprising'. During the early 1950s, in fact, some United Party members associated with the para-military extra parliamentary pressure group known as the 'Torch Commando' (see p.377). As it became clear that the Nationalist regime constituted no threat to monopoly capitalism, but was on the contrary guaranteeing the cheap labour system on which the rapid development of monopoly capitalism depended the UP's 'opposition' became increasingly muted. After the 1953 elections, in particular, it increasingly associated itself with the repressive measures being introduced by the Nationalist regime — supporting, for example, the banning of the ANC and PAC and the introduction of detention without trial. Indistinguishable from the Nationalists over many real issues the UP became a political irrelevancy. At every election since 1948 except 1970, the proportion of seats held by it declined as Table 3.1 shows:

Table 3.1:
Distribution of Parliamentary Seats 1948–74

Election	NP	UP	Others	
1948	79 (52.6%)	65 (43.3%)	6 (4.1%)	(Labour Party) *
1953	88 (58.7%)	61 (40.7%)	1 (0.6%)	" "
1958	97 (64.6%)	53 (35.4%)	—	
1961	99 (66.0%)	49 (32.6%)	2 (1.4%)	(Progressive Party, National Union)
1966	120 (75%)	39 (24.4%)	1 (0.6%)	(Progressive Party)
1970	112 (70%)	47 (29.4%)	1 (0.6%)	" "
1974	123 (76.4%)	41 (25.4%)	7 (4.2%)	" "

*See chart p.159. This Labour party is not to be confused with the 'coloured' Labour Party formed in 1966 see p.395.

The split in the UP in 1977 is discussed on p.146. The result was the strengthening of the PFP which became the official opposition, and the formation of two smaller opposition parties — the South African Party which later dissolved itself into the Nationalist Party, and the New Republic Party.
UP leader 1956-77: Sir de Villiers Graaff.

'White Politics' 1910–1982 Major Parties

Governing Parties

Opposition Parties

1910

South African Party

Leader L. Botha and, after 1919, J. Smuts. Represented alliance of mining capital and 'more prosperous' capitalist agriculture also represented commercial capital and incipient industrial bourgeoisie (initially).

Unionist Party

Authentic party of mining (imperialist) capital. Merged with SAP in 1920.

South African Labour Party

Party of white labour. Dominated from the outset by reformist, racist leadership but also including revolutionaries until First World War. The latter broke away during the war to form *International Socialist League* which became *SA Communist Party* in 1921. Leader F.H.P. Cresswell.

1914

Formation of **National Party** January 1914. Leader J.B.M. Hertzog former SAP cabinet minister. Represented smaller white landowners threatened by the process of transition to capitalism in South African agriculture. Also supported the aspirations of incipient industrial bourgeoisie i.e. became party of national capital. Called for policies of industrial protection and subsidisation for national capitalist interests against the 'free trade policies' favoured by imperialist capitalist interests and implemented by SAP government.

Unionist Party

South African Party

Lost 1924 elections to NP/LP 'Pact'. In opposition under Smuts.

Gesuiwerde Nasionale Party

(Purified Nationalist Party) formed 1934. Leader D.F. Malan. Represented an alliance of white petty bourgeois and Cape capitalist agricultural interests dissatisfied with the 'compromise' of 'fusion'.

SA Labour Party

Consisting of the bulk of the Labour Party who broke away from governing alliance with formation of 'fusion'. Leader W. Madeley.

1920

SAP

Unionists merged into SAP after 1920 election

1924

National Party Labour Party

'Pact' government elected in the wake of general strike and Rand Revolt of 1922. Pact implemented policies of protection and subsidisation which benefited capitalist agriculture and industrial capital. Also implemented a number of 'protective measures' (job colour bars) to benefit white labour. Introduced the so-called 'civilised labour' policy. Hertzog Prime Minister.

1934

United National South African Party

(United Party) formed through a 'fusion' of National Party and South African Party in the wake of the Great Depression and Gold Standard crisis. Represented a coming together of major bourgeois interests. Still pursued policies of protection and subsidisation but more concessions were made to demands of mining capital. Hertzog Prime Minister.

	United Party	SA Labour Party / South African Labour Party	Dominion Party	Herenigde Nasionale Party-Afrikaner Party	Afrikaner Party
1939	Outbreak of World War II and wartime economic policies led to desertion from UP of its former capitalist agricultural adherents. Became representative of alliance of industrial capital and mining capital. Hertzog resigned on outbreak of war and Smuts became leader and Prime Minister.	Entered governing coalition on outbreak of war. Madeley appointed Minister of Labour.	In governing coalition at outbreak of war. Represented predominantly imperialist oriented Natal sugar farmers and petty bourgeoisie.	(Reunited National Party) Becomes greatly strengthened by desertion of capitalist agriculture from UP. During war years built up a strong base among white petty bourgeoisie and white labour. But also riven by deep internal divisions.	OFS rural capital. Very weak. Led by N.C. Havenga, on 'Hertzogite' principals.
1948	Until its dissolution in 1977, the UP in opposition grew steadily weaker. Its 'race	(Disappears from political scene in 1958 elections when it failed to win any seats in	Natal sugar interests pro-imperialist, did not support 'fusion' and broke with SAP.	Coalition won 1948 election fought in the face of the heightened struggle by the popular masses of the war and postwar period. Promised a firm and decisive	

response to mass struggles as against the ambivalent and uncertain policies of the UP. Also promised to implement a number of policies to favour the particular interests of its constituent base — capitalist agriculture, non-monopoly industrial and financial capital, white petty bourgeoisie and white labour. Implemented policies of apartheid — intensified repression, segregation, job colour bars, influx control etc. Afrikaner Party merged with HNP in 1951 to form the *Nationalist Party*. D.F. Malan Prime Minister 1948-54; J.G. Strydom 1954-8; H.F. Verwoerd 1958-66; B.J. Vorster 1966-78; P.W. Botha 1978-

federation' policies were characterised by an opportunistic attempt to pick up all grievance votes against the NP and increasing right wing stance. Leaders: J. Smuts 1948-50; G.N. Strauss 1950-6; Sir de Villiers Graaff 1956-77.

parliament) until then in electoral alliance with UP. SALP collapsed when UP revoked this alliance in 1958.

1959 Nationalist Party

United Party

Progressive Party

Formed 1959 when a group of 'more liberal' United Party MPs broke away from UP accusing the latter of betraying principles. Supported by leading monopoly capitalist interests (e.g. H. Oppenheimer of Anglo American). Called for reforms in order to create a black supportive class for the bourgeoisie. Original proposals favoured a 'qualified franchise' open to those of all races who could meet certain minimum (high) property and/or educational requirements. Leader to 1971, J. Steytler, only MP Helen Suzman.

1961

National Union

Formed by disaffected NP MP who would not accept Bantustanisation. One MP in 1961, who then joined the United Party.

1969

Herstigte Nasionale Party   **United Party**   **Progressive Party**

(Reconstituted Nationalist Party) breakaway from Nationalist Party led by A. Hertzog (son of former Prime Minister J.B.M. Hertzog). Party of dissatisfied petty bourgeoisie and white labour factions which accused Vorster of making too many concessions to 'liberal' demands. Has thus far failed to win any seats in parliament but has remained a force in white (Afrikaner) politics.

1975

Reform Party

Split from UP and later joined PP to form *Progressive Reform Party*. Leader of PRP: Colin Eglin.

	Progressive Federal Party	New Republic Party	South African Party	Herstigte Nasionale Party
1977	Years of ineffective 'opposition' by the UP and the perceived need for the ruling class to make a more effective response to the crisis created by Soweto uprising, led to the dissolution of UP. A number of former UP MPs merged with Progressive Reform Party which became the 'official' opposition under its new name, PFP. Leader to 1979, Colin Eglin;	Created by factions of dissolved UP unwilling to merge with PFP. Both NRP and SAP more 'conservative' than PFP. Leader of NRP, Vause Raw; leader of SAP, J. Wiley.	SAP dissolved itself in 1980, and its leader (Wiley) joined NP.	

leader after
1979, F. van
Zyl Slabbert.
PFP can be seen
as the party of
'big business'
which wants
to make more
concessions to
black petty
bourgeois groups
in order to
develop a black
supportive class
for capitalism.
Prepared to
some extent to
make these at
the cost of some
'white privileges'.

Conservative Party of South Africa

Formed following the expulsion of 16 Nationalist Party MPs
for their refusal to accept 'healthy power sharing'. Is opposed
to the inclusion of 'non-whites' in central political structures.
However, unlike the HNP it does not favour a return
Verwoerd-style apartheid. Appears to have strong support in
rural and petty bourgeois constituencies, especially in the
Transvaal. Leader: A. P. Treurnicht.

1982

BIBLIOGRAPHICAL NOTE

General

Each of the political parties puts out programmatic and propaganda material too numerous to list here. A sketchy historical documentary overview up to 1960 is contained in Krüger, D.W., *South African Parties and Policies 1910–1960*, Cape Town, Human and Rousseau, 1960. The annual *Survey of Race Relations in South Africa* published by the South African Institute of Race Relations also gives information on the major programmatic and internal developments each year. The South African press is an invaluable source on white political parties. The political alignments of each of the major newspapers is indicated in the entry pp.406–14.

1. See 'General' above.
   Davies, R., Kaplan, D., Morris, M. and O'Meara, D., 'Class Struggle and the Periodisation of the State in South Africa', *Review of African Political Economy*, 7, 1976.
   Kaplan, D., 'The South African State: The Origins of a Racially Exclusive Democracy', *Insurgent Sociologist*, X, 2, 1980.
   Moss, G., 'Total Strategy', *Work in Progress*, 11, 1980.
   O'Meara, D., 'Muldergate and the Politics of Afrikaner Nationalism', *Work in Progress*, 22, 1982.
   Pahad, A., 'Reject Dummy Institutions', *Sechaba*, April 1983.
   Saul, J. and Gelb, S., *The Crisis in South Africa*, New York, Monthly Review Press, 1981.
   South African Institute of Race Relations *Handbook on Race Relations in South Africa*, Cape Town, Oxford University Press, 1949.
   South African Institute of Race Relations *Laws Affecting Race Relations in South Africa (to the end of 1976)*, Johannesburg, SAIRR, 1978.
2. See 'General' above.
   Adam, H. and Giliomee, H., *Ethnic Power Mobilised*, New Haven, Yale University Press, 1979.
   O'Meara, D., op.cit.
   O'Meara, D., *Volkskapitalisme: Class, Capital and Ideology in the Development of Afrikaner Nationalism 1934–1948*, Cambridge, Cambridge University Press, 1983.
   Schoeman, B.M., *Van Malan tot Verwoerd*, Cape Town, Human and Rousseau, 1973.
   Schoeman, B.M., *Vorster se 1000 Dae*, Cape Town, Human and Rousseau, 1974.
3. See 'General' above.
   Hackland, B., 'The Economic and Political Context of the Growth of the Progressive Federal Party in South Africa, 1959–1978', *Journal of Southern African Studies*, 7, 1, October 1980.
   Hackland, B., 'The Progressive Party, 1960–1980: Class Agents in a Capitalist Society', paper presented to conference on 'South Africa in the Comparative Study of Class, Race and Nationalism', SSRC, New York, 1982.
4. See 'General' above.
   O'Meara, D., 'Muldergate . . .', op.cit.
   Schoeman, B.M., *Vorster se 1000 Dae*, op.cit.

5. See 'General' above.
   Schoeman, B.M., *Vorster se 1000 Dae*, op.cit.
   Serfontein, J.H., *Die Verkrampte Aanslag*, Cape Town, Human & Rousseau, 1970.
6. See 'General' above.
   Heard, K., *General Elections in South Africa 1943-1970*, London, Oxford University Press, 1974.
   Thompson, L., *Politics in the Republic of South Africa*, Boston, Little Brown & Company, 1966.

4. State Structures and Policies

BASIC LAWS OF APARTHEID[1]

This brief summary rests on the fundamental proposition that the laws of apartheid can only be adequately understood as measures introduced by ruling class forces in the course of concrete class struggles to create and reproduce in South Africa a system of capitalist exploitation based on national oppression. The most basic laws of apartheid — racially discriminatory land laws, laws controlling the movement and settlement of blacks, laws excluding blacks from representative institutions of the state, 'industrial relations' and security laws — are all essentially measures aimed at creating or securing the rigidly controlled and highly exploitable black labour force on which the entire system of capital accumulation in South Africa depends. There are also a number of laws whose objective is to serve particular interests within the capitalist ruling class and its allies. These latter — such as job reservation laws and some measures relating to the movement of black workers from 'white' rural areas — have often been introduced at the expense of other particular ruling class interests and have been the subject of conflict within the ruling class and its allies. Unless understood in this way, apartheid laws may appear either as an incoherent list of esoteric regulations or (as often presented in liberal ideology) as the consequence of an attempt to impose some purely ideological and irrational vision of race separation.

This section provides a categorised summary of some of the major laws of apartheid, sketching their main provisions and functions.

Laws on Land Ownership and Occupation

These have served both to define and entrench property rights of white land-owners and to compel Africans to make themselves available to capitalist employers as wage labourers. Most of the basic measures came into force before the apartheid period (i.e. before 1948). Prior to union in 1910 (see p.132), a number of land laws and ordinances were in force in each of the four colonies, but the question of rights of land occupation was far from clearly defined.

After union, the land laws of the separate provinces were consolidated and tightened up in the 1913 Natives Land Act. This Act prohibited Africans, except those in the Cape, from acquiring land outside specifically demarcated 'native reserve' areas, constituting 7.3% of the land area of the country. It also severely restricted the number of African families permitted to remain on white-owned farms as rent-paying 'squatter peasants'. The implementation of this Act had a profound impact: it rapidly eliminated the small commodity-producing richer peasant strata that had begun to emerge on white-owned land with the expansion of the local market for agricultural commodities, following the development of the mining industry. These were forced by the terms of the Act either to make themselves available to white landowners as 'labour tenants' (a form of wage labour) or to move to the reserves — where overall conditions were such that inhabitants were compelled to seek work as migrant labourers.

The land laws were further consolidated in 1936 under the Natives Land and Trust Act, intended to 'settle once and for all' the racial land division in the country. This Act extended the area of the reserves to 13% of the total land area. It also prohibited Africans in the Cape from acquiring land outside of these areas, and empowered local Native Commissioners to limit the number of labour tenants residing on any white-owned farm to 'the estimated labour requirements of that farm'.

The basic land division entrenched in the 1936 Act was retained in legislation passed under the Nationalist regime after 1948. Amendments passed in 1954 and 1964 tightened up the clauses in the 1936 Act, providing for limitations on the number of labour tenants (which had not previously been extensively applied). Local tenant control boards were set up and progressively reduced the number of labour tenants. This corresponded with a process of increasing mechanisation of capitalist agriculture involving a reduced demand for labour and a consequent change from the labour tenant system (under which entire families resided and worked on the white farmers' land) to the contract labour system (under which the individual labourers came for a fixed contract period). Over the decade 1963–73 it is estimated that over a million people were removed from 'white' rural areas in terms of these laws.

More recently, during the Total Strategy phase of apartheid, various local consolidation committees and a national consolidation commission (the Van der Walt Commission) have made recommendations for modifications to the racial demarcation of certain specific areas. At the time of writing (December 1982) the Van der Walt Commission has completed its report but it has not yet been published. However, it is clear that its proposals will not alter the basic pattern of land ownership but rather have as their objective the 'consolidation' of 'self governing' or 'independent' Bantustans, often consisting of a large number of scattered parcels of land, into more 'viable' units (see pp. 197–217).

Laws Controlling the Movement and Settlement of Black Persons in 'White' Areas

These laws have as their objective the maintenance of a cheap labour system through: 1) restricting the freedom of movement of black persons so as to channel workers where employers need cheap labour; 2) enforcing employment contracts by making sure that workers stay where they are wanted as long as they are wanted; 3) policing the workers and allowing the 'weeding out' of the unemployed and 'troublemakers' and 4) confining and barricading the 'surplus population' (i.e. the unemployed) in the rural slums of the Bantustans.

The most important laws in this category are the notorious pass laws. The first pass laws were introduced as early as 1760, and applied to slaves in the Cape. During the 19th Century they were progressively but unevenly extended. With the development of the gold-mining industry at the end of the 19th Century, new stricter pass laws were introduced in the mining areas with the openly stated intention '. . . to have a hold on the native whom we have brought to the mines'.

Over the period up to 1948 such laws were maintained and extended, but were still applied variably from province to province, while certain categories of the African population were exempt, particularly women and specific 'professionals' (which latter nevertheless had to carry a document stating they were exempt).

After 1948, the Nationalist Party regime consolidated and extended the pass laws. This had the dual objective of increasing the controls over the African population to the benefit of the exploiting and privileged classes in general, and specifically of directing African labour to capitalist agriculture, which had suffered a 'haemorrhage' of African labour to the towns during the war years (see p.18).

Through the Natives Laws Amendment Act of 1952 and the Natives (Urban Areas) Amendment Act of 1955, 'influx control' was applied to all urban areas and to African women as well as men. Under Section 10 of the 1955 Act, only Africans who had resided in a particular urban area since birth, or had worked continuously for one employer in the area for a minimum of ten years, or for more than one employer for a minimum of 15 years and still resided in the area were given the automatic right to remain in the area. All others needed a permit to stay longer than 72 hours. Provision was also made for the establishment of local labour bureaux to control the movement into these areas of 'work seekers'. Local authorities were given powers to remove those Africans deemed 'surplus to requirements or who were habitually unemployed. or were leading idle or dissolute lives, or who had committed certain specified offences'.

Under the Natives (Abolition of Passes and Co-ordination of Documents) Act of 1952, the wide variety of passes which had previously been issued by employers and headmen (state appointed quasi-chiefs) as well as by the Department of Native Affairs, was replaced by a standard 'reference book' issued by the Department. Over the years, these were then issued on an area by area basis to women as well as men, and were to be produced on demand, serving as the basic document of control. During the same period, under regulations applying to labour bureaux in 'white' rural areas, officials had to ensure the 'labour conditions' in a certain area were 'satisfactory' from the standpoint of local capitalist farmers before permitting any African in that area to take up employment elsewhere. These 'efflux control' regulations were intended to alleviate the labour crisis confronting capitalist agriculture.

All these laws and regulations were tightened up and made more effective under amendments and new acts passed in the 1960s. More recently in the Total Strategy period of apartheid, the entire gamut of pass laws and influx control regulations was referred to the one-man Riekert Commission of Inquiry which reported in mid-1979. This commission, responding a) to demands from monopoly capital to permit greater 'horizontal mobility' of semi-skilled and skilled black labour and b) the perceived need by the ruling class to win over a supportive black middle class, recommended certain modifications. After some amendments the Riekert recommendations were embodied in the Orderly Movement and Settlement of Black Persons Bill presented to parliament in 1982 (and at the time of writing being considered by a Parliamentary Select Committee). Whilst purporting to be a measure of 'reform', this Bill drastically tightens up controls on Africans in urban areas. Africans who already have 'section 10 rights' (see above p.171), will be permitted to move to urban areas other than those in which they reside, but only if the state considers that accommodation and work are available. The Minister responsible can declare certain areas to be in a 'state of unemployment', in which case movement to them will be prohibited. Although those categories of the African population will 'enjoy' slightly greater rights of movement between urban areas, access to urban areas will be made more difficult for all other Africans. No provision is made for Africans who currently do not have 'section 10 rights' to acquire them automatically through residence, as there was in the past. Those who have resided ten years in an urban area and are South African (as distinct from Bantustan) citizens may apply to be considered urban residents, but the final decision rests with state officials.

Those Africans not defined as permanent urban residents will have to obtain authorisation to enter urban areas as 'work seekers'. This will only be granted if it is deemed that accommodation is available and the area is not classified as being in a 'state of unemployment'. Employers who employ 'illegal' blacks will be liable to a fine of R5,000 or 12 months imprisonment, and anyone who provides lodging to them, to a R500 fine or 6 months imprisonment. All forms of 'squatting' will be outlawed and 'unauthorised' Africans will not be permitted even to visit urban areas between the hours of 10 p.m. and 5 a.m. without special permission (thus forfeiting the 72 hour 'right' conceded under previous legislation).

In addition to laws controlling movement and access to urban areas, there are also laws zoning residential and business districts on a racial basis. A number of measures of this type existed before 1948 – notably the 1923 Natives (Urban Areas) Act (amended in 1945), certain pre-union ordinances in the Transvaal and Free State applying to persons of Asian origin, and two laws passed by the Smuts government in 1943 and 1946 (popularly known as the 'Pegging' and 'Ghetto' Acts) also applying to persons of Asian origin. However, the post-1948 NP regime introduced far more wide-reaching legislation, partly as a means of exerting greater control over oppressed classes in urban areas and partly in response to fears and prejudices on the part of petty bourgeois forces within the Nationalist Party concerning economic and social 'encroachment' from black petty bourgeois strata.

The major law here is the 1950 Group Areas Act frequently amended and re-enacted in Consolidation Acts of 1957 and 1966. This Act imposed control throughout the country over inter-racial property transfers. For this purpose the Act provided for the racial classification of companies (persons already being subject to a formal classification under the 1950 Population Registration Act). It introduced a complex procedure under which the responsible Minister, on advice from a Group Areas Board, could reserve specific areas in cities, towns and villages for particular race groups. Provision was also made for the compulsory vacating of such proclaimed 'group' areas by persons of other racial groups. The 1968 Community Development Amendment Act obliged traders operating in areas where they were 'disqualified persons' (but from which they had not yet been compulsorily moved) to obtain special permits before their trading licences could be renewed.

During the 'detente' period of the last years of the Vorster regime, a number of orders made under the Group Areas Act were relaxed as part of an exercise aimed at winning allies by alleviating 'petty apartheid'. This practice has continued – in respect of hotels, restaurants, sports facilities, places of entertainment etc – under the Total Strategy. There have also been hints that the Group Areas Act itself might be amended to permit access by African capitalists to central business districts. However, nothing concrete has yet emerged beyond the rejection of the first recommendations to emerge from the President's Council (see p.137) – that two areas reclassified as 'white' under the Group Areas Act be returned to their Asian and 'coloured' former inhabitants.

Laws Governing Relations between Capital and Black Workers

These date back to various Masters and Servants Laws passed in the different colonies between 1841 and 1904. These laws remained in force until 1977; they rendered a breach of an employment contract by a worker through *inter alia*, desertion, insubordination or refusal to carry out the command of an employer – a criminal offence subject to imprisonment; breach of contract by an employer, however, was a civil offence. Although these laws were formally applicable to all employees, over the years courts ruled that they should only be applicable to unskilled (i.e. black) workers. The principle of criminal liability for breach of contract by black workers was also entrenched in the Native Labour Regulation Act of 1911 governing the recruitment of African labourers, particularly for the mining industry.

As indicated on p.245 below, 'pass bearing natives' were specifically excluded from the official industrial relations machinery set under the 1924 Industrial Conciliation Act. This principle was maintained in the 1953 Native Labour (Settlements of Disputes) Act. Corresponding with the then strategy of 'bleeding the African unions to death', this Act prohibited strikes by African workers and made no provision for negotiation with unions including African workers as members. African workers were supposed to 'negotiate' in state and employer-dominated Works and Liaison Committees.

This situation changed somewhat after 1978: in response to the emergence of the democratic trade union movement after the mid-1970s, the ruling class embarked on a new strategy of attempting to incorporate the unions into the rigidly controlled and bureaucratic official industrial relations system. Legislation giving effect to this strategy (recommended by the Wiehahn Commission) was first introduced in 1979 through the Industrial Conciliation Amendment Act, amended several times since, and now renamed the Labour Relations Act (see p.325 for details).

Job Reservation Laws

These were introduced as a concession to various categories of white labour, often after militant struggles. They sought to 'protect' higher paid white wage earners from displacement by lower paid black workers. They have also excluded blacks from better paid, more skilled categories of work.

The first statutory job colour bars were introduced as clauses in mining regulations enacted at the end of the 19th Century. These provided that certain jobs were restricted to 'scheduled persons' i.e. whites in possession of a certificate of competence. These regulations were consolidated in a schedule appended to the Mines and Works Act of 1911 which specifically laid down that no 'coloured person' could acquire certificates of competency in the Transvaal or Orange Free State. The job colour bar provisions in this Act were ruled invalid by the courts in 1923, the year after the 1922 strike (see p.245). They were, however, restored under the Mines and Works Amendment Act passed by the Pact regime in 1926.

Other measures enacted prior to 1948 which had the effect of excluding Africans from more skilled jobs, were apprenticeship regulations (consolidated in the often amended 1922 Apprenticeship Act) and the 1937 Amendment to the Industrial Conciliation Act. The former did not formally exclude Africans, but it effectively prevented them from obtaining apprenticeship training by providing for minimum educational levels not normally attainable by blacks, and by allowing Apprenticeship Boards to restrict training to persons eligible to join racially exclusive trades unions. The 1937 Amendment empowered Industrial Councils to determine wage levels for all workers in an industry (and not just, as previously, those represented by a union on the Industrial Council). This allowed for the determination of 'high' minimum wages for certain categories of employment which acted as a deterrent to employers employing Africans in those positions. The Amendment also allowed for the negotiation of racially exclusive closed shop agreements.

The post-1948 Nationalist regime supplemented all the above measures by two new laws: the 1951 Native Building Workers Act and Section 77 of the 1956 Industrial Conciliation Act. The Native Building Workers Act imposed a statutory job colour bar in the building industry, whilst the latter measure provided for the establishment of an industrial tribunal with powers to make job reservation determinations in any industry or sector.

The post-1978 Total Strategy phase of apartheid (see p.37) has seen a number of modifications to these laws. Legislation following the reports of the Wiehahn Commission has repealed all job reservation laws and regulations (except those applying to the mining industry), prohibited racially exclusive closed shops and allowed Africans to be indentured as apprentices under certain conditions. However, job reservation determinations and the Mines and Works Act still remain in force in the mining industry. The official position is that they can only be repealed if there is a concensus among all parties — and there is little sign at present of the white mining unions agreeing to this (see p.261). Moreover, outside the mining industry, any group of workers which considers itself adversely affected by modifications to job colour bars can apply to the Industrial Court for an order prohibiting 'unfair labour practices'.

Laws Excluding Blacks from Representative Institutions of the State

One of the central aspects of the apartheid system of capitalist exploitation is the total exclusion of all blacks from access to any of the representative political institutions of the state. Indeed, a common definition of apartheid is one which sees only this total political exclusion and absence of any political rights in the central state. Under the apartheid form of bourgeois 'democracy', those few and steadily diminishing political rights which do exist are reserved exclusively for whites. The gamut of laws excluding blacks from the representative institutions of the state, together with the various modifications proposed by the 'new constitutional dispensation' are discussed pp.133-7.

Laws on Bantustan Administration

Under the racially exclusive political system generated by capitalism in South Africa, the only political 'rights' granted to the African majority of the population, are supposed to be exercised in one of the ten fragmented, so-called 'ethnic homelands' or 'national states' which make up the Bantustan system. According to apartheid theory, the African population are not 'South Africans', but rather nationals or citizens of one of these tribal 'states' created by apartheid. Each will eventually receive 'independence' and it is to these fragmented puppet regimes that the political demands of the majority of South Africans are supposed to be addressed. The operation and basic laws of the Bantustan system are discussed pp.197–217.

Repressive Security Laws of the Apartheid State

A number of such laws were in force before 1948, perhaps the most important being the Riotous Assemblies Act first passed in 1914 and amended several times since. This empowered the Minister to prohibit gatherings considered likely to 'endanger the public peace' or 'cause feelings of hostility between Whites and Blacks'.

These laws were considerably extended and rendered more Draconian under the Nationalist regime. The first major measure passed by the Nationalist regime as part of its assault on the organisations of the oppressed masses was the 1950 Suppression of Communism Act. This outlawed the Communist Party and made it an offence to propagate any doctrine in terms of an extremely broad and vague definition of 'communism'. The Act also empowered the Minister of Justice to remove from certain offices persons listed as communists, as well as to restrict any person to a certain area and/or prevent them attending gatherings.

In response to the Defiance Campaign launched by the ANC in the 1950s (see p.286) the Criminal Law Amendment Act of 1953 made it a criminal offence subject to long terms of imprisonment, fines or corporal punishment, to break any regulation 'by way of protest, or in support of any campaign against any law, or in support of any campaign for the repeal or modification of any law'.

Following the Sharpeville massacre, the ANC and PAC (see pp.283 and 297) were banned under the 1960 Unlawful Organizations Act, and detention without trial was provided for (first for 90 and then for 180 days) under successive amendments to the General Laws Acts. In 1967, in direct response to the launching of the armed struggle in Namibia by SWAPO, the regime passed the Terrorism Act. This Act made it an offence, with penalties ranging from a minimum of five years imprisonment to death, to participate in acts of 'terrorism' — so defined as to include activities ranging from participating in the armed struggle to 'embarrassing the administration of the affairs of state' or 'causing feelings of hostility between Whites and Blacks'. The Act also provided for the indefinite detention without trial of suspects on an order made by an officer above the rank of Lieutenant-Colonel of police in consultation with the Minister of Justice. The Act was made retrospective to 1962 and introduced a new principle in South African law in that the onus of proof was placed on the accused.

A number of the above mentioned Acts, most notably the Suppression of Communism Act and various General Laws Amendment Acts, were consolidated by the 1976 Internal Security Amendment Act. This retained all the major 'offences' under previous legislation and provided for restriction (banning) as well as indefinite 'preventive detention' of persons considered by the Minister responsible to be 'engaging in activities which endangered or were calculated to endanger the security of the State or the maintenance of public order'.

More recently, the whole gamut of security legislation was referred to the Rabie Commission of Inquiry which reported in February 1982. It recommended that in all major respects existing security legislation and practices be retained — taking pains, for example, to 'justify' detention without trial by referring to similar practices in other countries. It did, however, recommend both the introduction of certain review procedures to 'safeguard' the rights of detainees, and a distinction between the offences of 'terrorism' on the one hand and 'subversion' and 'intimidation' on the other. 'Terrorism' would continue to be widely defined to include 'offences' such as 'assisting terrorists' or 'failing to report the presence of terrorists to the police', and would remain subject to a maximum penalty of death. 'Subversion' (defined to include acts which did not actually involve violence) and 'intimidation' would be subject to maximum penalties of 25 years and 10 years imprisonment respectively. Legislation based on the recommendations of Rabie was enacted later in the year. The Minister of Police was renamed Minister of Law and Order and the Internal Security Act was amended.

The Amendment Act laid down *inter alia*, a procedure under which persons subjected to banning orders or detention could appeal to a Review Board and the Minister of Law and Order. However, most observers do not consider that the new procedures offer any significant check on the powers of the regime and a number of persons subjected to banning orders since the passage of the legislation have refused to appeal on the grounds that to do so would merely be to give credibility to the system. Moreover, rather than lessening the Draconian effects of the Terrorism Act, the main impact to date of the Intimidation Act has been to provide the authorities with further legislative ammunition to use against striking workers.

Other Discriminatory and Oppressive Laws

Such laws affect virtually every aspect of life of the oppressed masses and no attempt will be made to provide a comprehensive list here. Rather, mention will be made of just two areas — education and inter-racial sexual relations (laws on censorship and control of free expression are discussed pp.414–16).

Although education for Africans has always been far inferior to that available to whites, under a series of laws passed under the Nationalist regime (beginning with the 1953 Bantu Education Act amended several times and including the 1959 Extension of University Education Act) education at all levels was segregated. Education for Africans was made deliberately inferior on the assumption that its recipients would largely remain unskilled manual labourers. As the then Minister of Native Affairs, Dr H.F. Verwoerd explained when introducing the Bantu Education Act: 'He (the Native) must not be subject to a school system which draws him away from his own community and misleads him by showing him the green pastures of European society where he is not allowed to graze . . . there is no room for the Native in white South Africa above certain forms of labour'. These practices are enshrined in the existence of two separate education departments – the Department of National Education (for whites) and Department of Education and Training (for blacks). During the Total Strategy phase there has been some restructuring and a considerable expansion of educational facilities for blacks – partly because of the increased demand for more skilled black labour power by capital and partly because the Bantu education system had been the focal point of the struggles climaxing in the Soweto uprising. However, despite this and other minor modifications such as the token admission of some blacks to 'white' universities, the basic structure of segregated and inferior education remains intact. A proposal by the de Lange Commission of Inquiry to create a unified system was rejected by the regime after strong pressure from a *Broederbond* organised *Volkskongress* on education in 1981 (see p.270).

Sexual relations between African men and white women were prohibited under so-called 'black peril' laws dating back to 1902. In 1927, under the Immorality Act all extra-marital intercourse was prohibited between whites and Africans but not between whites and other blacks. These laws were considerably tightened up under the Nationalist regime. Under the 1949 Prohibition of Mixed Marriages Act, marriages between whites and members of other racial groups were made illegal, and the 1950 Immorality Amendment Act made any act of 'carnal intercourse' between whites and blacks liable to a penalty of up to seven years imprisonment. During the Total Strategy phase there have been a number of calls from liberal quarters of the bourgeoisie and abroad for these laws to be repealed as a 'test' of the sincerity of the Botha regime's 'reformist intentions'. However, all such calls have thus far been resisted – ostensibly because there is no unanimity among the churches as to what should be done in this regard. Moreover, it has become clear that if there is any change, these laws will, in official jargon, be 'improved' rather than repealed.

THE REPRESSIVE APPARATUSES OF THE APARTHEID STATE

The apartheid system depends for its continued existence on a high level of repression, both to enforce the wide range of regulations and controls over the exploited and oppressed masses and to respond to the growing challenge posed by the advancing liberation struggle.

The principle repressive apparatuses of the apartheid state include:
1) the military – known as the South African Defence Force (SADF) – embracing the Army, Air Force, Navy and Directorate of Military Intelligence (DMI);
2) the Police, including the Security Police;
3) the National Intelligence Service (NIS), successor to the Bureau of State Security (BOSS);
4) the courts and prisons, and
5) the security apparatuses of the Bantustans (armies, police forces, intelligence services, courts and prisons).

The Military – The South African Defence Force[2]

Currently the principal security apparatus of the apartheid state having replaced the Security Police and Bureau for State Security which previously held the dominant position. The period since the mid-1970s and particularly since P.W. Botha's accession to the premiership in 1978, has seen a rapid and extensive militarisation of the state. Through their strong representation on the State Security Council, which has effectively replaced the Cabinet as the highest decision making body in the state, top military commanders exert an increasing influence not only over security policy narrowly defined, but over the Total Strategy of the state.

This situation is partly a consequence of the rapid expansion of military forces in response to the advancing liberation struggle both within the country and in the southern African region. Between 1959/60 and 1977/8 the defence budget increased by over 1000% from R40 million to R1,654 million. Under the premiership of Botha it nearly doubled again between 1978/9 and 1982/3 to reach R2,688 million. As a percentage of the GNP, military spending rose from 0.75% in 1960, to roughly 5% in the 1980s.

The current militarisation of the state is also an outcome of struggles within the security apparatuses themselves, and linked to a struggle between different class forces within the governing Nationalist Party (see p.138). These struggles led to the formation of an alliance between the monopoly capitalist forces in the NP and top military commanders.

Under Botha's premiership, the Total Strategy of the monopoly-military alliance has become official state policy. It envisages, on the one hand, the further consolidation of a powerful and diversified military force and, on the other hand, a series of economic, political, social and ideological (psychological) measures designed to cultivate a supportive black middle class and create divisions among the oppressed masses.

South Africa now has a sophisticated military machine with particular capabilities for aggressive acts against neighbouring states. Through its Reconnaissance Commandos (Recces), its Ethnic Battalions and SADF-sponsored dissident groups (such as the MNR in Mozambique, UNITA in Angola and the Lesotho Liberation Army), the South African military has made numerous interventions in neighbouring states. Through the concept of 'area defence' it attempts to organise its permanent and conscript forces in a comprehensive integration of various components of the security services, aimed at combating the advancing liberation struggle.

However, the continued maintenance and expansion of this military machine also has contradictory effects. Rocketing defence spending is an increasingly heavy burden on the capitalist economy. So too are the increasingly longer call-ups of white males (who in the apartheid racial division of labour fill the bulk of managerial, technical, supervisory and skilled jobs). Moreover, both the protracted war in Namibia and the advancing liberation struggle in South Africa itself have had a demoralising effect on conscripts, resulting in a number of incidences of desertion.

The Role of the Military Prior to the 1970s

The apartheid state today is a highly militarised state; it not only has at its disposal a large and powerful military force but the military also plays the leading role in the co-ordination and execution of security policy and has an increasing influence in the formulation of all aspects of economic, political and social policy considered essential to the Total Strategy for the survival of the system. The military has not always played such a central role in the apartheid state, however. When the Nationalist Party took office in 1948, the principal repressive apparatus of the state was the police force rather than the military. The police enforced the wide range of regulations and controls over the masses and had to defend the system against any challenge by the oppressed classes. The Defence Force was essentially a conventional military force oriented towards external defence. Organised on the British model, it was designed to act as an auxiliary to the forces of the western powers in defence of the general strategic interests of imperialism in the region.

This basic definition of roles did not change fundamentally during the first phase of Nationalist rule prior to 1960. There were, however, a number of important changes in the structure of the military during the 1950s, the first being a major purge of senior officers. The old command structure had been dominated by officers who had fought in the Second World War: as South Africa's participation in the war on the side of the Allies had been opposed by the Nationalists, many senior officers were opponents of the new regime. Furthermore, democratic ex-servicemen's organisations such as the Springbok

Legion and Torch Commando (see p.377) had succeeded in mobilising strong extra-parliamentary opposition to various early actions of the NP. Faced thus with a potential threat to its rule, the Nationalist regime systematically removed a number of top commanders and replaced them with politically sympathetic officers, mainly *Broederbond* members.

The organisational structure of the armed forces was also changed by the NP regime in a concerted effort to modify the inherited British-type military system and develop a peculiarly South African defence structure. The Swiss and Israeli models were closely studied to develop a system in which the small regular 'Permanent Force' nucleus administrated, trained and provided leadership to a large part-time 'Citizen Force' and localised militia groups known as 'Commandos'. The foundations of the present system were laid down in the 1957 Defence Act which made all white males between 18 and 65 years liable for military service — although a ballot system calling up only a proportion of those liable remained in force until 1967.

While this restructuring of the 1950s did envisage a reserve role for the military in the event of 'internal disorders', the SADF still remained essentially orientated as a conventional force. This was evident, for example, in the sharp resentment expressed by some senior commanders at the use of troops to restore order when the police lost control following the demonstrations and massacres in Langa township of Cape Town in 1960.

With the launching of the armed struggle by *Umkhonto we Sizwe* in 1961 (see p.288) and the wave of decolonisation in Africa of the 1960s, the ruling class was faced with a new situation both internally and in the Southern African region. Although the ANC underground suffered a serious reversal with the Rivonia arrests in 1963, it was clear that it was reorganising in exile and would eventually re-emerge within the country. Within the region, South Africa remained until the mid-1970s surrounded by a protective barrier of 'buffer' states (the Portuguese colonies of Angola and Mozambique, its own colony of Namibia and settler-ruled Rhodesia). But the 1960s saw the onset of armed struggles in all of these territories, placing their colonial regimes under increasing pressure.

In response to the potential threat posed to the ruling class by this new situation, the armed forces were rapidly expanded, and developed new capabilities. The defence budget increased nearly sixfold from R44 million in 1960/1 to R257.1 million by 1970/1 and then nearly doubled to reach R472 million by 1973/4. Selective conscription through the ballot system was replaced by the call up of all physically fit white males in particular age groups in 1967. Increasing attention was paid to the development of 'counter insurgency' techniques and capabilities. In 1966 the SADF became involved along with the police in conflicts with SWAPO guerrillas in the Caprivi Strip. Following the 1967/8 Wankie Campaigns by joint ANC-ZAPU forces, it gave decisive support to the Rhodesian forces.

A further important development in the period was the initiation of arms production. The manufacture of ammunition began in 1961; in 1964 the South African state was confronted with a partial arms embargo. The state

Armaments Development and Production Corporation (ARMSCOR) was set up to manufacture arms within the country, and the Armaments Board, to purchase arms abroad (these were later merged to form the present ARMSCOR – see p.104).

Despite these developments, however, in the formulation of general state security policy, the military still remained subordinate to other security apparatuses, particularly the Special Branch and BOSS, which later became during the period the elite security apparatus of the apartheid state (see p.193). Moreover, until the mid-1970s, earlier notions that the SADF should remain basically an externally orientated conventional force were still prominent. As late as 1973, the Defence White Paper defined the priorities as the 'prevention or suppression of disorder instigated from *outside Africa*' and 'controlling and meeting any threats to its sea lanes'. Up to this point the state remained a police state rather than a military state. This was largely due to two factors: firstly, it was the Security Police and the forerunner of BOSS which had smashed the ANC underground in 1963; and secondly, given that the guerrilla threat had not yet gained an effective foothold on South Africa's own borders, there was still a relative complacency in military circles. Thus, an article in a prominent military journal in June 1973 stated that 'South Africa faces no real threat from its immediate neighbours. None of these are likely to launch an attack against South Africa or even countenance harbouring an "Army of Liberation" within their borders'.

Changing Conceptions in the Crisis of the 1970s
This complacency was shattered the following year: the overthrow of the fascist regime in Portugal in April 1974, followed by the independence of Mozambique and Angola – and the humiliating withdrawal of the South African intervention in Angola 1975-6 – coupled with the advancing liberation struggles in Zimbabwe and Namibia, together created a radically new situation in the region. At the same time the dramatically heightened mass struggle within South Africa itself (see p.32) faced the ruling class with a series of new internal challenges.

In these circumstances, defence spending was massively increased and the foundations of the current militarisation of the state were laid. The defence budget for 1974/5 was almost 50% higher than that for 1973/4. By the next year (1975/6) it was more than double the 1973/4 figure and by 1977/8 it had reached R1,654 million or over three-and-a-half times the R472 million of a mere four years earlier.

During the last years of the Vorster regime, security policy still remained dominated by the old BOSS network. The changed regional situation produced a hasty reformulation of regional policy, known as 'detente'. This was essentially a diplomatic offensive in search of allies within the Organization of African Unity. Arranged through contacts in the western intelligence service network, detente was fuelled by bribery and intrigue, and supplemented by the modification of some very minor forms of 'petty apartheid' (see p.43).

This detente policy did score some initial successes, but by the end of 1976 the policy was clearly in deep crisis. The major precipitating factor was the first South African invasion of Angola from August 1975 to March 1976. While interpretations over this invasion differ, it seems that the initial impetus to the South African intervention came from BOSS rather than the military. Senior military commanders reportedly favoured either a full-scale invasion or no intervention. They opposed the eventual limited intervention as potentially too damaging to South Africa's regional and international interests. In the event, the ignominious expulsion of the South African invasion force by Angolan and Cuban troops exposed South Africa as an aggressor and isolated it from a number of potential allies in Africa. Whilst some momentum to 'detente' still remained after the Angola debacle, this collapsed following the Soweto uprising of June-August 1976.

The Soweto uprising represented a crisis point internally, not only for the state and the ruling class in general (see p.33) but also specifically for BOSS itself. As indicated in the entry on BOSS/NIS (p.193) the elite security apparatus of the apartheid state was neither able to predict the Soweto uprising nor produce any coherent response to it. This had important effects on the conflicts within the ruling class. In particular it led to a strategic reconception by senior commanders of the role of the military both within the overall state apparatus and formation of state policy on the one hand, and in the actual conceptions of the strategy, role, formation and logistics of the SADF as a fighting force on the other hand.

Faced with the multiple and continuing crises after Angola and Soweto, senior officers became increasingly critical of existing security policy. Under the political protection of the then Minister of Defence and leader of the Cape Nationalist Party, P.W. Botha, they began to formulate alternative strategies. These were advocated first within the State Security Council — then an advisory body, set up in 1972 and embracing the heads of all security departments and senior cabinet ministers. However, in the context of the worsening crisis after 1976, and the patent political paralysis of the deeply divided Vorster regime and the Nationalist Party, the SADF chiefs increasingly canvassed support for their position publicly — and in the process became embroiled, through the Minister of Defence, in the intense factional conflicts within the government and ruling party (see pp.37-8).

The Military under the Botha Regime

The most explicit statement of the military's alternative strategy was published in the 1977 Defence White Paper. This called for the adoption of a 'Total Strategy' as the only means of saving the system from what was described as the 'total onslaught' against it (see p.38). These conceptions provided a basis for an alliance between top military commanders and the Afrikaner monopoly capitalist forces represented in the governing Nationalist Party (see p.144). With the triumph of this alliance in the accession to the premiership of Botha in 1978, the Total Strategy became official state policy.

The Angola fiasco moreover highlighted deficiencies in both the equipment and training of the South African army. Some of the equipment used in Angola, particularly the artillery, was of Second World War vintage, and the invasion force was badly outgunned by the Angolan and Cuban artillery and particularly demoralised by barrages from the 'Stalin Organ' rocket artillery. After this defeat, two important changes were introduced. Firstly, through the state-owned armaments company, ARMSCOR (see p.104), a crash armaments development programme was initiated; this had the objective of producing locally manufactured highly mobile and long-range weaponry, suitable to the types of aggressive military interventions made in Angola. The most notable result was the development of the 155mm G-5 long range howitzer, the G-6 mobile version of this artillery piece, and the Oliphant battle tank. These are claimed by the SADF to be the most advanced weapons of their type in the world. In the large-scale 'Operation Protea' invasion of Angola in late 1981, it was also claimed that 95% of the equipment used was locally produced. The Angola debacle secondly precipitated a strategic rethinking on the role of the Defence Force. Its aim was to increase the SADF's capacities as a highly mobile conventional invasion force to be used against neighbouring countries, whilst at the same time raising its capacity to fight a 'counter insurgency' war against guerrilla forces in Namibia and South Africa itself.

Under Botha's premiership the military apparatuses have been continually expanded and strengthened. Defence expenditure nearly doubled between the last budget of the Vorster regime 1977/8 and 1982/3 when it reached a massive R2,688 million (roughly equivalent to the GDP of Zimbabwe in 1978). 'Counter insurgency' and intervention capabilities directed at neighbouring states have been consolidated and developed, with the result that the apartheid war machine now possesses a range of capabilities for aggression against neighbouring states most of which have been well-tested in practice. These include: 1) Reconnaissance Commandos (Recces): specialist units containing a high proportion of mercenaries used for hit and run operations such as the Matola raid against ANC residences in Mozambique; 2) Ethnic Battalions: units stationed near the borders of neighbouring states composed of black soldiers of the same language/cultural group as the people of the neighbouring state, ready for raids into these territories as well as to support puppet groups; 3) puppet groups, such as UNITA, the MNR and Lesotho Liberation Army purporting to be indigenous 'resistance movements' and indeed drawing recruits from the country concerned, but supplied, led and directed by the SADF and 4) conventional forces deployed in Namibia and used for repeated massive strikes against Angola.

The military response to the advancing armed struggle internally is currently organised around the strategic concept of 'area defence'. This doctrine emerged as a response to the growing manpower shortage created by the advancing armed struggle. It aims at calling up more conscripts for longer periods whilst simultaneously economising on the use of manpower and facilitating a more effective specialisation and division of labour. It envisages 'on the spot defence' by local commando or guard forces made up of local residents such that 'in each area [these] will form the first line of defence aimed at containing terror attacks'. In this way, the fulltime forces will be able to assume fully the role of a 'reaction force' and 'deal with major incidents' that include striking at 'ANC sanctuaries in neighbouring countries' as well as watching the Mozambican and Zimbabwean borders.

At the same time, the basic organisation and discipline of the army has been reconceived in keeping with the perceived demands of counter insurgency war. In the past, emphasis was given primarily to the platoon and company structure and parade ground discipline and drill. The South African army had been disparagingly referred to by ex-Rhodesian mercenaries as an 'if it moves salute it, if it doesn't paint it' army. These practices are giving way to more 'functional' structures and discipline in which small combat groups, led by a corporal, receive primary attention.

Under Botha's premiership, the military has become not only the clearly dominant force in the co-ordination and execution of security policy narrowly defined, but has also become increasingly influential in the formulation of all aspects of state policy. This has manifested itself most obviously in the appointment of the former defence force chief and architect of the Total Strategy, Magnus Malan, as Minister of Defence in 1978, the first time in South African history that a serving officer had been appointed to the Cabinet. Moreover, the increasing importance of the State Security Council (SSC) has fostered military dominance over state policy. The Council was established in 1972 as a consultative body between the government and the chiefs of the security apparatuses. Under P.W. Botha, the Council is a military dominated body. In 1979 its role was redefined as to 'conduct' rather than to 'advise upon' the 'national strategic planning process', as in the past. The SSC has now clearly replaced the Cabinet as the most important policy formulation body of the state. Through a network of inter-departmental committees, it liaises directly with all government departments. It meets the day before weekly Cabinet meetings, and prepares the Cabinet's agenda. Not surprisingly, in a number of instances other government departments have been mobilised to act in support of military or quasi-military operations. One example is the way in which transport services have been used in support of destabilisation campaigns against neighbouring states.

As a result of these processes, South Africa now clearly possesses a formidable military machine (for details see p.186) and has become a highly militarised society. However, militarisation has not been without its own contradictions, but has involved a number of costs for the ruling class.

The continuing massive increases in military spending have become an increasingly heavy burden on South Africa's capitalist economy. The military budget today absorbs more than 15% of total government expenditure, at a time when revenue (due to the lower gold price) has declined.

Secondly, the increasingly longer call up period for white males, who fill the bulk of managerial, technical, supervisory and skilled jobs, is also involving an increasing economic cost for capital. This became clear in the wave of complaints from employers following the publication of the bill giving effect to the 'area defence' strategy. Reflecting this, the influential *Financial Mail*, urged in June 1982 that the 'economic aspects' of the new system be taken into account by the government as 'the new call up system is going to affect the vast majority of white men in SA and will certainly affect every business enterprise'.

Finally, it is clear that the protracted war in Namibia and the advancing liberation struggle in South Africa itself have produced a morale problem for the SADF. There have been a number of incidences of desertion and resistance to conscription (see entry on War Resisters, p.385). Between 1978 and 1982, 5,181 people were prosecuted for failing to report for military service. An unknown but large number of young men have gone into exile to avoid conscription. So acute has the problem become, that in early 1983 the regime conceded some ground by introducing a bill in parliament providing for forms of alternative 'service' for a limited range of 'consciencious objectors'. However, it refused to accept political objections to serving in the SADF as grounds for alternative service.

Top military commanders:
    Minister of Defence: Gen. Magnus Malan
    Chief of the Defence Force: Gen. Constandt Viljoen
    Chief of the Army: Lt. Gen. J.J. Geldenhuys
    Chief of the Air Force: Lt. Gen. M. Muller
    Chief of the Navy: Vice-Admiral A.P. Putter.

Statistical Appendix: The SADF in the 1980s

1. Estimated SADF Manpower 1960–1979

	1960	*1970*	*1974*	*1977*	*1979*
Permanent Force	11,500	13,000	21,500	28,000	40,000
National Servicemen	10,000	23,000	26,000	27,000	60,000
Citizen Force	2,000	30,000	120,000	180,000	230,000
Commandos	48,500	75,000	90,000	120,000	150,000
Civilians	6,000	8,000	11,500	12,500	14,000
Total	*78,000*	*149,000*	*269,000*	*367,500*	*494,000*
Standing Operational Force	11,500	42,000	47,500	105,000	180,000

Source: International Defence and Aid Fund (IDAF) *The Apartheid War Machine*, London 1980 p.41.

Few official figures are available on SADF strength. This table is an attempt to put together an estimation of the situation.

Different figures are given in other sources. Thus, citing *The Military Balance*, the SAIRR *Survey of Race Relations in South Africa, 1980,* Johannesburg, 1981, gives the following figures:

Standing Operational Force:
   in South Africa: 71,000 army
                          10,300 air force
                          4,750 navy
   in Namibia: 73,000
Total force capable of fielding: 404,000

2. Equipment

a) South African Army — Major Weapon Systems in Service

Type	Manufacturer	Number	Remarks
Tanks:			
Centurion Mk10	UK	150	Delivered from UK, Jordan and India (via Spain)
Merkava	Israel	30+	Believed to be on order
AMX-13	France/SA	80(approx.)	Sales unconfirmed
Sherman	US	?	Believed to be used for training purposes
Comet	UK	?	
Oliphant	SA/UK	?	Local development of British Centurion tank.
Armoured cars:			
Panhard AML-245/60	France/SA	800+	Manufactured under licence in SA
Panhard AML-245/80	France/SA	400+	Manufactured under licence in SA
Ferret	UK	100	460 delivered 1963–9; almost obsolete
Armoured personnel carriers:			
Saracen	UK	250	700 delivered 1956–66; almost obsolete
Commando V150	US/Portugal	100	320 believed ordered
M-113A1	US/Italy	150+	400 ordered via Israel
Ratel	SA	600+	In service since 1977; still in production
Artillery:			
Field:			
25-pounder (88mm)	UK	30	112 delivered 1951
Sexton s.p.g. (88mm)	Canada	30	180 delivered 1946
M.7 Priest s.p.g. (105mm)	US	?	World War II issue; rebuilt in SA

187

90mm FG	SA	150+	Still in production
5.5 inch (140mm)	UK	?	World War II issue; being replaced by 155mm
M109 s.p.g. (155mm)	US	20+	Delivered 1976
G5 155mm*	SA/Canada	100+	Being manufactured in SA with Canadian technology

Anti-tank:

17-pounder (76.2mm)	UK	100	234 delivered 1956
106mm Recoil-less Rifle	US	?	Delivered via Israel 1977
ENTACATGW	France	120	138 delivered 1955/6
Milan AT missile	France/FRG	?	To replace ENTAC

Anti-aircraft:

20mm 204GK	Switzerland	?
35mm twin K-63	Switzerland	?
40mm L-70	Sweden	?
3.7 inch (88mm)	UK	?

Surface-to-air missiles:(SAAF):

Cactus/ Crotale	France/SA	30+	Initially manufactured in France; now in production in SA
Tigercat	UK	54	Delivered via Jordan 1974

Source: IDAF, op.cit. pp.24–5.

*In mid-1982 ARMSCOR (see p.104) unveiled a new self-propelled version named the G-6. It is not known whether this weapon is yet operational, or in what quantities.

b) Estimate of South African Air Force Arms Inventory

Type	Role	No.	Manufacturer	Remarks
Landward air defence attack:				
Mirage F.1AZ	Ground attack fighter	60+	France/SA	32 delivered in parts from France; rest manufactured in SA; planned requirement 100+; equipped with EMD Aida II fire control system and laser range finder; a priority for ARMSCOR
Mirage F.1CZ	Interceptor	25+	France/SA	16F.1CZ delivered 1974-75 and more being
IIICZ		16	France/SA	manufactured in SA. Armed with R530 and R550.Magic air-to-air missiles; IIICZ now used as trainers
Mirage III BZ, DZ D2Z	Two-seater trainer	19	France	3BZ delivered early 1960s; 3DZ delivered 1965-66; 13 D2Z delivered 1972.
Mirage III RZ and R2Z	Tactical reconnaissance	10+	France	4 RZ and 4 R2Z delivered from France; 16 R2Z to be manufactured in SA
Mirage III EZ	Ground attack fighter bomber	38	France/SA	20 delivered 1965-66; 18 manufactured in SA; armed with Nord AS-20/30 air-to-surface missiles
CL 13B Sabre Mk6	Fighter	12	Canada	Now used as trainers at 85 AFS
BAC Canberra	Strike-reconnaissance	9	UK	Delivered 1962
Impala MB 326M Mk 1	Two-seater basic trainer	216	Italy/SA	16 delivered from Italy 1967; 10 delivered in parts 1967; 40 delivered in parts 1968; 150 manufactured in SA 1967-73
Impala MB 326 K Mk 2	Ground attack	122+	Italy/SA	7 delivered 1974-5; 15 delivered in parts 1975; 50 manufactured in SA 1976; 50+ on order for completion 1978

Maritime Command:

Buccaneer S Mk50	Maritime strike-reconnaissance	7	UK	Delivered 1965
HS Shackleton MR Mk3	Maritime patrol	7	UK	Delivered 1957; recently repaired; equipment up-dated
P.166 S Albatross	Coastal patrol and light transport	18	Italy	Nine delivered from Italy 1969; nine delivered 1973–4

Transport:

Lockheed C-130B Hercules	Heavy transport	7	US	Delivered from US, 1963
Lockheed L-100	Heavy transport	15	US	Civilian equivalent of C-130B; delivered from US for 'civilian purposes'
Transall C-160	Heavy transport	9	France/FRG	Delivered from France, 1969-70
Douglas C-47 Dakota	Medium transport	30	US	Delivered from US 1950s
HS 125	Light transport	4	UK	Delivered from UK early 1970s
Sweringen Merlin IVA	Light transport	7	US	Delivered from US 1970s

Utility/Liaison – Light Aircraft Command

Cessna CE-185	Light transport and reconnaissance	16	US	Delivered from US 1960s
Cessna 185 Skywagon	Light transport and reconnaissance	12	US	Delivered from US 1970s
AM.3CM Bosbok	Forward air control; tactical reconnaissance light transport casualty evacuation	40	Italy/SA	Delivered from Italy and manufactured in SA 1974-75

Atlas C4M Kudu	Forward air control tactical reconnaissance light transport casualty evacuation	40+	SA	Designed and manufactured in SA based on Bosbok
Helicopters:				
Alouette II and III (SE-313 and SE-316)	Light air support	110+	France	Seven II's delivered from France 1962; 54 III's delivered 1965-66; 16 III's delivered 1968; later orders unconfirmed
SA-330 Puma	Air support light transport	40+	France	20 delivered 1970-71; later orders unconfirmed.
SA-321 L Super Frelon	Medium transport	15+	France	16 delivered 1970-71; later orders unconfirmed
Westland Wasp	Light maritime support	12	UK	Delivered from UK 1966-74
SA-341 Gazelle	Light support	2	France	?
BO 105	Light support	?	FRG	?

Additionally: 30 HS Vampire trainers; 74 Rockwell; T-6 Harvard trainers; 1 BAC Viscount transport; 5 Douglas DC-4 transport.
There have been allegations that the SAAF also has the following:
40 Lockheed F-140 G Starfighters; 50 F-51D Cavalier; 25 Agusta Bell 205A Iroquois; 12 Lockheed P-2 Neptune; Pucara FMA IA.58.

Source: IDAF op.cit. pp.29-31.

c) South African Navy Inventory
  12   Israeli designed 'Reshef' missile strike craft
  3   French 'Daphne class' submarines
  3   Frigates (1 sunk February 1982)
  10   Minesweepers
  5   Patrol boats
  —   Various supply craft
  —   Unknown number of locally designed and produced 'Minister class';
       missile strike craft, derived from the Israeli; 'Reshef' craft

Source: Ibid *passim*

South African Police (SAP) and Security Police[3]

Previously the dominant security apparatus of the state, the police force's relative importance has now declined as that of the military has increased. Nevertheless, the SAP and its Security Branch continues to play a crucial role in the preservation of the system of apartheid. The absolute size of the police force has increased nearly threefold since 1960. Of the approximately 72,000 members of the police at the end of the 1970s, nearly 19,000 were white regulars, 15,820 were black regulars and the rest consisted of (mainly white) reserves in different categories.

The major functions of the police in the state today are:

1) The enforcement of apartheid laws and controls over the oppressed masses. One particular duty in this respect is the enforcement of pass laws (see p.171) which absorbs a large proportion of total police time and effort. Thus in 1979, 119,869 Africans were arrested by the police for pass law 'offences' (and a further 44,678 by Administration Board Officials).

2) 'Riot control'. As became apparent during the 1976 uprisings, the SAP now possesses a number of para-military units with armoured vehicles and other 'riot control' equipment, with which it intervenes to repress meetings, demonstrations etc. considered to constitute a challenge to the system. In fact, in the division of labour with the military, it is the police who are required first to do battle in townships, while the army and later air force are only called in the event of police being unable to restore control.

3) The Security Police (SP) are responsible for the arrest, detention, interrogation and prosecution of political opponents. Under the laws of apartheid, the SP have wide powers to detain whomsoever it sees fit until such time as the person concerned has answered all questions to the satisfaction of the police. The use of different forms of torture has now become routine in interrogation sessions. The names of a number of torturers have become notorious.

The Commissioner of Police is: J.J. Coetzee (formerly head of the Security Police).

Bureau for State Security (BOSS) – National Intelligence Service (NIS)[4]

The National Intelligence Service (NIS) is a successor to the Bureau of State Security (BOSS). Though still widely referred to by its former name, NIS was substantially restructured after 1978 and now plays a different role to the old BOSS.

BOSS was formally constituted in 1969. It replaced the Republican Intelligence (RI), which had functioned as a division of the Security Police since the early 1960s and which established its reputation by infiltration of the ANC/CP underground.

Under the premiership of B.J. Vorster (1966-78) BOSS became the 'elite' security apparatus of the state with a major influence on all aspects of security policy. It was involved in planting agents in a number of progressive and liberal organisations and engaged in bribery and 'dirty tricks' campaigns in South Africa, other African countries and abroad. It was also involved in organising diplomatic offensives into Africa during the 'outward looking' and 'detente' phases. However, according to defectors, it failed to penetrate on any significant scale either the ANC external mission or the emerging Black Consciousness organisations.

During this period BOSS created a number of enemies among important ruling-class forces. It acted as a partisan supporter of Vorster's centrist faction in the NP and *Broederbond*, provoking antagonism from both far right *verkramptes* and the Afrikaner monopoly capitalist forces dominating the Cape NP. It also provoked antagonism from top military leaders who saw its 'projects' as adventurist.

The demise of BOSS came during the crisis of the 1970s. Two major factors were of crucial importance. First, was its advocacy of the ill-fated South African invasion of Angola, in August 1975. Second, BOSS failed to either predict or propose an adequate response to the 1976 Soweto uprising. These failures gave opponents within the ruling class the opportunity to launch a campaign against it through the 'information scandal'.

After 1978 under Botha's premiership, BOSS was restructured and renamed (first the Department of National Security – DONS – and now the National Intelligence Service (NIS). In the formulation of strategy it is now subordinate to the military. It is currently supposed to concentrate exclusively on 'overseas operations' and act as an agency collecting and analysing intelligence. It was, however, implicated in the abortive Seychelles coup attempt of 1981, along with some officials in the military.

Formation and History of BOSS

The formation of a specific intelligence service within the security apparatus of the state dates back to the early 1960s. Following the Sharpeville massacre and the outlawing of the ANC as well as the PAC, the liberation movement had re-formed underground and launched the sabotage campaign. South Africa had just left the Commonwealth, thereby forfeiting the hitherto 'official and detailed co-operation' received from British intelligence. In these circumstances, the then Minister of Justice, B.J. Vorster, and Commissioner of Police, J.M. Keevy, decided 'there was a critical need for a sophisticated intelligence organization — one that could co-ordinate intelligence gathering and bring relief to the hard pressed Security Police'.

Republican Intelligence (RI) was formed to carry out these tasks, functioning initially as an undercover section of the Security Police. Its head was Col. H.J. van den Bergh, formerly head of the Security Police. RI's first priority was to smash the ANC/CP underground. Its basic *modus operandi* was to infiltrate agents, posing as students or journalists, into the underground organisation. It is generally regarded as having played a major role in smashing the underground during 1963-4. This considerably enhanced RI's reputation within ruling class circles along with that of the Minister of Justice, Vorster. Another event which is said to have increased RI's prestige was its involvement in the capture of an alleged Soviet spy, Yuri Loganov, (subsequently exchanged for a number of western spies captured in the Soviet Union).

With the elevation to the premiership in 1966 of the Minister responsible for RI, B.J. Vorster, its role was likewise enhanced. In 1969, the Public Service Amendment Act formally constituted the Bureau of State Security (BOSS). Basically as the RI renamed, BOSS was made accountable only to the Prime Minister. Its head, H.J. van den Bergh was promoted to General and came to be regarded as the second most powerful man in the country. Vorster formed BOSS to provide himself with a secure base during the deep divisions in the NP (see p.142); during his premiership (1966-78), BOSS became the elite security apparatus in the state.

According to defectors, during this period BOSS continued to try to infiltrate its agents, again largely posing as students and journalists, into anti-apartheid organisations both within South Africa and abroad. It achieved some successes, notably in penetrating NUSAS (see p.381) and, in a joint venture with the Security Police, the Geneva based International Universities Exchange Fund. However, again according to defectors, it failed to penetrate either the external mission of the ANC or the emerging Black Consciousness organisations. During the post-Rivonia decade of 'relative quiet' this did not create too many problems, but in the period of heightened mass struggle after 1972 it became a major liability and factor in the Bureau's subsequent demise.

BOSS is now also known to have been involved in a number of 'dirty tricks'. These included several murders of opponents within the country and abroad, by its 'Z squad'. Gen. van den Bergh boasted in 1978 having men who would kill at his whim. In conjunction with the Department of Information, BOSS also engaged in a number of 'projects' involving the bribery of influential persons and the financing of propaganda campaigns abroad, as well as in arranging secret diplomatic offensives into Africa during the so-called 'outward looking' and 'detente' exercises (see p.43).

During the course of this period, however, BOSS also created a number of powerful enemies within the ruling class. It was a partisan of Vorster's centrist faction in the Nationalist Party and the *Broederbond*. In this capacity, it acted in a number of ways against far right *verkramptes* and also blocked political initiatives by the monopoly capitalist forces dominating the Cape Nationalist Party. At the same time it provoked intense hostility from top military commanders. In part these were due to bureaucratic rivalries and jealousies. But more importantly, top military commanders viewed a number of BOSS's projects as adventurist and thus threatening to the overall security of the apartheid state. Furthermore, although the Bureau did see the need for some sort of 'hearts and minds' campaign to win black allies, when the crisis of the 1970s finally erupted, it could not produce any comprehensive alternative to the military's Total Strategy, which it nevertheless continued to block.

Demise of BOSS and Rise of NIS

The demise of BOSS came during the crisis of the 1970s; two events were of particular importance here. The first was the invasion of Angola from August 1975 to March 1976. This project was planned and pushed for by BOSS against resistance from the military. The eventual ignominious expulsion of South African forces by Angolan and Cuban troops was a big blow to the Bureau. The other event was the 1976 Soweto uprising: according to defectors, BOSS failed to plant sufficient agents in organisations of the oppressed masses, and the uprising took it completely by surprise. The elite state security apparatus was neither able to offer a coherent analysis nor to recommend a viable response – apparently suggesting at one stage that the whole thing was the result of a plot by the CIA in revenge for disclosures by South Africa about the Agency's involvement in the Angolan debacle.

These evident failures by the Bureau gave its rivals within the ruling class the opportunity to launch a campaign against both the BOSS leadership and the centre-right faction of the Nationalist Party behind it. This campaign was directed by leading forces within the military allied to the monopoly capitalist forces within the Nationalist Party, which had by 1977 formulated the essence of their Total Strategy. The particular mechanism here was the so-called 'information scandal'. Stripped of its moralistic rhetoric, the 'information scandal' was nothing more or less than the systematic 'leaking' by senior state officials (including, according to some BOSS defectors, P.W. Botha, the then Minister of Defence and leader of the Cape Nationalist Party) of 'damaging material' about the involvement of key centre-right rivals in secret projects with the objective of discrediting and politically neutralising them. The Secretary of Information, Eschel Rhoodie; BOSS head H.J. van den Bergh; Minister of Plural Relations and leader of Transvaal Nationalist Party, Connie Mulder and Prime Minister B.J. Vorster, to name the most important, were driven into political oblivion. Equally importantly, the process enabled P.W. Botha to emerge as Prime Minister at the end of 1978.

The Formation and Function of NIS

The 'information scandal' profoundly affected the whole of the BOSS organisation. Following the resignation of van den Bergh in September 1978, its name was changed to the Department of National Security (DONS). Until mid-1980 it was presided over by a former BOSS Deputy Secretary, A. van Wyk. This, however, was a caretaker appointment and it appears that the Department became much less active and possibly underwent a purge during this period. At this time a number of former BOSS agents defected and began publishing exposés.

In early 1980, however, the organisation was restructured. Increasingly, it was drawn into a new role within the now clearly military-led state security system. In February 1980 its name was again changed to the National Intelligence Service (NIS). At the same time, all security apparatuses were made accountable to a newly established Directorate of National Intelligence whose role was to scrutinise all security matters on behalf of the State Security Council. In mid-1980, Lukas Neil Barnard, a 31 year old former Professor of Political Science at the University of the Orange Free State, took over as head of NIS.

In May 1981, it was reported that a 'final decision' on the division of labour between NIS, Military Intelligence and the Security Branch of the police had been taken. NIS, which had hitherto had agents both within South Africa and abroad, would in future be concerned only with 'overseas operations', while the Security Branch would deal with 'internal security', placing its former overseas agents under the control of NIS. NIS would also 'liaise' and negotiate with foreign intelligence organisations. Military Intelligence, however, would retain its own special overseas contacts.

It is sometimes argued that NIS is now principally involved in the collection, evaluation, co-ordination and analysis of intelligence. It does, however, nevertheless still appear to have a certain 'intervention' capacity as evidenced by its active involvement, along with the military, in aspects of the planning and execution of the abortive Seychelles coup attempt in November 1981. Despite this debacle, however, NIS's final 'rehabilitation' was said to have occurred in May 1982, when it and its director were publicly praised by P.W. Botha for successfully arranging a 'spy swap' resulting in the release of a prisoner of war held by SWAPO. NIS now also functions as the secretariat of the State Security Council.

Director:
Lukas Neil Barnard

Other Repressive Apparatuses[5]

The Prisons Department: responsible for the incarceration of persons ranging from pass offenders to militants of the liberation struggle, as well as for the execution of those condemned to death. The prisons department had a staff of 16,064 in 1979 of whom 9,036 were whites and 7,028 blacks. An illuminating comment on the character of apartheid society emerges from the statistics for the daily average prison population. At over 100,000 persons this figure is over three times the level of Britain, which has twice the population. Broken down by 'population groups' the clear majority of prisoners are Africans – 73,538 in 1979 representing an average of 451 prisoners per 100,000 of the African population, compared to 4,316 whites representing 97 prisoners per 100,000 of the white population. In 1979, 133 people were executed – 98 Africans, 33 so-called coloureds, and two whites.

The Courts: responsible for handing out sentences to offenders against apartheid laws (see also pp.135-6).

The Pass Offices: responsible for issuing pass documents to Africans without which they cannot legally be outside their designated 'homelands'. The administration of the pass system has led to the creation of a vast bureaucracy now using modern imported equipment (ICL computers, Polaroid photographic equipment).

Administration Boards: responsible for the 'administering' of black urban areas including 'endorsing out' persons considered as undesirable or 'idle' i.e. unemployed. Administration Boards are increasingly involved as labour bureaux in the Bantustans, and a number have opened offices in various Bantustan areas. Each Board is headed by a superintendent and they also have their own 'location police'.

Security Apparatuses of the Bantustans: (see p.197-237).

THE BANTUSTAN SYSTEM

The Bantustans in Apartheid Policy – An Overview[6]

The Bantustans form a central prop of the apartheid form of capitalist exploitation in South Africa. Under apartheid, the Bantustans are the only areas of the country in which the majority of South Africans have any political 'rights'. First known officially as 'Bantu Homelands' and now as 'national states', the Bantustans are overcrowded, eroded and fragmented rural slums. Here the apartheid state barricades all those who are 'superfluous' to the immediate labour requirements of South African capitalism, and allows them out only when their labour is required by this or that branch of capitalist production.

Within South African capitalism, the Bantustans perform the crucial economic function of containing and dividing the reserve army of labour. Politically, they are likewise central to the maintenance of capitalist exploitation through national oppression – through the Bantustans, all Africans are stripped of their South African citizenship in a strategy which aims at the tribal fragmentation of the working class and the breaking up of any alliance of the nationally oppressed groups.

According to apartheid theory as it has developed over the years, the African majority of the population are not South Africans. Rather, they belong to different 'ethnic nationalities' each possessed of a 'distinct language, culture, life style, values and traditions'. Among the African population the regime distinguishes ten such different 'national groupings', each based on 'the traditional tribal homelands' which together comprise just over 13% of the total area of the country.

Apartheid policy is rooted in the principle that these ten separate 'nations' will be given their 'right to self determination' in their 'traditional areas' (see table p.218). The objective is that each will eventually emerge as an 'independent state'. The regime insists that the political demands of the African majority of South Africa's population can be channelled only through the Bantustans. Once these are all 'independent', as the responsible minister put it in 1978, 'there will be not one Black man with South African citizenship'. This neat semantic trick will therefore ensure that in the regime's view the national question has been resolved.

Crucial to this strategy is the creation of a tiny collaborative black bourgeoisie through the trappings of 'independent states' – a class force whose entire economic and political existence rests on the maintenance of apartheid. In recent years, Bantustan puppets such as the Matanzina brothers in the Transkei, the Sebe brothers in the Ciskei, Mpephu of Venda and Mangope of Bophuthastswana have become, for millions of South Africa's oppressed population, the real and most visible policemen of apartheid. The surrogate form of state repression channelled through the Bantustans (and therefore disclaimed by Pretoria) has emerged as one of the apartheid regime's central weapons against the rising challenge of the masses.

By the end of 1982, four Bantustan regimes (the Transkei, Bophuthatswana, Venda and the Ciskei) have been granted 'independence'; a fifth, KwaNdebele, was being prepared for 'independence'. As yet, these 'republics' are recognised only by the apartheid state which fathered them, together with the capitalists who require the migratory labour of their inhabitants from time to time, and those whites seeking the thrills of gambling, pornography and prostitution – banned in 'white' South Africa, but among the major industries of these 'states'. The other Bantustan leaders have all declined 'independence' on the grounds that they are South Africans and reject the necessary corollary of loss of South African citizenship which goes with 'independence'. More significantly, at every turn and through a wide variety of organisational forms, the overwhelming majority of South Africa's oppressed population have decisively rejected the Bantustans as a fraud designed to maintain apartheid and thwart the political demand for democracy in a unified South Africa. The various Bantustan puppet regimes have been able to sustain themselves only because, firstly, they are backed by the full repressive might of the South African state, and secondly, because the various legislatures' are dominated by nominated, government-paid 'chiefs', who virtually uniformly have toed the apartheid line.

This almost total rejection of the Bantustans and the loss of South African citizenship implicit in 'independence', has recently prompted a shift in the regime's concept of 'independence'. Under the Total Strategy, the 'independent' Bantustans were first selected to play the role of the 'inner core' of the proposed 'Constellation of Southern African States'. Since this latter proposal won almost no support in Africa, and in fact directly precipitated the formation of the Southern African Development Coordination Conference (SADCC), designed to reduce the economic dependence on South Africa of the states in the region (see pp.45-6), some rethinking has occurred. Now the regime is proposing a 'Confederation of Southern African States', comprising 'white' South African and the 'independent' Bantustans. Within this 'confederation' the separate 'states' will be autonomous, but perhaps share common passports and 'confederal nationality'. This is an attempt to still the powerful reaction against the loss of South African citizenship and to 'join together what apartheid has put asunder'.

The Bantustan policy developed historically, and continues today to be, a strategic response to a changing situation and growing mass challenge. Although the first Bantustan proposals were advanced by the regime in the 1959 Promotion of Bantu Self-Government Act, its roots go back to the last century. The Bantustans are based on what used to be called 'the Native Reserves' — those areas of land where peasant resistance had succeeded in preventing total colonial expropriation, and which were later designated as the only areas of the country in which Africans could own land (see p.170). As such, the reserves were the prop of the early segregation of development of South African capitalism (see p.8ff). As overpopulated and increasingly impoverished reservoirs of labour, they reproduced an accessible, cheap, migrant labour force for all sectors of capitalist production. Through the pass laws and legislation which restricted the access of Africans to the cities 'when they ceased to minister' to the needs of whites, the state attempted to disperse and control the political challenge of the oppressed (see p.171).

The Historic Origins of the Bantustans in the Segregation Period (1870–1948)
The first systematic implementation of a Reserves policy occurred in the
Natal Colony in the last third of the 19th Century. This policy was extended
on a national basis by the 1913 Natives Land Act – one of the fundamental
legislative props of the segregation period. The Act was designed to break
the relative economic independence of the African peasantry and drive them
into wage labour in the mines and labour tenancy arrangements on the farms
of emerging white capitalist farmers. It did so firstly by removing the vast
majority of rent paying squatter peasants from white farms, and secondly by
restricting African land ownership to the mere 8% of the total land area
designated as 'Native Reserves' (see pp.169–70). In terms of the 1936 Natives
Land and Trust Act the projected area of the Reserves was extended to just
over 13% of total land area (much of this additional land still remains in
white hands, however), and further measures were taken against labour
tenants. The highly fragmented land allocations of the 1936 Act remain the
basis of the 'national territories' envisaged in the Bantustan scheme (the
KwaZulu Bantustan for example consists of over 40 distinct parcels of land).

The reserve system in the segregation period provided the basis for the
later Bantustan strategies in the apartheid period. Its two necessary comple-
ments were the consolidation of tribally based, but state-installed, separate
political institutions for Africans, and the development of a system of control
of the influx of African workers from the reserves to the cities. The first of
these was established in the 1920 Native Affairs Act. This extended across
the country the system of tribally-based district councils first set up in the
Cape under the 1894 Glen Grey Act. The principle of separate, communally-
based political representation was extended by the 1936 Representation of
Natives Act. However, its full development in policy only occurred after the
election of the Nationalist Party on its apartheid programme in May 1948.

Secondly, the policy of influx control has a long history. Its clearest
statement was made by the Stallard Commission, which declared in 1922 that
permanent residence in the towns was the exclusive right of whites. Africans
were to be permitted in towns only to 'minister to the needs' of whites, and
were to be expelled to the reserves when they 'ceased so to minister'. A
system of pass laws would control the mobility of African labour, and house in
segregated townships those who worked in the cities. These principles were
enshrined in the 1923 Natives (Urban Areas) Act, which vested the powers of
control in local authorities. Amendments to this Act in 1937 and 1945
extended these powers of control over the influx into urban areas. However,
in contrast to later apartheid legislation, such control still remained with the
local authorities, and its implementation was not obligatory. In those cities
(such as Johannesburg and the other major industrial centres) where local
authorities were dominated by industrial interests concerned to maintain a
large pool of unemployed labour potentially on call in the cities, the
legislation was only intermittently enforced until the end of the 1940s.

Reformulation of 'Native Policy' in the 1940s

The 1940s were years of rapid economic development and intensified class
struggle (see p.16). They gave rise to both a well organised, militant African
trade union movement and severe divisions within the ruling class over the
appropriate response to the growing mass challenge to the system of segregation.
These divisions ranged over a wide gamut of issues. Of central importance was
the effective collapse of the capacity of the reserves to sustain the reproduction of a cheap migrant labour force and the consequent huge influx of
African labour into the cities. The growing impoverishment, erosion and
overcrowding of the reserves effectively proletarianised very large numbers
of rural dwellers. The urban African population more than trebled between
1921 and 1946 and the proportion of 'economically active' Africans officially
classified as peasants fell from over 50% in 1921 to just 8% in 1951. This
rapid proletarianisation generated acute urban and rural struggles, particularly
in the 1940s. The capitalist class was thoroughly divided over how state
policy should deal with this situation and particularly the question of migrant
labour.

The different class interests underlying these divisions are likewise discussed
on pp.17-20. However, it should be noted here that the overall party of
capital, the then ruling United Party, put forward a series of compromise
proposals enshrined in the Native Laws Commission 1946-8 (the so-called
Fagan Commission). This recognised the permanency of the urbanisation of
the African population as a result of the disintegration of production in the
reserves. It further supported the view that industry required 'a substantial
reserve of labour', and rejected a system of influx control designated to retain
the unemployed in the rural areas. It recommended that the Natives (Urban
Areas) Act be amended to allow workers and their families to settle permanently in the cities — a so-called 'stabilisation of labour'. However, it stopped
short of recommending the full-scale abolition of the migrant labour system.

The counter proposals of the then opposition *Herenigde* (reunited)
Nationalist Party were contained in the report of its Native Question Commission (known as the Sauer Commission). The report of the Sauer Commission represented the first programatic elaboration of the apartheid policy by
the Nationalist Party. It is important to realise that evolving apartheid policy
was a relatively flexible response, by an alliance of specific class forces, to a
changing set of conditions. It did not evolve as some of its critics have argued,
as a well developed 'Grand Vision', but as a series of programmatic adjustments to shifts in the class struggle. Since its formation in 1914, the Nationalist
Party had always had as one of its core principles a rigid segregationism.
Under the leadership of Gen. Hertzog (1914-34), this was ideologically
justified as 'Christian trusteeship' over 'our Native wards'. Following the
split in the old Nationalist Party in 1934, and the formation of the purified
Nationalist Party, both this new party and the secret *Afrikaner Broederbond*
began to devote some attention to 'the native question'.

However, this remained programmatically undeveloped throughout the
1930s and much of the 1940s. As late as 1944, a Broederbond sponsored

congress on 'The Race Question' declared that while apartheid was a desirable policy, it was still only a general principle which remained to be elaborated into firm policy proposals. This was the task of the NP's Sauer Commission prior to the 1948 election which brought the party to power. The report clearly reflected the pressing concern of capitalist agriculture with the effect of the efflux of labour to the cities and the growing labour crisis in agriculture. It also embodied the fear of strata of white labour and the white petty bourgeoisie that competition from semi-skilled African labour and the African petty bourgeoisie respectively would undermine their carefully carved out niches of privilege. The slogan of the NP in 1948 was the *oorstroming* (inundation) of the cities by an uncontrolled African proletariat. This threatened the interests of all class forces organised in the Afrikaner Nationalist alliance.

Like the Fagan Report, the Sauer Report addressed itself centrally to the question of the site and means of control of the industrial reserve army. While its proposals remained general, the Report committed the NP to the expulsion of unemployed Africans from the cities and a rigid system of influx control to retain surplus labour in the rural areas and admit only the employed into the cities. This was coupled with propsals for a national system of labour bureaux which would channel available labour according to the demands of the different branches of capitalist production. However, the Report made no mention of what later developed as the Bantustan strategy. At best it promised vaguely that 'the native will ultimately be able to find expression for his political aspirations in the reserves instead of having political rights in the white areas'.

The Early Implementation of Apartheid

The Nationalist Party came to power in May 1948 on this 'Apartheid' programme. However, in its first two years in office, the government produced various *ad hoc* measures but little substantive legislation besides a Prohibition of Mixed Marriages Act.

Following the appointment of Dr H.F. Verwoerd as Minister of Native Affairs in 1950, a more aggressive legislative programme was initiated. This set out to consolidate the three key aspects of what later turned into Bantustan policy: consolidation on the reserves, extension of tribally based separate political structures and stringent influx control measures. The 1951 Bantu Authorities Act imposed government appointed 'traditional chiefs' as the local administrators in 'tribal areas'. These chiefs were given extensive coercive powers under this 'retribalisation act'.

As the Secretary for Native Affairs told the new Bantu Authorities Chiefs in the Transkei: 'Under the Bantu Authorities which you constitute, you will be able to lead the people in the true sense. You will be able to tell them, not ask them, what to do. That is an important point'. Popular anti-apartheid Chiefs, such as Chief Albert Luthuli (then President of the African National Congress) were removed from office for refusing to implement Bantu Authorities. The Act aroused fierce popular opposition on the grounds that 'our chiefs are working against the people they are supposed to serve. They are being used by the government to deprive us of what is rightfully ours'. In some areas, such as Pondoland in 1960, opposition to Bantu Authorities led to open revolt.

The 1952 Native Laws Amendment Act severely limited the number of Africans with the right to live permanently in the urban areas to those who had been born or who had lived there continuously for 15 years or worked continuously for the same employer for ten years. All other Africans were only to be given the right of permanent residence in the overcrowded reserves. In the same year, the Natives (Abolition of Passes and Coordination of Documents) Act scrapped the myriad local varieties of passes and introduced a single standard document called a 'reference book', which all Africans over the age of 16 were required to carry at all times. For the first time, African women were now also obliged to carry passes — a recognition of their proletarian status which likewise promoted vigorous resistance throughout the 1950s (see p.171).

So far as policy towards the reserves was concerned, the 1951 Prevention of Illegal Squatting Act empowered the state to resettle in the reserves 'surplus' peasants still living in so-called 'black spots' on white-zoned land. Much concern was displayed with the reserves as a site for the reproduction of the reserve army of labour — to keep the unemployed away from the industrial centres. Verwoerd claimed to favour the establishment of 'economic farming units' in the reserves, in which 'full-time stock farmers or agriculturalists' would engage in commercial farming to sell their produce to the 'large non-farming native communities in the natives areas' — i.e. the unemployed. His predecessor had appointed the Tomlinson Commission to report on 'a comprehensive scheme for the rehabilitation of the Native areas with a view to developing within them a social structure in keeping with the culture of the Native and based on effective socio-economic planning'. The 17 volume report of the Tomlinson Commission recommended heavy state expenditure to 'develop' the reserves. It was in fact rejected by Verwoerd because Professor Tomlinson had interpreted apartheid too literally as a total separation of black and white, and based his recommendations on this assumption. This had never been the policy of the Nationalist Party; apartheid was designated rather to control the reproduction of a cheap migrant wage labour force within the reserves, to barricade the unemployed away from the industrial centres and to channel cheap labour to all sectors of capitalist production when and where required.

The legislation promoted by Verwoerd as Minister of Native Affairs in the 1950s largely succeeded in these aims. Through its various apartheid measures, and through extensive repression of all forms of popular organisation (see p.176), the regime succeeded in driving down the real wages of African workers throughout the 1950s. As such, it solved the various crises that had confronted different sectors of capitalist production in the mid- to late-1940s, and succeeded in raising the general rate of profit to the benefit of all capitals. However, it did so at the cost of provoking growing mass resistance. Throughout the 1950s, organised by the African National Congress, the various classes of the oppressed population joined together in increasingly more militant, non-violent resistance to the apartheid regime (see ANC entry pp.285–7). By the late 1950s, in the context of the indications of a rapid decolonisation in the rest of Africa, this challenge was beginning to pose a serious threat to the regime. It was forced to respond and the Bantustan policy was the result.

The Bantustans as a Strategic Response

The new Bantustan strategy of the apartheid regime was first announced in the Promotion of Bantu Self-Government Bill presented to parliament in May 1959. This new scheme provided for the restructuring of the Bantu Authorities system on the basis of eight Territorial Authorities (later expanded to ten and renamed 'Bantu Homelands'). It also envisaged their eventual 'independence' from South Africa. This new Bill was a hasty response to rising mass resistance – the NP had never before committed itself to 'independence' for the reserves. Verwoerd himself always limited his promises to 'self government' under Pretoria at the level of Territorial Authorities. Barely two months before the introduction of the Bill, Dr Eiselen, the Secretary of Native Affairs and close confident of Verwoerd (who had become Prime Minister in 1958), wrote an article arguing that apartheid (or 'separate development' as its proponents now termed it) was never intended to grant 'independence' to the reserves.

In 1961, Verwoerd acknowledged that 'in light of the pressure being exerted on South Africa', the Bantustans had been conceived as 'a form of fragmentation which we would not have liked if we were able to avoid it', but which he thought would succeed in 'buying the white man his freedom and right to retain domination in what is his country'. So hastily formulated was this response, that the Bill setting up the Bantustan scheme was not even disclosed to the Nationalist Party parliamentary caucus before being placed before parliament. Its reformulation of so-called traditional NP *'baaskap'* (white domination) policies provoked some opposition within the ruling party – leading to the expulsion of one of its MPs.

This strategic reformulation of apartheid into the new Bantustan policy immediately generated much activity dedicated to proving the 'morality' of this form of 'decolonisation'. It was perhaps best spelled out by the Minister of Native Affairs, M.D.C. De Wet Net. In introducing the Promotion of Bantu Self Government Act he argued that the Bantustan policy rested on three principles:

> The first is that God has given a divine task and calling to every People in the world, which dare not be destroyed or denied by anyone. The second is that every People in the world of whatever race or colour, just like every individual, has the inherent right to live and develop. Every People is entitled to the right of self-preservation. In the third place it is our deep convinction that the personal and national ideals of

every ethnic group can best be developed within its own national community. Only then will other groups feel they are not being endangered . . . This is the philosophic basis of the policy of Apartheid . . . To our People this is not a mere abstraction which hangs in the air. It is a divine task which has to be implemented and fulfilled systematically.

The Major Measures of the Bantustan Strategy

Stripped of such Calvinistic moralising rhetoric, as a response to a changing set of conditions, the developing Bantustan strategy after 1959 embodied a number of clear objectives.

i) Land Tenure Policies

In theory, the land in the Bantustans is communally owned, and every family has a right to a plot of land. In practice, the situation is very different. All these rural slums are hugely overcrowded, and totally unable to support the populations living in them, let alone those whom the apartheid regime still plans to move there. In the Bophuthatswana Bantustan for example, in 1977 there were 142,000 families living on land that, under present conditions, could only support 26,000 families. In the Transkei Bantustan, for the lucky ones who do have land, the average plot size per family in 1974 was between one and two hectares. In all the Bantustans, landlessness has been an acute and increasing problem for the last 40 years. Even in the 1930s, government commissions were already raising this as 'a critical problem', warning of 'appalling poverty' and the 'spectre of mass starvation'.

Such overcrowded land is rapidly worked out; soil erosion has been a gathering and terrible problem in these areas, spreading rapidly as the burden on the land increases. Under such conditions, production levels are inevitably very low, and falling. In 1977, the urban population within all the Bantustans was nowhere higher than 5%. Yet every one of them was forced to 'import' food from 'white' areas simply to prevent starvation levels from rising. With the rapid growth of 'administrative capitals' in the Bantustans since 1976, and the consequent rising urban population in these areas, the problem grows ever more acute. Though the situation varies between the ten Bantustans, the Transkei is fairly typical: in 1974, 60% of all households were unable to support themselves on the land, and a further 23% were able to do so in a 'good year' only; a mere 8.5% of households ever produced crops for sale, and a bare 0.1% produced exclusively for the market.

The overwhelming majority of this rural population is unable to subsist on the land and they are forced into wage labour to feed themselves. Yet there are desperately few jobs in these chronically underdeveloped areas. The jobs lie in the factories and mines and on the farms of the 'white' areas. But no African worker may simply leave a Bantustan to look for a job. They have to pass through a series of government labour bureaux which allocate employment to the chronically poor inhabitants of the Bantustans only where and when it is needed by the capitalist economy. Moreover, workers have an extremely limited choice of jobs. In effect they are compelled to accept whatever job contracts are offered by the labour bureaux — or else to migrate illegally to the 'white cities' and live there as fugitives, constantly threatened with arrest for not having the right stamp in their pass. At the end of the period of contract, workers are forced to return to the rural slums and begin the process anew.

The system of migratory contract labour rests on a three-legged pot of land laws which allocate 87% of South Africa to whites and 13% to blacks, and which create and sustain landlessness (see p.170); the labour bureau system, which channels labour according to the needs of the capitalist economy; and the pass laws and influx control measures which regulate the numbers of Africans allowed into the 'white areas' and controls them under highly repressive conditions while they are working there as 'temporary sojourners' (in the words of an apartheid minister — see p.171). Every adult African living or working in the 87% of South Africa designated as 'white areas' is required to carry at all times the hated pass — now renamed a 'passport' or 'citizenship document'. These must be stamped by the Labour Bureau or Administration Board which granted him or her 'permission' to enter a white area for a stipulated contracted period of labour. They must also be signed each month by the employer. Failure to produce one's 'dompass' (as the passes are popularly known), leads to instant arrest and prosecution. In 1976, 381,858 Africans were prosecuted under the influx control laws; most were fined and/or jailed and sent back to the Bantustans.

In this way, the Bantustans provide a permanent supply of cheap labour for capitalist production. The vast majority of the inhabitants of these rural areas are in no sense a peasantry. Unable to subsist through production on the land, totally dependent for their existence on the regular sale of their labour power, they constitute a huge proletariat — compelled by apartheid to rot in the Bantustans until their labour is required by this or that capitalist. Every member of this class not immediately required in production is forced by the state to live in the rural areas. This 'surplus population' thus remains barricaded in the Bantustans, under conditions of extreme and worsening poverty, at the beck and call of capital.

Here, too, is found an important sexual division of labour within this proletariat — it is the men who are driven out to seek wage employment. In 1974, i.e. before the current recession began to bite very deeply, 83% of the potential adult male labour force of the Transkei Bantustan were employed as migrant workers outside the Transkei. Such migrant workers may not take their families with them to the 'white' cities. In the words of a government minister, the men are 'labour units' who must not be burdened with such 'superfluous appendages' as wives and children. It is much more difficult for women to find jobs through the labour bureau system. So while the system of apartheid capitalism drives men to migrate, the women are forced to remain in these rural slums, scratching what existence they can from the overpopulated, tired-out soil, struggling against acute poverty to raise their children as the future reserve army of labour. Again using the Transkei as an example, 70% of the population between the ages of 15 and 44 were women at the time of the 1970 census. In 1974 there were only 66 men to 100 women living in the Bantustan. For the age group 25–29, the ratio was 28.9:100. The burden of production in these rural areas fails squarely on women. The position of rural African women as the most exploited, most oppressed and most degraded section of the South African population stems from these production relations which capitalism has generated in the Bantustans.

The intense pressure on the land and the growth of a reserve army of labour has been further heightened by the agricultural policies of the apartheid regime and their Bantustan puppets. The regime is quite explicit that it aims to reduce the numbers of what it terms 'small farmers' in the Bantustans — from 500,000 to 50,000 said a deputy minister in 1973. It is trying to build up a rich African peasantry, together with a class of African capitalist farmers, leaving the bulk of the population as a vast rural proletariat to supply labour for the white areas, while a few work on the farms of their new black masters. In the Bophuthatswana Bantustan, this process is relatively advanced. A number of African entrepreneurs are operating farms of more than 1,000 hectares, while the number of privately owned tractors jumped from less than 10 to over 1,000 between 1970 and 1977. At 'independence' in 1977, the Bophuthatswana 'Department of Agriculture' was explicit in its aim to reduce the number of farmers to '25,000 viable units', each with a minimum annual income of R1,600. The 120,000 'surplus farmers' would have to 'change their attitudes' and be 'persuaded' to relinquish their customary rights to land.

The agricultural policies, subsidies and betterment schemes of the regime are all geared to this clearly stated aim. Through the 'registration' of plots and the introduction of leasehold, the remaining forms of communal land tenure are giving rise to a rapid concentration of land in a few hands. Already, land which the government has bought from white farmers previously living in these 'black' areas has been sold to large-scale operators or rentiers, mainly the Bantustan leaders themselves and their cronies.

This tendency was further assisted by the policies of the first two 'independent' Bantustans — the Transkei and Bophuthatswana. Immediately after 'independence', taxes on huts, cattle and other domestic animals were increased by as much as 3,000%, to 'persuade' these 'surplus farmers' to relinquish their rights to land. This is one of the ways in which the sham-independence of the Bantustans has enabled the aspirant capitalists who man the 'governments' of these regions to speed up their own accumulation.

The land question in the Bantustans reveals the real relations of production in South Africa, and the unique fact of a huge, nationally dispossessed proletariat forced to live in the rural areas. The conditions of life in the Bantustans are inextricably linked with the overall conditions of the South Africa proletariat under this particular form of capitalist exploitation based on national oppression. Because their families are forced to live in the Bantustans, and because the large unemployed portion of the proletariat is also compelled to live there, migrant workers are vitally concerned with conditions in the rural areas. The waves of struggles against the break up of the various 'squatter' town-

ships around Cape Town since 1976, and the state's continuing attempts to deport these workers to the Transkei Bantustan, highlights the linkage between urban and rural struggles. This is seen even more clearly in the 'resettlement' aspect of Bantustan policy.
the 'resettlement' aspect of Bantustan policy.

ii) Resettlement and Control

Bantustan policy after 1960 gave rise to an accelerated programme of mass forced removals of Africans from the rural and urban areas of 'white' South Africa. This programme has dumped in the Bantustans — in the words of one Bantu Affairs Commissioner — those

> redundant people [who] could not render productive service in an urban area . . . men who had lost their jobs and could not find new employment; old and infirm people, unmarried mothers.

In the years 1960–70 alone, almost two million people were forcibly moved into the Bantustans.

Various apartheid provisions accounted for these removals. Thus, 340,000 people were moved under sections of the 1936 Natives Land and Trust Act (see p.170) which provide for the abolition of labour tenancies on white farms; a further 656,000 were transported for 'illegal squatting' on white farms. The programme to eliminate so-called 'black spots' in the rural areas removed a further 97,000, whilst the resiting of urban townships in the neighbouring Bantustans accounted for another 327,000. The 'endorsement out' of the urban areas under pass law offences of those who did not enjoy Section 10 rights (see p.171) and other legislation controlling the lives of urban Africans, saw a further 400,000 'superfluous' Africans dumped in the Bantustans.

These removals were carried out with great brutality and no concern for the capacity of the Bantustans to provide a living for those dumped there. As the responsible apartheid minister announced in 1969: 'the removal of these superfluous Bantu from the white homelands is not dependent on the development of the Bantu homelands'. Most of the people so removed are dumped in so-called 'resettlement' camps. Today, one third of the population of all the Bantustans — a total of nearly 4 million people — live in the crude shelters of the 'resettlement' camps. They have been described in one study as 'a demoralised group of people with a general feeling of despair'. Conditions in these camps are appalling; the South African Institute of Race Relations has published statistics showing that one in four babies born in these camps dies during its first year of life. Some such camps, such as Limehill, Dimbaza, Stinkwater and others, have become international synonyms for the callousness of and intense human suffering induced by apartheid. At the Limehill resettlement camp in early 1969, out of a previously healthy community of 7,500, over 70 people died of various gastro-intestinal diseases, caused by appalling living conditions, within five months of being dumped there. The

then Minister of Health (himself a medical doctor) claimed in parliament
that this was not an unusual death rate and was in no way attributable to
resettlement, but to 'malnutrition and ignorance'.

The resettlement and removal programme continued in the 1970s; apart
from 'black spot' removals, 'endorsement out' under pass laws, and the
uprootings of tenants, the so-called 'consolidation' of the Bantustans provided
a further impetus to these removals, most notoriously in the Winterveldt
district of the Bophuthatswana Bantustan. Any resistance to removals was met
with instant violence by the state, highlighted by the unprovoked shooting of
Saul Mkhize by a policeman in April 1983 as he led the resistance of the
residents of Driefontein against a scheme to remove them to a resettlement
camp. Almost a million people were forcibly removed under these various
procedures in the 1970s, bringing to three million the total number forcibly
moved between 1960 and 1979.

Complementary to this, controls over the urban African population have
been greatly extended. The 1971 Bantu Affairs Administration Boards Act
finally removed control over the administration of African housing and influx
control from local authorities. The administration of all matters relating to
urban Africans was brought directly under the central apartheid state through
16 local Bantu Administration Boards. A number of these are now extending
their activities into the Bantustans themselves – acting as primary channels of
labour recruitment. Since 1978, the alleged reforms of the Total Strategy
period have proposed a rigid division of the African population into those
already employed who enjoy the 'right' of residence in the 'white' cities (but
in segregated townships of course), and the army of unemployed who will
remain perpetually imprisoned in the impoverished Bantustans and let out
only as contract labourers. First proposed by the 1979 Riekert Report, this
principle has now been embodied in the Orderly Movement and Settlement of
Black Persons Bill, introduced in parliament in 1982. This Bill further
drastically curtails rights of urban residence and establishes the most rigid
set of influx controls ever introduced in South Africa (see p.172).

iii) Deprivation of Citizenship
The corollary to this system of removals and controls has been the systematic
stripping of South African citizenship from all Africans. Apartheid theory
considers all Africans to be members of one of the ten distinct 'national
groups' identified by its anthropologists. The 1970 Bantu Homelands Citizenship Act provided that all 'Bantu' in South Africa would be made 'citizens'
of one of the Bantustans, even those who had never lived outside of the
'white' areas. Every African was to be issued with a certificate of such
'citizenship'. Until 1976, this implied a form of dual citizenship, as Bantustan
'citizens' retained South African citizenship. However, the 'citizens' of the
four Bantustans which have now become 'independent' since 1976 (the
Transkei, Bophuthatswana, Venda and the Ciskei) have all been unilaterally
deprived of their South African citizenship. Introducing an amendment to
this Act in 1978, the responsible apartheid minister declared: 'If our policy

is taken to its logical conclusion so far as black people are concerned, there will not be one black man with South African citizenship'. This is perhaps the single most important reason given by other Bantustan leaders for so far refusing to accept 'independence'. This issue has likewise aroused intense mass anger. P.W. Botha's 1982 proposals for a 'Confederation of Southern African States' incorporating South Africa and the 'independent' Bantustans (the so-called SABCTV countries), have sometimes been interpreted as a plan to contain this opposition to the deprivation of South African citizenship by creating a wider 'confederal nationality'.

iv) Bantustan Repression

The vehement opposition to citizenship deprivation, and the whole Bantustan system in general, points to a further basic objective of this strategy. By barricading a large part of the proletariat in dispersed, fragmented and eroded rural slums, and stripping all Africans of their South African citizenship, the Bantustan strategy has sought to contain the mass challenge to apartheid in areas far removed from the industrial centres, and to destroy such opposition by dividing any alliance of nationally oppressed class forces along tribal lines.

This has implied not only intensive policies of 'retribalisation', but as importantly, the systematic use of ever more extensive forms of mass repression within the Bantustans. Based on the notorious Proclamation R400 issued in the Transkei to contain the rural uprising known as the 'Pondo revolt' in 1960, repressive measures have been extended to all the Bantustans. The 1979 Black States Constitution Act gives the 'governments' of all the Bantustans wide powers of detention without trial, and the right to ban meetings, individuals, publications and organisations. These powers have been extensively used by every single Bantustan leader. The so-called 'independent' Bantustans have either simply taken over 'South African' security legislation, or substituted even wider repressive powers under their own 'legislation'. Thus, for example, the 1977 Transkei 'Public Security Act', besides incorporating all the basic provisions of South African repressive legislation, further makes it an offence equivalent to treason to refuse recognition of Transkeian 'independence', or to advocate that it forms 'part of another country' (i.e. South Africa). A maximum sentence of the death penalty is provided for.

There are two sides to the repressive apparatuses in the Bantustans. On the one hand, these apartheid-derived powers are widely used by the Bantustan ruling groups against their perceived internal enemies. The action of the Ciskeian para-military 'green berets' to sniff out the real and imagined opponents of 'President' Lennox Sebe, have gained particular notoriety. On the other hand, the repressive systems of the Bantustans have in fact developed into a crucial part of the wider repressive strategy of the central apartheid state. The 'unsophisticated' Bantustan leaders have been used to engage in forms of particularly brutal and sadistic repression which the central apartheid state can no longer afford to be seen to be implementing itself – and for which it can thus disclaim all responsibility. The most recent examples of this are the particularly violent and bloody campaign of the Ciskei 'Central Intelligence Service' against the South African Allied Workers' Union (see p.222), involving mass detentions, torture, fire bombings and shootings in which a number of people associated with the union have been killed – and the brutal response of the Venda authorities to an ANC attack on a Venda police station.

Over and above this particular repressive role, in each of the Bantustans which have accepted 'independence', the apartheid regime is training 'a national Defence Force' which will be assigned important counter-insurgency roles in the overall South African military strategy. To date, the history of these 'armies' has been a mixture of farce and vicious repression against their own populations. The Transkei army has been used to quell student unrest, whilst that of Bophuthatswana has carried out raids against squatters and 'non-Tswana' traders in the Winterveldt region of this Bantustan.

These armies are officered largely by white South Africans and white mercenaries. The former commander of the Rhodesian Selous Scouts, Lt. Col. Ron Reid-Daly, is Commander in Chief of the Transkei Defence Force. His former counterpart in Bophuthatswana (since promoted to Minister of Defence'), a South African brigadier, H.B. Riekert, has declared the Bophuthatswana-Botswana border an 'operational area'. Riekert argues that: 'The enemies of South Africa are also the enemies of Bophuthatswana. We work in close collaboration with the South African Defence Force'. There have been complaints from the Kingdom of Lesotho that its territory has been attacked by the Transkei army.

v) Cultivation of an 'Alternative' Leadership
The early formulations of the Bantustan strategy clearly recognised that if it was to succeed in its objective to divide potential allies in the national liberation struggle, apartheid had to win for itself black allies who could offer a credible and effective alternative leadership to that provided by the popular mass organisations, particularly the ANC. However, until the Total Strategy period (i.e. 1978), the state remained to some extent trapped in the illusions of its own ideology. It appeared to believe that the 'real leaders' of the African people were the reactionary and collaborating tribal chiefs created by its own Bantu Authorities system. Thus, rather than seeking an alternative black leadership amongst the urban petty bourgeoisie (as in one thrust of the Total Strategy), after 1959, the emerging Bantustan strategy threw its full political weight behind these already thoroughly discredited and unpopular collaborator chiefs. This move alone ensured that no significant social force within the African population could support the Bantustan scheme.

The political dominance of these chiefs has been secured through the institutions erected by the South African state in the Bantustans. Since Bantustan 'elections' have monotonously produced either a very low poll or large majorities for anti-Bantustan parties, the rule of the chiefs is sustained by reserving at least an absolute majority of seats in all the Bantustan 'legislative assemblies' for appointed chiefs or their nominees. The actual proportion of seats thus reserved for the chiefs ranges from 50% in Bophuthatswana to 100% in KwaNdebele (see Table 4.1, p.219). Relying on the full coercive weight of the apartheid state, the groups which dominate the political apparatuses of the Bantustans have been able to sustain their rule without any need to cultivate a wider political base for themselves. The only possible exception to this is Chief Catsha Buthelezi. As 'Chief Minister' of the KwaZulu Bantustan, he has attempted to create a mass-based vehicle for his wider personal political aspirations through his 'National Cultural Liberation Movement'— *Inkatha yeNkululeko yeSizwe* (see entry p.387). However, *Inkatha* remains a tribalist organisation, and widespread complaints from within KwaZulu indicate that *Inkatha* is used to enforce unquestioning loyalty to Buthelezi and his politics of 'collaborative opposition' from the Bantustan's population.

vi) Industrial 'Decentralisation' Fostering a Collaborator Black Bourgeoisie

Over and above its consolidation of the political power of the Bantu authorities chiefs as an alternative political leadership, Bantustan policy has likewise clearly sought to cultivate a very small collaborator black bourgeoisie and petty bourgeoisie within the homelands. While the Bantustan policy in no way begins to meet the minimum demands of all oppressed classes, in its attempt to contain these demands, the regime was forced to make available to the Bantustan leaders various resources which were not available to Africans in the earlier years of apartheid. Thus, it has created the space for the consolidation within apartheid of a small collaborating bourgeoisie and petty bourgeoisie, whose position is totally dependent on the maintenance of the apartheid system.

There are a number of aspects to this. Firstly, the erection of elaborate apparatuses of 'states' manned by local bureaucracies, has clearly expanded employment opportunities for an emerging petty bourgeoisie within those regions. Thus, by early 1979 the number of permanent posts on fixed establishment in seven 'non-independent' Bantustans (i.e. excluding the Transkei, Bophuthatswana and KwaNdebele) stood at 27,625. Various bursary and training schemes maintain a trickle of potential recruits to this stratum. Such new Bantustan bureaucrats administer the operation of the Bantustan system for Pretoria and are dependent for their advance on the successful operation of apartheid.

The second element of this chosen group of collaborators is a small group of local capitalists cultivated by the Bantustan system. More often that not this group is interlinked with the senior politicians and bureaucrats within the Bantustans. Since the introduction of the Bantustan system, state policy towards this group has undergone a number of changes.

Prior to 1959, a major objective of apartheid policy had been to prevent the development of a black commercial petty bourgeoisie in both urban and rural areas. However, with the recognition of the need to cultivate a group of black collaborators as an alternative leadership to the liberation movement, the Bantustan strategy envisaged the use of state funds to set up and capitalise a number of small entrepreneurs within the Bantustans. In 1959 the Bantu Investment Corporation (BIC) was established for this purpose. At the same time, however, apartheid policy made it increasingly difficult for even small African traders to operate outside the Bantustans. The ultimate proclaimed objective was to drive all African commerce out of the so-called white areas into the Bantustans.

In its first ten years of existence, the BIC concentrated on buying out petty white commercial operations in the Bantustans. These were then rented or sold to African businessmen — sometimes known as a 'bottle store bourgeoisie' — themselves usually financed by BIC loans. Between 1959 and 1970, loans totalling almost R6 million were made to 798 African business-men. In this period, these types of operation of the corporation were concentrated in the Transkei — where in 1966 the subsidiary Xhosa Develop-ment Corporation was established. Such subsidiaries were later initiated in the other Bantustans as well. Through these means, the slow development of a class of small petty capitalists was fostered.

However, as the regular and loud complaints of even the most pliant homeland puppets against the BIC revealed, the bulk of the BIC efforts and capital after 1965 were devoted to creating investment incentives in the Bantustans for the re-siting and expansion of 'white' industrial and other undertakings then located in the major industrial centres. The major aim of the Bantustan 'development corporations', as stated by the (white) managing director of the Transkei variant, is to protect white industrialists investing in the area. This policy has been through a number of phases.

Prior to 1969, Bantustan policy forbade new investment by white capitalists in the Bantustans. This, explained Prime Minister Verwoerd, was to prevent these one-day-to-be independent 'states' from being 'exploited by neo-colonialists'. Rather, the state favoured the erection of labour intensive 'border industries' close to the Bantustans which would provide employment away from the major industrial centres to 'homeland commuters'. As Verwoerd explained in 1965, this border industry programme was designed to ensure that white factories on the perimeter of reserved African areas would make full use of 'tribal' African workers who would thus be absorbed there in the service of 'white people'. A wide range of, *inter alia*, tax conces-sions, capital grants, low interest long term loans and exemption from mini-mum wage legislation were intended to attract capital into these areas. Measures of compulsion were also used. The 1968 Physical Planning and Utilization of Resources Act provided that any capitalist proposing to employ extra labour, expand existing production facilities or set up new factories, required the permission of the Department of Planning. In effect, new or expanding labour-intensive operations would only be approved if sited in the border areas, while capital-intensive projects would be confined to the existing 'white' industrial areas.

The border industries programme was not a·success. The few major centres all developed near already large cities (e.g. Rosslyn near Pretoria) and created almost no employment anywhere near the main Bantustan areas. In the words of a former economic adviser to the Prime Minister in 1979:

> It is often said that the border areas have negative influence on the development of the Bantu areas. I have a lot of sympathy with this point of view because the border industries are situated close to the Bantu areas and yet the Bantu are not allowed to do skilled work.

The relative failure of the border industries programme led to a shift in state policy in 1969. Whilst border industries would still be encouraged, white capitalists would now be allowed to invest in the Bantustans on an 'agency' basis. Under this scheme, long term contracts of between 25 and 50 years would be given to 'white' firms to act as 'agents' of either the BIC or the local Bantustan development corporation. All concessions available in the border industries programme were also applied to the agency scheme, and the BIC itself offered additional concessions. Initially four so-called 'growth points' within the Bantustans were envisaged. The BIC announced a new 'five year plan' to spend R86 million in the South African Bantustans, and a further R18 million in those of Namibia. The breakdown of this planned expenditure is illuminating. Slightly over 75% was intended for the development of infrastructure at the 'growth points' and the building and development of undertakings available for 'agency' investment by South African capitalists. Less than 25% was earmarked to erect business premises and provide credit for African businessmen cultivated by the Bantustan system. In the period 1959–74, the BIC made loans totalling R77 million. Only 18% of these were made to African-owned enterprises, whilst white-owned enterprises received 56% of BIC credit, and the subsidiary development corporations the remainder. In fact, the total loan capital provided to African businessmen was considerably lower than the African deposits in savings banks set up by the BIC. Moreover, BIC credit policy towards Africans was very strict; only 14% of African loan applications by 1968 were approved. Those loans which were approved were furnished on terms far less favourable than those offered to white investors and none of the 'agency' concessions were granted to African businessmen.

The somewhat contradictory objectives and function of the BIC to foster on the one hand, the development of small African-owned enterprises, whilst on the other hand, protecting the supremacy of the interests of white investors, led to loud complaints from the very group of collaborators the Bantustan strategy sought to cultivate. The 'Chief Minister' of Bophuthatswana complained of the BIC in 1972: 'I would like this corporation to render a service to us more than make a profit of us'. The KwaZulu 'Chief Minister' demanded of the border industries policy in 1974: 'What do we get out of all of this? Can anyone deny that we are being reserved for the sole exploitation by people other than our own entrepreneurs?' In this way, BIC policy revealed very clearly the limitations of the Bantustan objective to cultivate a small class of collaborating capitalists. While it did provide loans, training and other incentives previously unavailable to black businessmen, it did so on such a meagre scale, under such stringent restrictions, and so patently functioned to protect first and foremost the interests of white investors, that it effectively hindered the development of this class. Its operations were still further proof that black capitalists would be totally subordinated to the wider interests of apartheid capitalism and would not be permitted to emerge as large scale entrepreneurs. Thus, while this emerging group of Bantustan petty capitalists were totally dependent on the handouts of the apartheid system, such were the conditions of these handouts that they were not won as real allies of the ruling class. The broader democratic demands of the national liberation movement remained highly attractive to them.

A recognition of these limitations in its own tactics led the apartheid regime to modify aspects of this policy between 1975 and 1977. The BIC's functions were decentralised into 'national development corporations' for each of the various Bantustans. In 1977, the BIC itself was renamed the Corporation for Economic Development (CED). Most importantly, the old 'agency' system and bar on direct investment by white enterprises were scrapped, and white and other capital was given fairly free entry into the Bantustans. The clear objective of this change was to forge closer links of economic and political dependency between investing white monopolies and local capitalists. The latter would now sit on the boards of the enterprises of the former, rather than seek to establish their own petty undertakings in the face of control by 'external' monopolies.

The lifting of these racial proscriptions also freed CED to finance any undertaking in the Bantustans. In effect too, this has meant that funds are consolidated into larger undertakings. These changes have to some extent been successful. Amongst the dominant groups in the Bantustans, CED is no longer attacked as the agent of 'exploitation by people other than our own entrepreneurs'. In reality, however, the level of industrial investment in the Bantustans remains derisory. The most important large scale undertakings to have emerged are mining operations (mainly in Bophuthatswana) and various existing and planned casino and entertainment centres. The latter explicitly provide an almost exclusively white clientele with a range of gambling and sexual 'services' banned outside the 'independent' Bantustans. The development of these kinds of enterprise does not foster the interests of any but a small group of the Bantustan petty bourgeoisie and bourgeoisie. The majority of the petty bourgeoisie and those capitalists outside these narrow leadership circles remain trapped in an extremely contradictory position, still potentially available to support the broad democratic demands of the national liberation struggle.

vii) The Move Towards 'Independence'
Finally, the strategy has moved into the phase of granting 'independence' to various Bantustans. During its first ten years, the policy developed slowly. Only the Transkei region was given a form of 'self-government' in 1963. In 1971 the Bantu Homelands Constitution Act empowered the President to

confer 'self-government' on the other Bantustans. The following year, the Ciskei, KwaZulu and Bophuthatswana Bantustans had various executive functions devolved to them under this Act, and the other Bantustans followed. Responding to the growing crisis of the mid-1970s (see p.32) the state pressurised Bantustan leaders to accept 'independence'. The Transkei acceded in 1976, Bophuthatswana in 1977, Venda in 1979 and the Ciskei in 1981 (the latter despite the findings of its own 'Quail Commission' that the vast majority of its inhabitants were totally opposed to 'independence'). It has further been announced that KwaNdebele is being prepared for 'independence'.

Conclusion

The Bantustan strategy emerged in the late 1950s as a response to rising mass resistance to apartheid. It sought to consolidate South African capitalism through the division of the oppressed and the creation of a small collaborative black leadership without any power to challenge the existing order. It also sought to mystify and conceal the exploitative relation between capital and the mass of migrant workers in the Bantustans be redefining it as a freely contracted relationship between independent states.

To some extent that strategy has succeeded. It has placed as actors on the political stage a group which had not existed before — the collaborating rulers/capitalists of the Bantustans. Within the old reserves, which became the Bantustans, the overwhelming majority of the population remained trapped in poverty as unemployed migrant workers unable to scratch a living from the overcrowded, worked out land, simply waiting for employment in 'white' South Africa. In these areas, the peasantry has virtually ceased to exist as a surplus producing class which reproduced itself through agrarian production. A notable feature of 'self-government' in almost all of these Bantustans has been a slow process of centralisation of land, and more importantly control over commercial networks, in the hands of people linked with the Bantustan administration — usually the 'chiefs'. In this way too, the Bantustan policy has consolidated the interests of a small ruling group of collaborators.

At a wider level, however, the Bantustan strategy has failed dismally in many of its central objectives. The fraudulence of 'independence' for these parts of South Africa, the implacable opposition of most of the oppressed population to these schemes, and the total rejection of 'independence' by the international community is well known, and we shall not dwell upon it here. However, it should be noted that the pathetic failure of the 'independence' strategy has compelled strong opposition to the scheme from even the other Bantustan puppets themselves. In 1980, the leaders of the 'non-independent' Bantustans presented the apartheid state with a list of 'non-negotiable' principles. These included:

1) — preference for a unitary state as a first option, but qualified willingness to consider other alternatives;

2) — non-negotiable rejection of independent black homelands;

3) — non-negotiable abolition of all forms of statutory racial discrimination;

4) – non-negotiable dismissal of the 1913 and 1936 Land Acts as the basis of land division between black and white;

5) – non-negotiable retention of South African citizenship and the right to a South African passport.

These 'non-negotiable' demands by apartheid's collaborators may yet prove to be eminently negotiable. However, the regime itself has made a number of blunders which have strongly alienated their own political creations. Most importantly, the cavalier disregard of the expressed wishes of 'national assemblies' in 1982, when without consulting the Bantustans involved, South Africa offered the whole of KaNgwane and part of KwaZulu to Swaziland, produced bitter opposition, and eventually a defeat for the regime (see p.224).

Clearly, the Bantustan strategy is in deep crisis. The upsurge of various forms of mass struggle against the regime in the 1970s and 1980s finally destroyed whatever credibility the Bantustan leaders retained. Recent proposals of a 'Confederation of Southern African States' have been welcomed by them as a means of ensuring that a wider 'confederal nationality' as South Africans is retained. In the final analysis, however, whatever semantic twists and petty concessions are made, both the regime and its Bantustan puppets are faced with the fact that the Bantustan strategy can never hope to accommodate the very basic demands of all oppressed classes for full democratic rights in a unitary state, the abolition of all forms of discrimination and the resolution of the land question. They cannot escape the present impasse.

Bophuthatswana[7]

(See: a) Tables 4.1a and b; b) Map, p.220; c) Introductory essay to this section.)

The so-called Tswana homeland, 30% of its population is classified as 'non-Tswana' by the apartheid regime. The Bantustan was granted 'independence' in December 1977. Its 'President' is Chief Lucas Mangope.

The 'independence' of Bophuthatswana was preceded by a state of emergency to allow the ruling group to contain the vociferous popular resistance to its collaboration with apartheid. At the height of this resistance, during the general uprising of June 1976, students burned down the newly built 'legislative assembly'. The strong repressive measures taken against Mangope's opponents continued after 'independence'. Most notorious here has been the campaign of raids, arrests and general harrassment against 'non-Tswana' traders in the sprawling Winterveldt area of the Bantustan. The 'national army' was used in this exercise and has also come to play an important role in South Africa's counter insurgency war. A number of armed clashes, and in one case near Rustenburg in 1978, a prolonged engagement, have been fought between ANC guerrillas and Bophuthatswana forces.

The Bantustan is 'ruled' by the Bophuthatswana Democratic Party led

Table 4.1a
The Bantustans — Basic Information[8]

Bantustan	'Tribe'	Area (1000ha)	Number of pieces	Total African population 1976 (thousands)	De jure population 1976 (thousands)	Percentage of de jure population in the Bantustan	Population density 1976	'Chief Minister' or 'President'	Capital
Bophuthatswana	Tswana	3,800	7	1,154	2,103	29	30.4	Chief Lucas Mangope	Mmabatho
Ciskei	Xhosa	533	18	475	872	58	89.1	Chief Lennox Sebe	Bisho
Gazankulu	Shangaan (Tsonga)	675	4	333	814	29	49.3	Professor Hudson Ntsanwisi	Giyani
KaNgwane	Swazi	370	3	209	590	14	–	Enos Mabuza	Louisville
KwaNdebele	S. Ndebele	75	1	150	–	–	–	Simon Skosana	Siyabuswa
KwaZulu	Zulu	3,100	44	2,891	5,029	41	86.8	Chief Gatsha Buthelezi	Ulundi
Lebowa	N. Sotho N. Ndebele & Pedi	2,200	14	1,388	2,234	42	63.1	Dr Cedric Phatudi	Lebowakgomo
QwaQwa	S. Sotho	58	1	91	1,698	1	189.6	Chief T.K. Mopeli	Phuthaditjhaba
Transkei	Xhosa	4,100	3	2,391	4,250	39	56.5	Chief Kaizer Matanzina	Umtata
Venda	Venda	650	3	339	449	53	52.2	Chief Patrick Mphaphu	Thohoyandou

Table 4.1b
Bantustans — Details: Assembly Members, Revenue, etc.

Bantustan	Date of 'independence'	Proportion of elected members in the Assembly 1979	GDP 1974 (R1000)	Direct expenditure by SA government in 1975-6 (R1000)	Grants from SA State Revenue Fund 1975-6 (R1000)	Internal Bantustan Revenue 1975-6 (R1000)	Percentage contribution from internal revenue 1975-6	Number of contract workers employed in SA outside the Bantustan in 1976	GDP per capita 1976 (R)	Number of permanent posts on fixed establishment 1978	Number of SA officials seconded to the Bantustan administration in 1978
Bophuthatswana	1977	48	150,977	17,996	38,419	11,952	17.5	51,100	155	n.a.	n.a.
Ciskei	1981	43	45,971	19,422	25,974	7,760	14.6	24,900	99	3,646	151
Gazankulu	–	38	24,364	6,368	9,108	4,791	23.6	72,500	73	3,523	70
KaNgwane	–	0	–	–	–	–	–	7,700	57	697	58
KwaNdebele	–	0	–	–	–	–	–	–	–	–	–
KwaZulu	–	44	135,399	55,482	71,996	20,590	13.9	273,400	78	10,692	343
Lebowa	–	40	91,094	19,356	25,605	13,338	22.9	196,900	78	6,108	289
QwaQwa	–	33	4,529	2,688	1,999	4,829	50.7	11,000	74	1,388	27
Transkei	1976	50	n.a.	25,272	71,080	18,730	16.3	343,300	107	n.a.	n.a.
Venda	1979	50	15,361	3,894	11,459	3,111	16.8	57,900	74	1,571	92

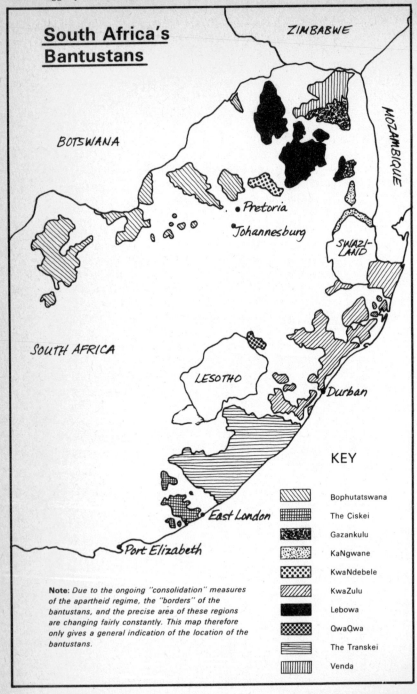

South Africa's Bantustans

KEY

Bophutatswana

The Ciskei

Gazankulu

KaNgwane

KwaNdebele

KwaZulu

Lebowa

QwaQwa

The Transkei

Venda

Note: *Due to the ongoing "consolidation" measures of the apartheid regime, the "borders" of the bantustans, and the precise area of these regions are changing fairly constantly. This map therefore only gives a general indication of the location of the bantustans.*

by Mangope. This party had split in 1974 from Mangope's old Bophuthats-wana National Party over a dispute within the 'Cabinet'. In 1975, the latter party joined the opposition National *Seoposengwe* (United) Party led by Chief T. Pilane, who was later displaced as party leader by the leader of the old BNP, Chief H. Maseloane. The NSP opposed Mangope's 'independence' plan. In a very low poll in the 1977 elections, it won only four of the 48 elected seats in the 'national assembly', with Mangope's party taking the remainder.

Bophuthatswana is occasionally portrayed as the only Bantustan with any prospect of economic viability, given the relatively large scale mining operations undertaken there. In 1976, mining and quarrying accounted for over 50% of the 'GDP' of the Bantustan. Its economy is likewise well known for the prominent place occupied by the 'Sun City' casino/entertainment complex owned by the South African Breweries monopoly. Sun City has come to epitomise the 'casino independence' of the Bantustans and their subordination to the economic interests of monopoly capital. In the late 1970s, Mangope became embroiled in a row with local chambers of commerce affiliated to the National African Federated Chambers of Commerce (see p.119), which had opposed 'independence' and which further sought to build up African business in the Bantustan to the exclusion of competition from large white undertakings. Mangope's close co-operation with monopoly interests is strongly resented by smaller and aspirant capitalists. (Mangope used to be known amongst 'Tswanas' in Johannesburg as 'Vorster's firstborn'.)

The co-operation with white capital is also reflected in the composition of the Bophuthatswana 'Cabinet'. Whites occupy at least three key posts. The 'Minister of Finance' rejoices in the traditional Tswana name of Sir Cyril Hatly. The 'Minister of Defence' is a South African brigadier, H.B. Riekert, while in 1982 Mangope appointed as 'Minister of Manpower Utilisation' a man who has specialised in governmental appointments in unrecognised 'states' — former Rhodesian minister and Ciskeian 'presidential adviser', Rowan Cronje.

The 'independence' of the Bantustan has intensified struggles within it. A considerable process of centralisation of landholdings in the hands of individuals has been reported. The protracted struggles over the Winterveldt area and attempts by the Mangope regime to drive out 'non-Tswana' traders has also led to deep tension in the region.

The Ciskei[9]

(See: a) Tables 4.1a and b; b) Map, p.220; c) Introductory essay to this section.)

The Ciskei is one of two so-called 'Xhosa homelands' (the other being the Transkei). It was granted 'independence' in December 1981 under particularly farcical conditions. The year prior to 'independence', the 'Quail Commission' appointed by the Ciskei administration found that 90% of 'Ciskeians' living both within and outside the Bantustan were totally opposed to 'independence'. However, following a rapidly summoned and rigged 'referendum' the next year, the 'Chief Minister', Lennox Sebe claimed majority support for 'independence'. The apartheid regime itself disputed Sebe's claim that he had negotiated a unique 'independence' settlement which would allow 'Ciskeians' to retain their South African citizenship. At the 'independence celebrations' themselves, during the raising of the flag of the new 'state' the flagpole first collapsed and then broke and finally had to be held up by South African soldiers. It was reported that the laughter of the crowd drowned out the 101 gun salute and the 'independence address' by Sebe. The head of the regime's security police said he 'did away with' the Ciskeian corporal in charge of the flag raising ceremony.

The Ciskeian administration is led by 'President' Lennox Sebe and his brother 'General' Charles Sebe, head of the Ciskei 'Central Intelligence Services'. The regime has become particularly notorious for its extremely repressive and brutal rule. Detention without trial is extensively used to stifle all dissent — extending even to minor squabbles in Sebe's Ciskei National Independence Party. The para-military 'green berets' regularly break up meetings, beat up Sebe's real and imagined opponents and generally intimidate any potential troublemakers. Since 1980 the regime has launched a particular wave of terror against the South African Allied Workers Union (SAAWU — see p.337) whose major base lies in an East London township technically incorporated in the Bantustan. Hundreds of SAAWU members have been detained, and a number of people associated with the union have died in arson and shooting attacks. 'General' Sebe has announced he will have 'no mercy' on SAAWU. In 1983 the Ciskei regime announced its intention to introduce 'punishment camps' for Ciskeian contract workers who strike or break their contracts and so 'discredit' the Bantustan. The 'Minister of Manpower', Chief Maqoma, said that labour was Ciskei's 'black gold'. His comments were described by the general secretary of the Food and Canning Workers' Union as worthy of a 'slave trader'.

An interview granted by Charles Sebe (sometimes characterised as South Africa's answer to Idi Amin) one year after 'independence' is revealing of his conception of the meaning of this process. Asked if the 'promise of independence' had been fulfilled, and whether he saw 'this first year of independence as a success', Sebe replied:

> There is an enormous difference between what the Ciskei was before independence and what it is now. Take my department for instance. We never had a Department of State Security before independence. After Independence the Department is manned by well over 887 men. My surplus budget is R1,800,000, which is outstanding because I am going to have to use this money hurriedly now because there are only two months to go till the end of the financial year. The total budget of the Department of State Security was plus-minus R12 million. Yes, there is no doubt the first year has been a great success.

The Bantustan is 'ruled' by the Ciskeian National Independence Party, presently the only group represented in the 'national assembly'. Since its formation in 1973, the CNIP has been characterised by a number of quarrels and divisions, with some of its leaders going into 'exile' in the Transkei. However, all the various 'parties' formed out of these squabbles have found their way back into the CNIP.

The 'economy' of the Ciskei has little worthy of note beyond the fact common to all Bantustans that it remains basically a reserve in which unemployed 'Xhosas' are dumped. The Ciskei National Development Corporation has set up a number of small 'industries' which, together with those established under the 'agency' system, employed a total of 2,989 African workers in less than 50 undertakings in 1979. The Bantustan regime's promotional material to lure investment into the region emphasises the availability of cheap labour. Significantly, most of the very few wage labourers employed in the Ciskei are women — whose labour power comes even cheaper than that of the men who are forced to leave their new 'republic' to seek work in 'foreign' South Africa.

The Ciskei is unrecognised by its sister Xhosa 'republic' of the Transkei, which claims hegemony over its territory.

Gazankulu

(See: a) Tables 4.1a and b; b) Map, p.220; c) Introductory essay to this section.)

The so-called Tsonga/Shangaan homeland, part of whose population lives close to the south-western border of Mozambique. The territory was granted 'self-governing status' in 1973. Its 'legislative assembly' consists of 42 nominated and 26 elected members. There seems to be very little political activity in the Bantustan, which to date lacks even a single political party. Led by 'Chief Minister' Professor Hudson Ntsanwisi, its administration has vocally refused either to accept 'independence' or recognise the 'independence' of those Bantustans which have chosen this option.

This reflects something of the vacilating position of 'Chief Minister' Ntsanwisi. Prior to assuming his current office, he was a well known Shangaan literary and cultural figure who taught at the tribal college known as 'the University of the North' (Turfloop). His work was characterised by a strong Shangaan cultural chauvinism, in keeping with his later role as collaborator with Pretoria's attempted 'retribalisation' of African politics and culture. However, in refusing the proferred 'independence', Ntsanwisi has made much of the 'birthright as South Africans' of the 'non-independent states'. Yet he has also used tribalistic arguments in an attempt to beg more money from Pretoria. Thus in 1980 he made representation to the government comparing the area and population of Gazankulu with that of the now 'independent' Venda. Though the former is larger than the latter on both counts, Venda's receipts from the South African government in 1979 were more than twice those of Gazankulu (R104 million : R49 million).

The economy of Gazankulu has virtually nothing to characterise it as anything other than a labour reservoir. The Tsonga/Shangaan Development Corporation has initiated a number of petty projects of little consequence. Less than 16,000 people were engaged in paid employment within the Bantustan in 1978, and 15% of these were employed in the actual Bantustan administration (not including its police force). The rest of the inhabitants are either unemployed or dependent on the remitted wages of migrant workers.

KaNgwane[10]

(See: a) Tables 4.1a and b; b) Map, p.220; c) Introductory essay to this section.)

The so-called South African Swazi homeland, KaNgwane is best known for its part in the prolonged saga of the 'land offer' made by South Africa to Swaziland in 1981–2. The total disregard shown by the South African regime for the wishes of its Bantustan collaborators in this 'national state', reveals the real conception of 'national rights' underlying the Bantustan strategy. As one commentator put it: 'in the apartheid scheme of things, nations are created and nations are taken away.'

KaNgwane was granted 'self-governing' status in 1978. Since then its internal politics have been characterised by sharp conflict between two factions. The first, led by the present 'Chief Minister', Enos Mabuza, represents an alliance between an emerging intelligentsia and petty bourgeoisie in the Bantustan on the one hand, and the majority of 'chiefs' on the other. This group is now organised into the *Inyandza* (United) National Movement. In general it has sought to win for itself as many as possible of the material benefits of collaboration with the regime whilst opposing 'independence' and hanging on for its 'rights as South Africans'. The other faction, led alternatively by David Lukele and Chief Johannes Dlamini, draws support from a smaller group of more traditionally-minded chiefs, and has identified its interests more closely with the Swazi kingdom. Its 'party', *Inyandza ye Mswati* (Union of Mswati) in fact emphasises a Swazi ethnic unity.

Control of the KaNgwane 'legislative assembly' since 1977 has passed from Dlamini to Mabuza back to Dlamini and again back to Mabuza as the two brought legal suits and counter suits against each other. After 1979, however, Mabuza appeared to consolidate his position.

In 1981, the legislative assembly requested that it be given 'Chapter 2' powers of 'self government', but emphasised to the apartheid regime that it was not interested in 'independence'. After some stalling and a lot of pressure on both Swaziland and Mabuza's party, the South African regime eventually refused this request and made the unprecedented suggestion that KaNgwane seek incorporation into the Kingdom of Swaziland. Early in 1982, as part of its proposed land deal with Swaziland — in which Swaziland would be ceded both KaNgwane and the Ingwavuma part of the KwaZulu Bantustan — the

224

apartheid regime took the further unprecedented step of dissolving the KaNgwane 'legislative assembly'. This ignored the vociferous opposition to the scheme from the majority Mabuza faction of the Bantustan's political leadership. For this group, the land deal threatened possible loss of employment, reduction of salaries and a general reduction of status and benefits under the royalist form of rule in the Swazi kingdom. The pro-incorporation group, led by Chief Dlamini, clearly sought to gain from its close alliance with Swazi royalism.

The detailed chronology of this saga is not important here. It should simply be noted that the very strong opposition to the deal from virtually all groups in the Bantustan, not to mention in the wider South African state, coupled with the particularly inept tactics of the apartheid regime and finally the death of Swazi king Sobhuza in August 1982 appear to have stalled the implementation of this deal. In late 1982 the KaNgwane legislative assembly was reinstated. The matter has been referred to the Rumpf Commission on which each of the interested parties is supposed to be represented (but the apartheid regime refused to accept the nomination of liberal law professor John Dugard as the KaNgwane delegate). When the Swazi Prime Minister, Prince Mabandla Dlamini, was dismissed in March 1983 for — amongst other reasons — opposing the land deal, he is alleged to have advised Enos Mabuza over the issue.

Like all other Bantustans, KaNgwane is primarily a labour reservoir. Its 'GDP' is amongst the smallest of all the Bantustans and almost no industrial activity takes place within it. Recently, high grade anthracite deposits have been discovered, but the exploitation of these has not begun. The vast majority of its population are dependent for their existence on migratory labour.

KwaNdebele[11]

(See: a) Tables 4.1a and b; b) Map, p.220; c) Introductory essay to this section.)

The so-called South Ndebele homeland, KwaNdebele is the newest and second smallest Bantustan.

When the original list of eight Bantustans was drawn up in 1959, no provision was made for the 'south Ndebele'. A separate 'homeland' was established in 1975, a first-stage 'legislative assembly' of purely nominated members was set up in 1979, and 'self-government' granted in April 1981. Under 'Chief Minister' Simon Skosana, the Bantustan 'Cabinet' has already opted for 'independence' and begun negotiations on this with the apartheid regime.

KwaNdebele is an arid, overpopulated area with almost no agriculture and no industry. It has no water supplies — most water is delivered by tanker. The few existing economic activities consist almost exclusively of various commercial undertakings, mostly owned by the 'Cabinet' and members of the 'legislative assembly'. KwaNdebele functions almost entirely as a dormitory for the unemployed and 'commuters' travelling to work in the various towns of the giant Pretoria-Witwatersrand-Vereniging industrial complex.

Its establishment as a separate Bantustan in 1975 was in fact virtual recognition of its status as a dormitory and labour reserve. Given its relative proximity to South Africa's major industrial complex, large numbers of the 'citizens' of other Bantustans have drifted to KwaNdebele as the closest they can get to the industrial heartland without incurring the risk of harassment under the pass laws, uprooting and dislocation. Thus research by the regime's Human Sciences Research Council indicates that 55% of its inhabitants came to the Bantustan from 'white' farms, and a further 30% from the Bophuthatswana Bantustan.

There are no political parties in KwaNdebele, and not even Bantustan type elections have been held. Its leaders are refreshingly frank about their own collaborator status. KwaNdebele 'strongman' and 'Interior Minister', P.M. Ntuli admits: 'All the homeland leaders have to take independence. They are all driving government cars on the government road to independence'. Reports on the leaders who strove to get Ndebele recognised as a separate 'nation' by Pretoria indicate that they keep tight control over the commercial life of the Bantustan. All the territory's liquor licences are held by Bantustan 'ministers', and 'nearly all the new shops belong to government officials or members of their families. Licence holders are nearly all related to members of the tribal authorities'. This ruling collaborator clique has opted for 'independence' in the hope of securing accelerated 'development aid' from Pretoria. Admits 'Interior Minister' Ntuli: 'Dr Koornhof [the responsible apartheid minister] says the man who accepts independence receives the most help from Pretoria. We want the central government to look at us'.

KwaZulu[12]

(See: a) Tables 4.1a and b; b) Map, p.220; c) Introductory essay to this section; d) Entry on *Inkatha yeNkululeko yeSizwe*.)

The so-called homeland of the Zulu – largest of the ten 'ethnic nationalities' identified by apartheid theoreticians. KwaZulu is led by the controversial Chief Gatsha Buthelezi who maintains a one party system through his 'national cultural liberation movement', the tribalist *Inkatha yeNkululeko yeSizwe*.

The KwaZulu 'legislative assembly' was established in 1972, and Buthelezi elected 'Chief Executive Councillor'. This final agreement to participate in the Bantustan system followed years of resistance to the Bantu Authorities system inside Zululand. In 1977 the territory became 'self-governing' under 'Chief Minister' Buthelezi. However, both Buthelezi and the KwaZulu 'legislative assembly' have been vocal opponents of 'independence' for the Bantustans, laying strong rhetorical claim to their status as South Africans – whilst nonetheless consolidating a strongly tribalist form of political organisation in *Inkatha*.

The politics of KwaZulu and *Inkatha* are discussed at length, pp.387-95.

However, a number of points bear repeating here. Buthelezi's dominant political position within the Bantustan rests on a sometimes uneasy alliance between the KwaZulu petty bourgeoisie (many of them physically located in the two Durban 'townships' — KwaMashu and Umlazi — which form part of KwaZulu) and various strata of the chiefs. KwaZulu is the most fragmented of all the Bantustans, consisting of over 40 separate pieces of land in 1980. As such, it clearly cannot fulfil the political and economic aspirations of anything but a very small group. Hence the support of its petty bourgeoisie for Buthelezi's more ambitious political strategy to act as the national representative of the African petty bourgeoisie and demand 'power-sharing' in the existing system — whilst at the same time gathering to itself the fruits which the Bantustan system holds out to its collaborators.

There have been sharp political divisions between the Zulu chiefs since the mid-1880s. Buthelezi's aristocratic descent and chieftainship of the dominant Buthelezi clan have placed him in a strategic position to win the support of the majority of the chiefs for his dual track policy of consolidating their power within KwaZulu on the one hand, whilst seeking greater power within the central South African state on the other hand. However, since at least the mid-1970s, KwaZulu politics have also been marked by a sharp conflict between Buthelezi and the Zulu King, Goodwill Zwelithini, with sporadic attempts to form a 'king's party' in opposition to Buthelezi. The 'Chief Minister' has alleged that these were sponsored by the South African state embarrassed by his rhetorical opposition to apartheid and eager to remove him. Basing himself in the 'legislative assembly', Buthelezi has progressively reduced the power of the King and subjected him to humiliating restrictions. The King is now not allowed to give interviews, nor travel outside of the royal village without the express permission of the KwaZulu 'Cabinet' (i.e. Buthelezi). In 1980, in an attempt to escape these restrictions, the King tried to join the South African Defence Force. His application was referred to Buthelezi who rejected it with contempt.

In this alliance between the petty bourgeoisie and the chiefs, elements of the petty bourgeoisie have also been restive. Buthelezi's strategy seeks essentially to win the support of monopoly capital for his demand for access to the institutions of power within the state. To this end he has, on more than one occasion, threatened to 'unleash my people'. Yet this strategy does involve close economic co-operation with large capitalist enterprises. Under his 'tripartite' economic strategy — previously labelled 'African Communalism' — a number of large enterprises have been admitted into KwaZulu, in partnership with the KwaZulu Development Corporation (KDC), and with KwaZulu shareholders. On one occasion in 1975, the opening of a supermarket by the large Checkers chain aroused strong opposition from the local chamber of commerce. It took Buthelezi some time to bring them under control, again through a mixture of threats and concessions.

The various challenges to Buthelezi's position in the mid-1970s, particularly from the King, but also from some small traders, coupled with the increasingly virulent attacks on his politics of participation in the Bantustan system by the

Black Consciousness Movement (see entry p.302), led to his recognition of the need for an organised political base. Consequently, *Inkatha* was revived in 1975. Since then it has been imposed on the Bantustan to create a virtual one party state. Elections were delayed on various specious excuses until *Inkatha* was organised. Widespread compulsion has been used to force people in KwaZulu to join *Inkatha*. The KwaZulu 'legislative assembly' formally requested the apartheid state to outlaw any other political parties in KwaZulu — a request which the white minority regime refused as 'undemocratic'.

The fragmentation of KwaZulu makes a mockery of any discussion of its 'economy'. In 1981, 56% of its economically active population were employed outside the Bantustan. In the same year 300,000 migrant workers and 400,000 so-called 'commuters' (residents who commute daily to work in 'white' areas) from KwaZulu were employed in the 'white' areas of South Africa. A total of 58,895 people were engaged in wage employment within the Bantustan itself. Probably a majority of these were directly employed by the KwaZulu 'government'. The KwaZulu Development Corporation has put forward various 'development proposals', but there is little industrial production inside KwaZulu. A number of small mining undertakings, together producing less than R1 million in 1980, are also in operation.

Given the total integration of KwaZulu into the economy of the Natal Province, in 1980 amidst much publicity, Buthelezi set up the 'Buthelezi Commission'. Staffed predominantly by the representatives of capital and conservative white academics, it was to investigate the 'requirements for stability and development in KwaZulu and Natal'. The commission recommended an integrated 'mixed market economy' and a form of 'consociational democracy' which would treat Natal and KwaZulu as one region. These proposals have been widely discussed in the non-Nationalist Party press in South Africa as offering a possible guide to the resolution of 'racial conflict' in a way which does not seriously challenge the existing structure of power — particularly economic power. It also signifies Buthelezi's and *Inkatha*'s search for a more meaningful role in the existing system (see *Inkatha* entry, p.394).

Lebowa

(See: a) Tables 4.1a and b; b) Map, p.220; c) Introductory essay to this section.)

The Lebowa Bantustan is a fragmented hold-all which is supposed to function as the 'ethnic homeland' of three groups identified by South Africa's anthropologists — the North Sotho, North Ndebele and Bapedi. It is ruled by 'Chief Minister' Cedric Phatudi and the Lebowa People's Party (LPP).

Lebowa was granted 'self-govering status' in 1973. Prior to this it had been ruled by Chief Maurice Matlala as 'Chief Minister' of an 'interim legislative assembly'. In the elections for the new 'Chief Minister', Chief Matlala was narrowly defeated by Dr Cedric Phatudi — who represented an alliance of petty bourgeois elements and certain chiefs ranged against Matlala's bloc of chiefs.

However, the ruling alliance in Lebowa has been a fragile one. In the period shortly after 'self-government' a number of liberal petty bourgeois elements, grouped around the 'Minister of the Interior' and LPP deputy-leader, Collins Ramusi, tried to reduce the power of the chiefs. With Phatudi's backing, a commission headed by Ramusi recommended a constitutional change to push the chiefs into a fairly powerless 'upper house'. The chiefs appealed to their apartheid masters, who, alarmed at the prospect of a possibly anti-apartheid petty bourgeoisie marginalising the chiefs and using the Bantustan as a political base (as appeared to be Ramusi's strategy), refused the amendment on the grounds that nothing would be done to 'weaken the Chiefs'. Much pressure was then put on Phatudi. A number of chiefs threatened to withdraw their support unless he remove Ramusi who was accused, *inter alia*, of 'disrespect for the Chiefs'. In July 1975 Ramusi was dismissed; the LPP split into pro-Ramusi and pro-Phatudi factions, each of which 'expelled' the other and claimed the assets and mantle of the LPP. The issue was finally resolved in the 1978 elections when the Phatudi faction won what many observers termed 'a surprising victory'. However, Phatudi himself had lost much support from the chiefs and narrowly avoided defeat by Chief Matlala in the elections for the 'chief ministership'.

The fragility of the politics of Lebowa have been characterised by a number of other conflicts. There has been strong local resistance to forced removals carried out under the apartheid regime's plan to 'consolidate' Lebowa's fragmented territory from 15 blocks to five. In 1980 this spilled over into open violence when a group calling themselves 'the Congress People' (after the ANC) refused to accept the authority of Chief Matlala. Two people were reported killed in armed clashes with the Lebowa police. Phatudi's 'government' has also been involved in a protracted dispute with the Gazankulu Bantustan over border and other issues. On a number of occasions this conflict has been referred to the apartheid state. Phatudi has also proposed the merger of Lebowa with KwaNdebele in a bid to stop secessionist moves by 'North Ndebele' chiefs — some of whom have been detained and charged with incitement.

Given this fragile internal base, Phatudi has attempted to consolidate support by adopting an increasingly strong anti-independence rhetoric. Whereas in 1976 he announced that he might request 'independence' if his land claims were met, by 1979 he was attacking any notion of 'divorcing from one's country'. In 1976 he was involved in the abortive 'Black Unity Front' together with other Bantustan leaders (see p.404). Phatudi likewise rejected the proposed 'Constellation of Southern African States', arguing that the proper solution for South Africa would be a federation of 'self-governing' states enjoying complete internal autonomy but a common South African citizenship. Phatudi's self-assessment and weak political base are well illustrated in the dispute over the name for the new Lebowa 'capital'. In 1979 he announced that the 'Cabinet' had 'unanimously' decided to name the new capital 'Phatudi'. This was rejected in 1980 in a twice prorogued session of the 'legislative assembly', which chose the name Lebowakgomo. Phatudi then announced that the name would remain 'Phatudi City' because it was 'necessary for a nation to honour its leaders'. The 'legislative assembly' decision has, however, prevailed and little more has been heard of 'Phatudi City'.

In common with the other Bantustans, Lebowa is primarily a labour reservoir for South Africa's capitalist economy. In 1981, according to official figures, Lebowa had 139,000 migrant workers and a further 58,000 'commuters' absent working in South Africa. Their wages made up 75% of the 'GNP' of this Bantustan. Within Lebowa itself, in 1981 just over 47,000 people were in wage employment; of these, 11,500 were working on the Bantustan's 21 mines which together produced a value of R60 million. A further 7,000 people were employed in 40 small industrial undertakings, whilst the majority of the remainder were employed by the Bantustan administration.

QwaQwa

(See a) Tables 4.1a and b; b) Map, p.220; c) Introductory essay to this section.)

The so-called South Sotho homeland and the smallest Bantustan. It is ruled by 'Chief Minister' Kenneth Mopeli and the *Dikwankwetla* ('strong men') National Party (DNP). The territory was given 'self-governing' status in 1980.

The total area of this 'national state' is 58,000 hectares, over 20,000 of which are mountainous and uninhabitable. The number of people living in the Bantustan rose from 24,000 in 1970 to over 200,000 in 1979. This rapid rise was caused by a large influx of low-paid agricultural workers from other parts of the Orange Free State, who sought to use QwaQwa as a base from which to secure employment on the mines (apartheid laws forbid agricultural workers to leave the 'white' rural areas of South Africa to seek urban employment). By 1979 the population density stood at over 400 per square km.

Given this high population density, little agricultural production, or indeed any kind of productive activity takes place. QwaQwa remains a labour reservoir pure and simple. In 1981, 6,781 people were engaged in wage employment in the Bantustan — most working for the 'administration' — while over 40,000 were working as migrant labourers in South Africa. The Bantustan's 'ministers' complain that land zoned for agricultural production has to be used to settle and house the rapidly rising population. A 1978 study by the apartheid research organisation, Benso, concluded that given the minute size of QwaQwa, the total absence of natural resources, and the severe overpopulation, unless the Bantustan were given more land — which Benso concluded was politically 'unfeasible' — its only prospect of any kind of economic development was to be turned into a 'city state' administering all 'South Sotho' in South Africa. Should this not occur, QwaQwa should lose its status as a 'South Sotho Homeland'.

This plan was rejected by Mopeli's 'government'. The extreme overcrowding and stark poverty in QwaQwa are used by the Mopeli administration in its attempt to acquire more land. The major policy platform of the ruling group in QwaQwa consists of strident land claims on the South African state — Mopeli has claimed half of the province of the Orange Free State together with land from other Bantustans, particularly the Transkei. This has led to tribalist conflict between Mopeli and other Bantustan leaders, as the QwaQwa leader claims that 'his' South Sotho people are oppressed in other areas. He regularly cites figures of the number of 'South Sotho' living in other Bantustans who 'wish to be incorporated into QwaQwa'. Thus, Transkei 'independence' in 1976 was declared a 'day of mourning' in QwaQwa because of the 'enslavement' of 'our South Sotho brothers' in that region. A number of South-Sotho speaking chiefs in the Transkei have in fact been detained by the Matanzima regime for advocating unification with QwaQwa. The Mopeli 'administration' has rejected any notion of 'independence' until its land claims are met. In 1976, the 'Chief Minister' predicted that ultimately QwaQwa would merge with Lesotho.

The first elections in QwaQwa were held in 1975. Mopeli's DNP won 19 of the 20 elected seats, and Mopeli replaced Chief Wessels Mota as 'Chief Minister'. In true Bantustan tradition, the DNP has since been wracked by a series of squabbles over the crumbs of Bantustan office, leading to a split in 1979 when Mopeli dismissed two senior ministers. These then called a special conference of the DNP and 'expelled' Mopeli. However, the conference was declared 'unconstitutional' and the two dissident ministers then formed their own *Matla a Sechaba* (Power of the Nation) party. In the 1980 elections Mopeli's DNP won all seats. The DNP is currently the only party represented in the 'legislative assembly'. For a while it was also a member of the South African Black Alliance (see p.403) but has since withdrawn from this grouping.

The Transkei[13]

(See: a) Tables 4.1a and b; b) Map, p.220; c) Introductory essay to this section.)

> The larger of the two so-called Xhosa Homelands (the other being the Ciskei). The Transkei was the first Bantustan to opt for 'independence' (in October 1976). It is ruled by 'President' Kaiser Matanzima and his younger brother 'Prime Minister' George Matanzima. The Matanzima brothers are the longest serving open collaborators of the apartheid regime amongst the Bantustan leaders.

For many years the Transkei provided the laboratory for various apartheid policies and particularly the Bantustan strategy. As far back as 1894, the Glen Grey Act set up a series of tribally-based district councils dominated by the chiefs. These councils were then extended to other regions under the 1920 Natives Affairs Act. When the Nationalist Party regime introduced the Bantu Authorities Act in 1951, the Transkei was the first region in which a Territorial Authority was established in terms of the Act. With the announcement of the Bantustan strategy in 1959, the Transkei Territorial Authority again provided the model for the 'constitutional development' of the other Bantustans. The Transkei was the first Bantustan to be given 'self-government' in 1963 — the others followed suit only in the 1970s. It was likewise the first of the Bantustans to be granted 'independence' in October 1976. In other respects too, the Transkei has functioned as a model for apartheid. Following the 1960 peasants' revolt in Pondoland (which forms part of the Transkei), emergency repressive measures were granted to the Bantu authorities under the notorious Proclamation R400. The chiefs were given the right to ban meetings and detain persons without trial. These powers were widely used by the Matanzima regime prior to 'independence', when Proclamation R400 was replaced by the even more Draconian Transkei Public Security Act (see p.210). However, with the accession to 'self-government' of the other Bantustans, the provisions and powers of Proclamation R400 were extended to these areas and their rulers.

The political history of the Transkei is instructive in the functioning of the Bantustan system. It is also inextricably tied up with the position of the Matanzima brothers in conflicts between Transkei chiefs. Kaiser Matanzima was appointed Chief of the AmaHala clan in 1940, subject to the overrule of the Paramount Chief of the Tembu. In 1955 he entered the Transkei Territorial Authority (known as the Bunga) because he saw the Bantu Authorities Act and the tribalist structure it created as 'the foundation of the eventual independence of the African people'. In this he was strongly opposed by his nominal superior and long-standing political arch-foe, the Paramount Chief (sometimes called the 'King') of the Tembu, Chief Sabata Dalindyebo — who was an opponent of the Bantu Authorities system. From then dates Matanzima's growing collaboration with the apartheid regime. In order to consolidate his position in the Territorial Authority, and in strong contradiction to the 'traditional' practices apartheid theory claimed to be promoting, the South African state made Matanzima Regional Chief of Emigrant Tembuland over the opposition of Paramount Chief Dalindyebo in 1958. In 1966, when Matanzima's inferior position to Dalindyebo in 'traditional' matters became an increased political embarrassment, the apartheid regime conjured up the non-existent 'traditional' office of 'Paramount Chief of the Emigrant Tembu' for their most pliant puppet, thereby giving him 'equal status' with Dalindyebo. Matanzima's enmity with Dalindyebo continues. In 1979, when Dalindyebo was leader of the opposition in the 'National Assembly', Matanzima had him arrested, convicted under security legislation and stripped him of his Paramountcy. Dalindyebo then fled the Transkei, was invited to Swaziland by King Sobhuza, and joined the ANC in exile.

In the Transkei elections preceding the granting of 'self government' in 1963, Matanzima's Transkei National Independence Party (TNIP) was trounced. On a platform of opposition to the Bantustan system, multi-racialism and the assertion of a common South African citizenship for all, the Democratic Party (DP) won 33 of the 45 seats. However, Matanzima emerged as 'Chief Minister' with the support of 42 of the 58 government-paid chiefs, who on their own constituted a majority in the 'assembly'. Once in office, Matanzima's regime began a policy of harassment and bannings of the Democratic Party under Proclamation R400. The DP's representation declined with each succeeding election – partly because the petty bourgeoisie which had supported the DP virtually *en bloc* in 1963, slowly began to go over to the TNIP as its control over the economic favours which apartheid offered to its Bantustan puppets, and its monopolisation of power contrasted with the impotence of the DP under its articulate but ineffectual leader, Knowledge Guzana. By the 1973 elections, the ruling TNIP had won not only a majority of elected seats, but a 55% majority of votes cast in a low poll (34% of registered voters). The DP began a debate of its policy of 'multiracialism' which its 1974 congress blamed for its declining fortunes. Early in 1976, Guzana was replaced as party leader by Hector Ncokazi, who was strongly influenced by the ideology of Black Consciousness. This was a revolt of the rank and file of the party against its representatives in the 'legislative assembly'. Guzana and most of these representatives then split away to form the New Democratic Party. The more 'radical' DP was severely weakened when, one week before the closure of nominations for the pre-'independence' elections, 15 of its leaders were detained.

In the three years which followed, a series of other 'opposition' parties emerged, based mainly on factionalist splits and tribalist rivalries in the ruling TNIP. In 1979, however, Chief Sabata Dalindyebo succeeded in uniting all surviving opposition groups into a new party, the Democratic Progressive Party (DPP). Observers argued that the DPP posed a real threat to the TNIP in the next elections. During this period, and specifically the years 1979 and 1980, the TNIP was itself badly shaken by a series of tribalist splits and divisions, particularly losing support in its crucial base in East Pondoland as the powerful Sigcau chiefs (whose father Botha Sigcau was the first Transkei 'President') switched their allegiance to the DPP. During this period Kaiser Matanzima gave up the 'prime ministership' to his brother George – previously 'Minister of Justice' – and acceded to the 'presidency' of the Bantustan. George Matanzima's heavy handed attempts to exercise personal political control shattered the delicate tribal alliances which brother Kaiser had laboriously constructed, and produced a protracted political crisis. It was ended through the proven method of intensified repression. Besides Dalindyebo, many other important opposition leaders were detained, including a number of disaffected former 'Cabinet Ministers'. The heads of the Transkei army and police were likewise detained (leading to the appointment of Lt.-Col. R. Reid-Daly, former head of the infamous Rhodesian Selous Scouts, as head of the Transkei 'army'). The 'Minister of the Interior' announced that a planned *coup d'etat* in the police force had been foiled. All possibility of a coup was strongly denied by George Matanzima. The 'Minister' was dismissed and detained; he died in prison two days later. Armed clashes between the police and peasants were reported, and in 1980 a State of Emergency was declared. Eventually, this repressive response broke the organised opposition; many of the TNIP defectors returned to the fold. In the 1981 elections, the opposition DPP won only one seat, that contested by its new leader, Caledon Mda. The TNIP held 148 elected and appointed seats because, following the banning of Chief Dalindyebo, all the chiefs went over to the Matanzima party.

These intensely tribalist and repressive politics aside, the 'Republic of Transkei' is characterised by a number of other distinct and farcical political features. It has laid claim to large parts of South Africa. When the apartheid regime refused to hand over the East Griqualand area to the Transkei in 1978, the Matanzima brothers 'broke off diplomatic relations', with the only state in the world recognising Transkei 'independence', revoked 'the non-aggression pact', and threatened 'armed struggle' to recover the land. The Transkei leaders have also claimed the Ciskei Bantustan as their territory and do not recognise the 'independence' of the 'sister Xhosa Republic'.

The administration of the Transkei is in a shambles. A pro-apartheid news-paper reported in 1979 that the Bantustan was bankrupt. It was saved only by an additional grant of R73 million from the South African government (with whom it had 'severed diplomatic relations') — this was in addition to the R113.5 million grant already made for the year 1979/80. Corruption within the region is so rife, that in 1980 the South African state assumed a measure of control over the administration of the budget of this 'independent' state. Corruption runs through all levels of the state bureaucracy. However, its prime exponents and major beneficiaries are the Matanzima brothers themselves. There have been numerous reports of the Matanzima brothers buying hotels, farms and other undertakings from first the Xhosa Development Corporation and then the Transkei Development Corporation at prices substantially lower than those at which these bodies first acquired such properties. In 1979 Matanzima tried to shift the blame for corruption onto the South African head of the TDC. His successor, a Briton, was himself fired (and another Briton whom he had hired as the Transkei's 'roving ambassador', was severely assaulted by the regime's security police) when he tried to dismiss 'incompetent' white South Africans employed by the TDC. In the past, a number of senior 'army' officers, including the 'Chief of Staff' have been charged with fraud.

Like all the other Bantustans, the Transkei is a labour reservoir for South African capitalism. Its 'economy' is sustained by the remittances of the more than 500,000 migrant workers from the Transkei working in the industrial centres of South Africa. In 1973, for example, their income comprised 70% of the Bantustan's 'GNP'. The incidence of migrant labour is shown in other striking figures: in 1974 there were only 66 men to 100 women living in the Transkei; for the age group 25-29, the ratio was 28.9:100.

Attempts by the apartheid regime to generate industry within the region have not been very successful. The first six years of its incentives to industrialists attracted only one bag factory. This was followed by a number of small consumer goods industries, employing a total of 4,050 mainly female workers in 1975. In this year, a total of 47,400 people were engaged in wage employment in the Transkei. Over 20,000 of them worked directly for the 'government'. The overwhelming majority of the Bantustan's population are in fact proletarianised producers, forced by apartheid laws to remain on the land, but unable to scratch a living from the overcrowded, worked-out soil. The average maize yield per hectare was one to three bags in 1974, compared with over 100 on most capitalist farms in South Africa. A 1974 study found that while 83% of households were engaged in some kind of farming, only 8.4% produced a surplus for sale 'in a good year', while only 0.1% produced exclusively for the market. Perhaps the most important cash crop in the region is marijuana, commonly known as *'dagga'*. Estimates of the value of the illegal trade in this crop on the South African market range from R120-R600 million per annum. The chiefs are deeply involved in this lucrative illicit traffic and many of them openly advocate its legalisation.

Since 'independence', the agricultural policies of the Matanzima regime have sought to consolidate large-scale private land ownership by using massive tax increases (in some cases of up to 1,000%) to force small producers to sell their cattle and leave the land. As the groups around the collaborating chiefs consolidate their hold on such private land, forms of capitalist farming are being introduced. However, such measures have not really succeeded in consolidating a significant rural bourgeoisie. The Transkeian bourgeoisie, such as it is, is essentially a commercial — trading and bottle store — bourgeoisie, highly dependent on the regime for trading and liquor licences. The other main social category which had benefited from 'independence' has been the bureaucracy, whose numbers have risen from 2,446 in 1963, to 19,800 in 1979.

The economy of the Transkei has also gone 'the Casino route', and the regime aims at a substantial increase in tourism. However, based as it is fundamentally on migrant labour, this 'economy' is in the final case sustained by huge grants from the apartheid regime (with whom 'diplomatic relations' were quietly restored in 1980). Between 1978 and 1980 these grants totalled R572.77 million.

Venda[14]

(See: a) Tables 4.1a and b; b) Map, p.220; c) Introductory essay to this section.)

The so-called Venda homeland and the third Bantustan to accept 'independence' (in September 1979), Venda is ruled by 'President' Patrick

Mphephu, whose regime is noted even amongst the Bantustans for its repression and brutality.

The Territorial Authority of Venda was changed into a 'legislative assembly' in 1971, and Venda was granted 'self-governing' status in 1973. Chief Patrick Mphephu, a self admitted 'conservative traditionalist' was elected 'Chief Minister' in an election which carried all the hallmarks of Bantustan politics. The opposition (and then anti-Bantustan) Venda Independence People's Party (VIPP) won 13 of the 18 elected seats. There was much doubt as to how the chiefs who comprised the rest of the 60 member assembly would vote. Mphephu loaded the chiefs into a bus, took them on a trip to the Manyelleti game reserve, plied them with alcohol, and, through offers of rewards and favours, won the support of 37 of the 42 non-elected members.

The following year Mphephu formed his own party, the Venda National Party (VNP), as 'traditionally oriented and concerned with preserving the powers and functions of the chiefs'. The VNP favoured independence if its land claims were met. However, for some time the uneasy alliance of chiefs which Mphephu had cobbled together against the VIPP remained fragile. In 1974-5 a steady drainage of chiefs away from the VNP to the VIPP reduced Mphephu's majority from 24 to six. Again, through a process of bargaining and favours, this drift was halted. By 1976 the VNP majority was again reported to be around 20 seats.

The rather comfortable jockeying for position between the petty bourgeois VIPP and Mphephu's party was shaken in 1977 by large-scale student demonstrations and boycotts against Bantu Education and the Bantustan system. Students in Venda stoned the 'legislative assembly' building and burnt down other government buildings. New security legislation was enacted giving Mphephu the power of banning and detention without trial. He closed over a hundred schools in Venda and thousands of pupils were sent home.

These developments shook the vacillating VIPP, confronted with genuine mass resistance to apartheid, it moderated its previous rhetorical opposition to the Bantustan system. When Mphephu announced that Venda would become 'independent' in 1979, the VIPP abandoned its opposition to 'independence' and adopted a 'neutral' position in the forthcoming elections, leaving it 'to the people to decide'. In the event the party still won 31 of the now 42 elected seats in a 52% poll. Again, there was strong speculation that Mphephu would lose the election for the 'chief ministership' in the assembly. To prevent this, 12 VIPP representatives were detained and the party boycotted the election. Mphephu was 'elected' unopposed. The VIPP abandoned its boycott when its representatives were threatened with the loss of their R7,000 annual salaries (the per capita income of Venda then stood at R171). By 1981, its leader (Baldwin Mudau), himself seeking a 'Cabinet' post, called for a merger of the VIPP and VNP, which Mphephu scornfully rejected. The opportunist politics of the VIPP were highlighted by Gilbert Bakane who took over as VIPP leader on Mudau's death in 1981. In a situation of intense repression, Bakane claimed that 'Venda is democratic'. Its problems, he said, stemmed from the fact that his party was ignored: '. . . we are not being used at all. The frustrating thing is not being able to exercise any influence in Venda'.

Mphephu has taken other steps to strengthen his still shaky position. To consolidate his hold over the chiefs, the apartheid state invented for him the non-existent 'traditional' title of 'Paramount Chief of the Venda'. Far more seriously, to stifle open mass discontent, the Mphephu regime has responded with a brutality notable even among the Bantustans. Following an armed attack by the African National Congress on a Sibasa police station in 1981, the regime instituted what a number of journalists referred to as a 'reign of terror'. There were large-scale detentions and a number of clergymen, including those of the pro-apartheid Dutch Reformed Church (see entry p.271), were expelled from Venda. Torture was widely reported and one detainee died in detention.

Venda is distinct from the other Bantustans in the sense that a relatively high proportion, around 65% of its *'de jure'* population – those whom the apartheid state decrees should be 'Venda citizens' – actually live in the Bantustan. Thus it was estimated in 1979/80 that just over 50,000 people were 'employed' in Venda. However, over 43,000 of these were listed as 'agricultural labourers'. In an area in which large-scale capitalist agriculture based on wage employment is relatively underdeveloped, this figure does not point to a high level of wage employment. Venda was also reported to supply 35,000 migrant and 'commuter' workers to 'white' South Africa. Their earnings made up some 70% of the 'gross national income' of Venda. The Venda Development Corporation has instituted some small-scale projects, mainly commercial undertakings. As yet there exists hardly any industry in the region. The regime also set up a casino and greyhound-racing operation to lure thrill seekers from 'white' South Africa. This, however, went bankrupt in 1983. During court cases it emerged that the Mphephu regime had staked future revenue due to be paid to it by Pretoria as security for the purchase of expensive gambling equipment. In 1981, grants from the South African state accounted for 75% of the budget of 'The Republic of Venda'. Among other 'development projects' undertaken by the Bantustan are a palace for 'President' Mphephu costing R588,000, and houses of R88,000 for each 'Cabinet Minister' – whose annual salaries of R27,000 are higher than those paid to any cabinet minister in any country in southern Africa (including South Africa itself).

BIBLIOGRAPHICAL NOTE

General

As in other chapters much information was gleaned from a regular reading of the following newspapers: *Rand Daily Mail, The Star, Financial Mail, Sunday Tribune, Sunday Times, The Sowetan, The ANC Weekly Newsbriefing* and *South African Pressclips* (produced by Barry Streek, Cape Town). Moreover, the Annual Surveys of the South African Institute of Race Relations synthesise various developments covered in this chapter.

1. See 'General' above.
   Hellman, E., (ed.) *Handbook on Race Relations in South Africa*, Cape Town, Oxford University Press, 1949.
   Lacey, M., *Working for Boroko*, Johannesburg, Ravan Press, 1980.
   Sachs, A., *Justice in South Africa*, Brighton, Sussex University Press, 1973.
   South African Institute of Race Relations, *Laws Affecting Race Relations in South Africa (to the end of 1976)*, Johannesburg, SAIRR, 1978.
2. See 'General' above.
   International Defence and Aid Fund, *The Apartheid War Machine: The Strength and Deployment of the South African Armed Forces*, London, IDAF, 1980.
   'Paratus: Official Periodical of the South African Defence Force' Republic of South Africa Department of Defence, *White Paper on Defence and Armaments Supply* 1977, 1979 and 1982.
   See also the publications of the Stockholm International Peace Research Institute; The Institute for Strategic Studies, *The Military Balance*, London, annual and, for a pro-regime view, the publications of the Institute of Strategic Studies of the University of Pretoria, especially its journal, *Strategic Review*.
3. See 'General' above.
   International Defence and Aid Fund, op. cit.
4. See 'General' above.
   Articles by defecting BOSS agent, Arthur McGiven, *Observer*, London, January 1980, and the 4 part series, 'The BOSS/DONS Story' by Mervyn Rees, *Rand Daily Mail*, February 1980.
   Winter, G., *Inside BOSS*, Harmondsworth, Penguin, 1981.
5. See 'General' above.
   Moss, G., *The Wheels Turn: South African Political Trials 1976–79*, Geneva and London, n.d.
   Sachs, A., op. cit.
   Students for Social Democracy, *Repression in South Africa*, Cape Town, n.d.
   See also sections on 'Trials' and 'The Courts' *Work in Progress*, Johannesburg, *passim*.
6. See 'General' above.
   Desmond, C., *The Discarded People*, Harmondsworth, Penguin, 1971.
   Greenberg, S., and Giliomee, H., 'Labour Bureaucracies and the African Reserves' *South African Labour Bulletin*, 8, 4, February 1983.
   Maré, G., *African Population Relocation in South Africa*, Johannesburg, South African Institute of Race Relations, 1979.
   Mbeki, G., *South Africa: The Peasants' Revolt*, Harmondsworth, Penguin, 1964.
   Report of the Department of Cooperation and Development for 1978–9, Pretoria, RP102/1979.
   Rogers, B., *Divide and Rule: South Africa's Bantustans*, London, International Defence and Aid Fund, 1980.
   South African Congress of Trade Unions, *Land and Labour in South Africa*, 1979.

South African Research Service/Development Studies Group (hereafter SARS/DSG), Information Publication No.6, *'Homeland' Tragedy: Function and Farce*, Johannesburg, 1982.
7. See 'General' above.
Financial Mail Special Report 'Bophuthatswana Going it Alone' 2 December 1977.
8. See 'General' above.
Buro vir Ekonomiese Navorsing Samewerking en Ontwikkeling (hereafter Benso), *Surveys*, Pretoria.
Report of the Department of Cooperation and Development, op. cit.
Rogers, op. cit.
9. See 'General' above.
Green, P., and Hirsch, A., 'Manufacturing Industry in the Ciskei', SARS/DSG, op.cit.
10. See 'General' above.
SARS/DSG Information Publication No.7, *The Swaziland-South Africa Land Deal*, Johannesburg, 1982.
11. See 'General' above.
Rand Daily Mail, 15-18 June 1982.
12. See 'General' above.
The Buthelezi Commission, *Requirement for Stability and Development in KwaZulu and Natal*, Durban, H and H Publications, 1981.
13. See 'General' above.
Innes, D., and O'Meara, D., 'Class Formation and Ideology: The Transkei Region', *Review of African Political Economy*, 7, 1976.
Leeuwenberg, J., *Transkei: A Study in Economic Regression*, London, Africa Publications Trust, 1977.
Southall, R., *South Africa's Transkei: The Politics of an 'Independent' Bantustan*, London, Heinemann, 1982.
Streek, B., and Wicksteed, R., *Render Unto Kaiser: A Transkei Dossier*, Johannesburg, Ravan Press, 1981.
Transkei Study Project, *Transkei (In)Dependence*, Johannesburg, 1976.
14. See 'General' above.
Badat, M.S., 'Profile of a Bantustan: Venda', SARS/DSG Information Publication No.6, op.cit.

Index

AAC, *see* Anglo American Corporation
AB, *see* Afrikaner Broederbond
Abrams, G: 308
accumulation: 51, 113, 115, 119; high rate under apartheid, 2, 9; changing pattern of in 1960s, 28-9
Acts of Parliament, *see* Legislation
Administration Boards: 35
AFCWU, *see* African Food and Canning Workers' Union
AFL-CIO, *see* American Federation of Labour
African Bank of South Africa: 120, 124, 125
African Food & Canning Workers' Union (AFCWU), *see* Food & Canning Workers' Union
African Mine Workers' Union (AMWU): 292, 322-3, 346
AFRICAN NATIONAL CONGRESS (ANC): **Entry, 283-90**; 16, 17, 26, 28, 34-5, 36, 46, 83, 100, 103, 142, 146, 158, 176, 181, 182, 184, 185, 193, 194, 202, 211, 217, 237, 291-4, 295-9, 302, 304, 307, 313, 329, 331, 367, 368, 377, 378, 379, 391, 393, 394, 413
African Peoples' Democratic Union of South Africa (APDUSA): 313
African Resistance Movement (ARM): 379
African trade unions, *see also* Democratic trade unions: 17, 21, 33, 34, 40-1, 109, 116
African workers: 31, 116-9, 122
AFRIKAANSE HANDELSINSTI-
TUUT (AHI): **Entry, 114-6**; 79, 112, 113, 125
Afrikaners: as bearers of racial prejudice, 2; impact of capitalism on, 15
AFRIKANER BROEDERBOND (AB): **Entry, 266-70**; 14, 72, 73, 79, 80, 83, 84, 96, 114-6, 140, 143, 145, 152, 155, 178, 193, 195, 201, 256, 259, 270-1, 272, 273, 276, 277, 377, 393, 411, 416-8, 420; attempt to take over trade unions, 19, 247-8
Afrikaner capital: 57, 58, 96, 106, 109, 114-6, 117, 118, 119, 120; non-emergence prior to 1939, 15; in NP class alliance, 19-20, 141-5, 154; growth fostered by NP after 1948, 23-4; entry into mining, 28; interpenetration with non-Afrikaner capital, 28-9, 37
Afrikaner economic movement: 19-20, 72, 80, 114-6, 139-40, 266, 268, 274
Afrikaner nationalism: 11, 13, 15, 84, 114-6, 155-6; new class alliance in 1948, 18-20; changing class base in 1960s, 30; split in class base post-1976, 37-8; in Total Strategy, 39; organised through NP, 138-45; in labour movement, 247-8; role of Broederbond, 266-70; role of churches, 272-6
Afrikaner Party: 161, 162, 412
Afrikaner petty bourgeoisie: 30-1, 37, 114-6; key force in NP class alliance, 19; measures taken by

241

NP to advance it, 25-6
AFRIKANER STUDENTEBOND
(ASB): **Entry, 278-9**; 280
AFRIKANER WEERSTAND
BEWEGING (AWB): **Entry, 156**;
279
Aggett, Dr N: 254, 328, 343, 346,
380
agriculture (capitalist): 30, 98, 115;
early development, 5-6, 11-13;
based on national oppression, 11;
class struggles around, 11-13;
deserts UP in 1948, 18-19;
measures taken by NP to advance
it, 24; changes in 1960s, 29;
penetration by monopolies, 56;
organisation of, 116-9; mechanisation, 118
AKSIE EIE TOEKOMS (AET):
Entry, 155-6; 151, 267
Alexander, R: 342, 366
All African Convention (AAC):
311-3
American Federation of Labour –
Congress of Industrial Organisations (AFL-CIO): 345
ANC, *see* African National Congress
ANGLO AMERICAN CORPORA-
TION (AAC): **Entry, 65-70**; 28,
29, 56, 57, 58, 61, 62, 71, 73, 76,
87, 89, 106, 107, 108, 111, 122,
123, 124, 142; relation to PFP,
146, 148-9, 162, 407, 408
Anglo-Boer war: 7, 10, 11, 132
ANGLOVAAL: **Entry, 85-7**; 29, 58,
63, 70, 71, 76, 103, 108, 124
Angola (Peoples Republic of): 32, 36,
44, 46, 100, 104, 106, 146, 180,
182, 183, 184, 193, 195, 297
Anti-Cad: 311-13
apartheid: 111, 113, 115, 116, 120,
123; conventional explanations of,
1, 2; as product of capitalist
exploitation, 2, 11; as system of
cheap labour, 2-3; class basis of, 2;
as NP policy, 20, 140-5; doctrine
of, 19-20; early implementation,
21-2; restructures class relations
to benefit all capitals, 21, 22;
first phase, 22-6; second phase,
27-32; golden age of, 28, 92;

1970s crisis of, 32-7; basic laws of,
169-78; role of bantustans,
197-237; theological rationalisa-
tion of, 273-6
APDUSA, *see* African Peoples Demo-
cratic Union of South Africa
APRP, *see* Azanian Peoples Revolu-
tionary Party
Argus Group: 406-10
ARM, *see* African Resistance Move-
ment
ARMSCOR: **Entry, 104-5**; 55, 58,
61, 77, 182, 184
ASB, *see* Afrikaner Studentebond
ASSOCIATION OF CHAMBERS OF
COMMERCE (ASSOCOM):
Entry, 111-4; 120, 125
AWB, *see* Afrikaner Weerstand
Beweging
Azania: 298, 301
AZANIAN PEOPLE'S ORGANISA-
TION (AZAPO): **Entry, 308-10**;
308, 399, 405
Azanian Peoples' Revolutionary
Party (APRP): 301
AZANIAN STUDENTS ORGANISA-
TION (AZASO): **Entry, 370**; 303,
309, 383

Baard, F: 343, 366
Bakane, G: 236
Bankorp: 71, 79, 94-6
BANKS: **Entry, 94-6**; 120
Bantu education: 33
Bantu Investment Corporation (BIC):
212, 213, 214, 215
BANTUSTANS: **Entry, 197-211**;
29-30, 31, 40, 46, 117, 118, 119,
120, 137, 170, 171, 175-6;
individual bantustans, 217-37
Barclays National Bank, *see also*
Banks: 61, 64, 65, 94-6
BARLOW RAND: **Entry, 75-8**; 29,
56, 57, 58, 62-3, 65, 66, 70, 71,
81, 96, 104, 108, 196, 407
BAWU, *see* Black Allied Workers'
Union
BCM, *see* Black Consciousness
BCMA, *see* Black Consciousness
Movement of Azania
Bell, F: 105

321-50
Trade Union Advisory and Co-
  ordinating Council (TUACC):
  324, 327, 334
TRADE UNION COUNCIL OF
  SOUTH AFRICA (TUCSA):
  Entry, 250-5; 125, 249, 256,
  257, 264, 265, 321, 323, 320,
  321
TRANSKEI (the): **Entry, 231-35**;
  198, 202, 205, 206, 209, 210,
  211, 212, 213, 215, 216, 218,
  219, 222, 231, 312, 391
Transkei National Independence
  Party (TNIP): 233-5
TRANSVAAL ANTI SA-INDIAN
  COUNCIL COMMITTEES:
  Entry, 294-6
Treurnicht, Dr A.P: 73, 139, 145,
  149-53, 155, 267, 270, 275
Trotskyism: 292, 310, 311, 312,
  313, 379
Tshabala, V: 125
Tutu, Bishop D.M: 421, 422

UF, *see* Urban Foundation
uMkhonto we Sizwe (MK): 26, 103,
  283, 284, 288-9, 291, 293, 294;
  after Soweto, 34-5, 181
UMSA, *see* Unity Movement
unemployment: 30, 31, 55, 107
Unionist Party: 159, 160
Unita: 46, 180, 184
United Kingdom South Africa Trade
  Association: 122
United Nations: 18
UNITED PARTY: **Entry, 157-8**;
  12, 15, 24, 67, 98, 106, 112,
  117, 118, 146, 160, 161, 162,
  163, 164, 201, 259, 268, 377,
  409, 420; loses capacity to
  organise capitalist class, 17-20
United States of America (USA):
  46
UNITED WOMEN'S ORGANISA-
  TION: **Entry, 368-70**
UNITY MOVEMENT OF SOUTH
  AFRICA: **Entry, 310-14**; 293,
  295, 304, 309
UP, *see* United Party
URBAN FOUNDATION: **Entry,**

122-125; 67, 84, 120, 307, 380
Urban Training Project (UTP): 324,
  327, 345
UWO, *see* United Womens Organisation

van den Bergh, Gen. H.J: 194, 195,
  196
van der Horst, Dr J.G: 81, 82
van der Walt Commission: 170
van Huyssteen, D.P.S: 80
VENDA: **Entry, 235-7**; 40, 198, 209,
  211, 216, 218, 219, 223
Venda National Party (VNP): 236
Venda Independence Peoples' Party
  (VIPP): 236
verligte/verkrampte: 30, 73, 142, 143,
  149-55, 193, 195, 269-77, 411-3,
  417-8
Verwoerd, Dr H.F: 30, 43, 73, 83,
  84, 115, 141, 142, 143, 152, 154,
  162, 178, 202, 203, 213, 269,
  274, 276, 288, 411, 417,
Viljoen, Gen. C.L: 186
Viljoen, Dr G. van N: 73, 270, 277
Viljoen Commission: 113, 115
VOLKSKAS: **Entry, 79-80**; 23, 29,
  58, 63, 70, 71, 73, 82, 83, 94, 95,
  96, 124, 141; position advanced
  by NP after 1948, 24
Vorster, B.J: 38, 44, 73, 113, 116,
  122, 142, 143, 144, 150, 154
  162, 173, 182, 183, 184, 193,
  194, 195, 269, 392, 397, 401,
  418

Waddell, G.H: 67, 70, 148, 149
wages: 33, 106, 110; mine wages for
  blacks cut 1897, 9; rising African
  wages in World War II, 17; falling
  African wages under NP rule,
  21-2, 203; wage gap in 1960s,
  31; constancy of mine wages
  1897-1970, 105
wage labour: first emerges in mining
  industry, 8; emergence in agriculture, 11; position advanced by
  NP post 1948, 24-5
WAR RESISTERS: **Entry, 385-6**
Wassenaar, A.D: 72, 73, 75
Western Province Federation of
  Trade Unions: 249

255

AFRICA TITLES FROM ZED PRESS

POLITICAL ECONOMY

DAN NABUDERE
Imperialism in East Africa
Vol I: Imperialism and Exploitation
Vol II: Imperialism and Integration
Hb

ELENGA M'BUYINGA
Pan Africanism or Neo-Colonialism?
The Bankruptcy of the OAU
Hb and Pb

BADE ONIMODE
Imperialism and Underdevelopment in Nigeria:
The Dialectics of Mass Poverty
Hb and Pb

MICHAEL WOLFERS AND JANE BERGEROL
Angola in the Frontline
Hb and Pb

MOHAMED BABU
African Socialism or Socialist Africa?
Hb and Pb

ANONYMOUS
Independent Kenya
Hb and Pb

YOLAMU BARONGO (EDITOR)
Political Science in Africa: A Radical Critique
Hb and Pb

OKWUDIBA NNOLI (EDITOR)
Path to Nigerian Development
Pb

EMILE VERCRUIJSSE
Transitional Modes of Production:
A Case Study from West Africa
Hb

FATIMA BABIKIR MAHMOUD
The Sudanese Bourgeoisie —
Vanguard of Development?
Hb and Pb

NO SIZWE
One Azania, One Nation:
The National Question in South Africa
Hb and Pb

BEN TUROK
Development in Zambia: A Reader
Pb

J.F. RWEYEMAMU (EDITOR)
Industrialization and Income Distribution in Africa
Hb and Pb

CLAUDE AKE
Revolutionary Pressures in Africa
Hb and Pb

ANNE SEIDMAN AND NEVA MAKGETLA
Outposts of Monopoly Capitalism:
Southern Africa in the Changing Global Economy
Hb and Pb

CONTEMPORARY HISTORY/REVOLUTIONARY STRUGGLES

AQUINO DE BRAGANCA AND IMMANUEL WALLERSTEIN (EDITORS)
The African Liberation Reader: Documents of the National Liberation
Movements
Vol I: The Anatomy of Colonialism
Vol II: The National Liberation Movements
Vol III: The Strategy of Liberation
Hb and Pb

EDWIN MADUNAGU
Problems of Socialism:
The Nigerian Challenge
Pb

MAI PALMBERG
The Struggle for Africa
Hb and Pb

CHRIS SEARLE
We're Building the New School!
Diary of a Teacher in Mozambique
Hb at Pb price

CEDRIC ROBINSON
Black Marxism:
The Making of the Black Radical Tradition
Hb and Pb

MAINA WA KINYATTI
Thunder from the Mountains:
Mau Mau Patriotic Songs
Hb

EDUARDO MONDLANE
The Struggle for Mozambique
Pb

BASIL DAVIDSON
No Fist is Big Enough to Hide the Sky:
The Liberation of Guinea Bissau and Cape Verde: Aspects of the African
Revolution
Hb at Pb price

BARUCH HIRSON
Year of Fire, Year of Ash:
The Soweto Revolt — Roots of a Revolution?
Hb and Pb

SWAPO DEPARTMENT OF INFORMATION AND PUBLICITY
To Be Born a Nation:
The Liberation Struggle for Namibia
Pb

PEDER GOUWENIUS
Power to the People:
South Africa in Struggle: A Political History
Pb

HORST DRECHSLER
Let Us Die Fighting:
The Struggle of the Herero and Nama Against German Imperialism
(1884-1915)
Hb and Pb

GILLIAN WALT AND ANGELA MELAMED (EDITORS)
Mozambique: Towards a People's Health Service
Pb

ANDRE ASTROW
Zimbabwe: A Revolution that Lost its Way?
Hb and Pb

GILLIAN WALT and ANGELA MELAMED
Mozambique:
Towards a People's Health Service

RENE LEFORT
Ethiopia: An Heretical Revolution?
Hb and Pb

TONY AVIRGAN AND MARTHA HONEY
War in Uganda: The Legacy of Idi Amin
Hb and Pb

LABOUR STUDIES

DIANNE BOLTON
Nationalization: A Road to Socialism?
The Case of Tanzania
Pb

A.T. NZULA, I.I. POTEKHIN, A.Z. ZUSMANOVICH
Forced Labour in Colonial Africa
Hb and Pb

JEFF CRISP
The Story of an African Working Class
— Ghanaian Miners' Struggles, 1870–1980

LITERATURE

FAARAX M.J. CAWL
Ignorance is the Enemy of Love
Pb

KINFE ABRAHAM
From Race to Class
Links and Parallels in African and Black American Protest Expression
Pb

OTHER TITLES

A. TEMU AND B. SWAI
Historians and Africanist History: A Critique
Hb and Pb

ROBERT ARCHER AND ANTOINE BOUILLON
The South African Game:
Sport and Racism
Hb and Pb

WOMEN

RAQIYA HAJI DUALEH ABDALLA
Sisters in Affliction:
Circumcision and Infibulation of Women in Africa
Hb and Pb

CHRISTINE OBBO
African Women:
Their Struggle for Economic Independence
Pb

MARIA ROSE CUTRUFELLI
Women of Africa:
Roots of Oppression
Hb and Pb

ASMA EL DAREER
Woman, Why do you Weep?
Circumcision and Its Consequences
Hb and Pb

MIRANDA DAVIES (EDITOR)
Third World — Second Sex:
Women's Struggles and National Liberation
Hb and Pb

Zed press titles cover Africa, Asia, Latin America and the Middle East, as well as general issues affecting the Third World's relations with the rest of the world. Our Series embrace: Imperialism, Women, Political Economy, History, Labour, Voices of Struggle, Human Rights and other areas pertinent to the Third World.

You can order Zed titles direct from Zed Press, 57 Caledonian Road, London, N1 9DN, U.K.

WOMEN IN THE THIRD WORLD: TITLES FROM ZED PRESS

BOBBY SIU
Women of China:
Imperialism and Women's Resistance, 1900–1949
Hb and Pb

INGELA BENDT AND JAMES DOWNING
We Shall Return:
Women of Palestine
Hb and Pb

MIRANDA DAVIES (EDITOR)
Third World — Second Sex:
Women's Struggles and National Liberation
Hb and Pb

JULIETTE MINCES
The House of Obedience:
Women in Arab Society
Hb and Pb

MARGARET RANDALL
Sandino's Daughters:
Testimonies of Nicaraguan Women in Struggle
Pb

MARIA MIES
The Lacemakers of Narsapur:
Indian Housewives Produce for the World Market
Pb

ASMA EL DAREER
Woman, Why do you Weep?
Circumcision and Its Consequences
Hb and Pb

RAQIYA HAJI DUALEH ABDALLA
Sisters in Affliction:
Circumcision and Infibulation of Women in Africa
Hb and Pb

MARIA ROSE CUTRUFELLI
Women of Africa:
Roots of Oppression
Hb and Pb

AGNES SMEDLEY
Portraits of Chinese Women in Revolution
Pb

RAYMONDA TAWIL
My Home, My Prison
Pb

NAWAL EL SAADAWI
Woman at Zero Point
Hb and Pb

ELISABETH CROLL
Chinese Women
Hb and Pb

ARLENE EISEN
Women in the New Vietnam
Hb and Pb

Zed press titles cover Africa, Asia, Latin America and the Middle East, as well as general issues affecting the Third World's relations with the rest of the world. Our Series embrace: Imperialism, Women, Political Economy, History, Labour, Voices of Struggle, Human Rights and other areas pertinent to the Third World.

You can order Zed titles direct from Zed Press, 57 Caledonian Road, London, N1 9DN, U.K.